Fred Meijer

STORIES OF HIS LIFE

Fred Meijer

STORIES OF HIS LIFE

Bill Smith & Larry ten Harmsel

William B. Eerdmans Publishing Company

Grand Rapids, Michigan / Cambridge, U.K.

Published 2009 by

Wm. B. Eerdmans Publishing Co.

2140 Oak Industrial Drive N.E., Grand Rapids, Michigan 49505 /
P.O. Box 163, Cambridge CB3 9PU U.K.

Printed in the United States of America

Library of Congress Cataloging-in-Publication Data

Smith, Bill.
    Fred Meijer: stories of his life / Bill Smith & Larry Ten Harmsel.
      p.   cm.
    ISBN 978-0-8028-6460-4 (pbk.: alk. paper)
    ISBN 978-0-8028-6486-4 (cloth.: alk. paper)
    1. Meijer, Fred, 1919- 2. Meijer Inc. — History. 3. Merchants —
Michigan — Biography.   I. Ten Harmsel, Larry, 1945-   II. Title.

HF5469.23.U64M4559   2009
381'.141092 — dc22
[B]

                                                 2008053910

www.eerdmans.com

Contents

Foreword

His red hair has gone white, but he is still Fred. He is husband of long standing to Lena — "Toots," sometimes, in that context — father of three, grandfather of seven, employer and colleague of thousands. Nearly nine decades on, he comes to his office nearly every workday. It's a little harder to visit stores, which is what he would be doing much more often if he could.

In the office he tells stories, so it's fitting that this book should talk about him that way — in stories. He lives his life with a remarkable consistency, considering how differently things could have turned out if this or that gamble had not paid off, considering where he started and where that life has led.

He was once quoted as saying he could be happy living in a double-wide mobile home, and I have absolutely no doubt that would be the case. His world is social and relational more than either material or spiritual. Who people are and what they can do — their inherent worth and dignity — are what counts. His curiosity has propelled him. With no background — no prior interest, really — in contemporary sculpture, he has built one of the most significant collections in the world. (With no thought but to share it, of course.) Ideas surface, not from expertise but from thoughtful questions, from asking Italy's most prominent sculptor, "What was the one project you always wanted to do but never did?"

Curiosity he came by naturally. His father, Hendrik, who opened his first grocery store in 1934, when Fred was fourteen, brought wide eyes and an open mind to his immigrant experience in America. When Hendrik decided to become a grocer, Fred was at his elbow from the first. Together they asked questions, scouted competitors, learned everything they could from every salesman with something to offer. Hendrik pushed Fred forward — partly, perhaps, to give Fred the experience, partly also because the immigrant still spoke in a heavy Dutch accent. In either case, the son came of age quickly.

It should be said that, physically, he took after his mother, Gezina, more than his father; but her austere and earnest ways were tempered in him by the restless expansiveness of his father. Fred likes to downplay his academic performance, but records show that these things are relative. It was simply that his big sister, Johanna, was an exceptional student, and he would always be her little brother.

The Great Depression was the defining moment of Fred's youth, as it was for so many of his generation. The Northside Grocery cum Thrift Market cum supermarket was Hendrik's response to the hardship of the times. "Thrift" was an abiding virtue.

Hendrik managed to be an imposing figure in Fred's life without being an intimidating one. Fred gave up thoughts of college to become Hendrik's partner, and they became inseparable in their business lives. They shared an office. Their desks faced one another for a time. One assistant — Pam Kleibusch, of whom more in this book — worked with both.

It was a relationship that could not be duplicated a generation later, as Fred and Lena raised three sons. They had only recently moved to Grand Rapids, because that was the nearest big city, the place where the future lay. Yet even as he built a business, Fred was as involved a father as any son might wish for. He worked hard, socialized little, but was quick to staff a booth at a PTA carnival. He built a serious tree house out back, and he constructed a stile over the barbed wire atop the golf course fence behind the house so that in winter we could climb over with our sleds and slide down the steepest fairways. We took up skiing and so did he — and he installed our bindings in the shop in the basement.

Ours was never a household where the job was left behind when you came home from work. Fred's career permeated our lives. Lena was a pillar of patience. (They had met when Hendrik hired her as a cashier in that first store, so she understood Fred's world.) Sundays were marked less by piety than by family pilgrimages — to Meijer stores that had begun to open further afield, in Holland or Battle Creek or Muskegon or Kalamazoo. My brothers and I would clamber from the back of the station wagon for Sunday dinner of sorts, the offering depending on the food service available at a particular big store. There were vending machines in Kalamazoo, and we liked to pick out sandwiches there. If we went out at night, we drove past competing supermarkets to see how many checklanes were open.

Car trips also took us to more distant points — Washington or Boston, Tahquamenon Falls or the Wisconsin Dells. Lodging was almost invariably a modest motel — cabins when we could find them, one room with the boys fighting to see who got to sleep in the rollaway bed — and almost always Dad was touring stores along the way.

Fred and Lena lived for forty years in the ranch house on Grand Rapids' northeast side where they raised their sons. Again a consistency, a stability, in the flux and uncertainty of a burgeoning business. Here routine prevailed. Fred and Lena had their chairs. Fred tried to keep up with his reading at night. There was something of a formula to this life that set a tone for the organization that Meijer Inc. was becoming. Fred was ready with respect and empathy, and you could — can — count on him.

Although today he hunches a little over his walker, the man who once hiked the Milford Track in New Zealand still gets about — and almost always, it seems, with a double mission: to work with people and to solve problems. In his world, the second cannot be accomplished without the first, and the first cannot be contemplated without the thoughts and opinions of others. It was what he grew up watching his father do. It is a direct reflection of a Dutch homily he keeps on a plaque in his office: "Niet ik, niet jij, maar wij" ("Not I, not you, but we").

My brothers and I could not hope to replicate the relationship Fred had with his father, but we were included every step of the way. I am told of my anxiety as a little boy flying over Kalamazoo in a single engine plane as my dad scouted real estate. Brother Doug was barely in his teens when he accompanied our dad on a buying trip to Hong Kong. Mark was still in my mother's arms when Fred and Hendrik and

Miss Michigan cut the ribbon on a store that would later become a pioneer supercenter.

Fred embodies the contradictions of his life — and of a Dutch heritage of peaceableness and schism. He is a puritan with a rebel's disdain for convention. He combines an obsession with safety, sanitation, even security with a delight in risk and adventure. He is a bundle of opinions and a seeker of consensus.

For all the routine, stories abound. As they have been collected and edited by Bill Smith and Larry ten Harmsel, they come to comprise far more than a miscellany of anecdotes. They add up to a remarkable life.

HANK MEIJER

Acknowledgments

The authors wish to thank many people for their support and encouragement during the process of putting this book together. Among them are Joyce De Graaf, who typed much of the manuscript through several revisions; and Amy Fahner, who also did a good deal of typing. Jane Smith, Rebecca Smith, and Paul Mason served as a focus group for Bill. Jim Vanden Bosch, Mieke ten Harmsel, and Dorothea Schneider offered Larry important suggestions about his work. Bob Strodtbeck, Dave Meinke, and David Hooker helped with photos; Todd Gray assisted Bill with parts of the interview process; George Zain supplied many old photos, together with valuable insights about Meijer company history; Bryan Richards and Michael Ross helped with research and documentation; Sheryl Mason provided delivery service; Reinder Van Til, as editor and friend, excelled at making the crooked straight and the rough places plain. Pam Kleibusch assisted in many aspects throughout the project.

And we offer a special thanks to the scores of people from every walk of life who contributed their stories about Fred. This book would not have been possible without the constant help and encouragement of the Meijer family. Mark, Doug, and Hank were generous in contributing stories from their youth. Most important, of course, were Fred and Lena. They have patiently sat through lengthy interviews over the past two years, and their acquaintance has been felt for five decades in Bill's life, and for nearly three decades in Larry's. It is both an honor and a pleasure to count them as friends.

Key to Frequently Cited Books

IHOW   *Fred Meijer, In His Own Words.* Eerdmans, 1995.

TY   *Thrifty Years: The Life of Hendrik Meijer,* by Hank Meijer. Eerdmans, 1984.

Chapter One

A Depression-Era Childhood

Here at our sea-washed, sunset gates shall stand
A mighty woman with a torch, whose flame
Is the imprisoned lightning, and her name
Mother of Exiles. From her beacon-hand
Glows world-wide welcome; her mild eyes command
The air-bridged harbor that twin cities frame.
"Keep, ancient lands, your storied pomp!" cries she
With silent lips. "Give me your tired, your poor,
Your huddled masses yearning to breathe free,
The wretched refuse of your teeming shore.
Send these, the homeless, tempest-tost to me.
I lift my lamp beside the golden door!"

— Emma Lazarus

They were Dutch immigrants, from Hengelo in the province of Overijssel, close to the German border. It was a grimy, hard-working city, surrounded by poor farms, its skyline dominated by faceless factories, where many of their friends and relatives toiled. The industrial revolution in the eastern provinces of the Netherlands had brought most of the workers little more than a grim sort of poverty, along with aspirations for something better. Two young Netherlanders who yearned to get out were Hendrik Meijer and Gezina (Zien) Mantel.

Don Koster

My father came over from The Netherlands in 1906 on the *Nieuw Amsterdam*, a ship that had been recently built, on its maiden voyage. The ship was 615 feet long and carried 2,886 passengers, most of them poor. During the voyage almost everyone became sick on account of the new paint and being confined to small cabins in the lower decks. Hendrik Meijer came over on this same ship a year later.

Hendrik Meijer arrived in America in 1907. For the next few restless years he worked at whatever he could find: first in Holland, Michigan, among other Dutch immigrants; then as a laborer in Chicago; then clear across the country in Yakima, Washington, for a while; then back to Chicago, where he studied at the New Method Barber School, achieving certification in that trade in August 1911. All the while he was writing letters to Zien, describing the new country to her and dreaming in those letters about when she could join him in America, yet always putting off the date of her arrival — at least the way she impatiently saw it — so that he could see just a bit more of the world. Zien, treading water with her family in Hengelo, feared that he was becoming a vagabond.

But finally Hendrik was ready to settle down, and she joined him in 1912. Two weeks after her arrival in the United States, they were married by a justice of the peace

Gezina and Hendrik, around 1920

Hendrik (foreground) in his barbershop

in Grand Haven, Michigan. And though their life would be rather peripatetic for a few years, they eventually settled quite comfortably in Greenville, Michigan, a bustling town of about 5,000 inhabitants, several prosperous factories, and a surrounding sprawl of lakes, rivers, and relatively fertile farmland.

The year 1919 was a significant one for the Meijers. After a couple of Hendrik's career ideas didn't work out as planned — sales and installation for the Holland Furnace Company, followed by brief forays into secondhand furniture and haircutting in Muskegon — he returned to an earlier career: a reliable trade in a barbershop that he purchased on the north side of Greenville.

Along with the barbershop they bought sixteen acres just outside of town, and there the small family — mother Gezina, father Hendrik, and three-year-old Johanna — tried to build a prosperous life for themselves. That spring Hendrik bought his first cow, the beginning of what was to become a small dairy operation. Zien quickly learned to milk the cow while caring for their toddler. And another addition was on the way: she was expecting a baby by the end of the year.

When we hear of immigrant farmers in small-town America, we often think of their lives as rather narrow, constricted by poverty, hard work, and the uncertainties of a foreign language. But Hendrik wasn't just a farmer (nor is any other farmer in America, one suspects): he was a budding entrepreneur, even though he may not have been entirely convinced of the virtues of capitalism. For some years he had been the American correspondent for *Recht Door Zee* ("all the way to the sea"), a Dutch anarchist newspaper, and he occasionally wrote articles that were critical of his newly adopted homeland. He was not entirely convinced about the American way, but he was still capable of jumping into it with both feet.

Where politics was concerned, he knew that most of his customers in the barbershop were conservative, but he didn't temper his opinions for their taste. "I tell them," he said, "that if an anarchist . . . wants to get rid of someone with a crown on his head, the whole world wants to see him dead. But when that monster with the crown gets it into his head to kill thousands and thousands of people, then you are supposed to agree with him, because your country is telling you to." (*TY*, p. 102)

Hendrik displayed the fierce patriotism frequently seen in immigrants, but his love for America demanded that he try to describe it honestly. He was critical of the authorities when Eugene V. Debs was sent to jail for opposing World War I, and at one point he went so far as to write that in America "the real friends of the people are behind bars." (*TY*, p. 103)

Nor did Hendrik's wife, Gezina, fit stereotypical images of the immigrant farm wife. Very likely no one really fits those stereotypes entirely, but Zien was certainly a special case. A vegetarian and a teetotaler, a feminist pacifist whose family in the Netherlands encouraged her radicalism, she had no trouble expressing her opinions. Shortly before she came to America, an organization in Hengelo mounted a production of Henrik Ibsen's unsettling new drama about a woman's need for independence, *A Doll's House*. Zien played the lead role of Nora, a character who scandalized a generation of European playgoers when she slammed the door as she left her boorish and controlling husband for an independent life.

The Danish immigrant farmers in the mid-Michigan community of

Greenville, like their Dutch counterparts, had fled poverty and injustice in their homeland. But it is hard to imagine that many of them had had such wide experience of the world or such boundless energy as this poor but strangely cosmopolitan young couple. Like Puritans, they did not smoke or drink or use strong language, and they distrusted frivolous forms of entertainment. They insisted on respecting all people, regardless of race or social class. The Meijers had little use for organized religion, but they looked at the world through intensely moral eyes, and they always hoped to encourage a sense of fairness and justice around them as the world tried to rebuild itself after the devastation of the Great War.

As hostilities ceased, European politics in 1919 experienced a series of convulsions, many of which would have been intensely interesting to Hendrik and Gezina. In late June of that year the Treaty of Versailles was signed, ending World War I, but inexorably ripening the conditions that would lead to World War II. The Netherlands had successfully defended its neutrality in the war (which had not yet acquired a Roman numeral). But now the Kaiser was seeking refuge there, and despite Allied attempts to extradite him, the Dutch allowed the Kaiser to stay, infuriating the Allies.

Kaiser flees German revolution

BERLIN, Germany, Nov. 9, 1918—Kaiser Wilhelm II abdicated today and fled to Holland. Pressure from the spreading revolution in Germany, caused by the collapse of the German armies, brought about his abdication.

Efforts are being made to form a new government under Friedrich Ebert. He is leader of the German Socialists.

The revolution started among German soldiers at the port of Kiel.

The Kaiser first sought refuge with the army. He found no protection there, so he had to leave the country.

In middle Europe, the Hapsburg Kingdom, which had ruled the Austro-Hungarian Empire for five centuries, came to an end, and there was no certainty about what would replace it. Turkey embarked on a deadly process of ethnic cleansing, trying to get rid of its Armenian and Greek minorities. Throughout Europe it must have seemed as though the aftermath of the "War to End All Wars" had not brought peace so much as widened the differences between the right and the left, the old world not quite dead and the new world not quite born. In Italy, Benito Mussolini founded the Fascist party. Six months later, Adolf Hitler presented his ideas for the National Socialist (Nazi) party in Munich. In Moscow, the first Communist International met, while the Red and White Russian armies were still at war over the future of Russia, soon to become the Union of Soviet Socialist Republics.

In the United States, labor unrest resulted in the lynching of an Industrial Workers of the World union representative, and in the founding of the American Communist party.

In January, as Prohibition went into effect in the United States, the League of Nations was being founded in Geneva.

The Nineteenth Amendment to the U.S. Constitution, giving women the right to vote, was approved by Congress and sent to the states for ratification.

Late in that year of 1919, on December 7, a date that would later be

Gezina,
Johanna,
and Fred, 1921

Fred (age four)

etched in American's collective memory in connection with Pearl Harbor, Frederik Gerhard Hendrik Meijer was born in the family farmhouse in Eureka Township, a mile or so north of Hendrik's barbershop. Ellis Ranney, whose family owned the Ranney Refrigerator Factory, and a longtime friend (and customer) of Hendrik, sent flowers to celebrate the occasion. The baby's Dutch uncle, Frans Mantel, wrote: "I can see little Fred. Ger. Henry become a big farmer over there in America. But who knows ahead of time what will become of such a little boy." (*TY*, p. 107)

Several of Hendrik's earlier jobs hadn't worked very well, but his Greenville barbershop prospered, and before long he was able to put up his own building in the city, using the basement for haircutting and renting out the other floors. He was a budding capitalist, though he was still rather suspicious of rich people, a suspicion he and Zien shared with their children. Zien not only worked on the farm and raised the children; she also helped out in the barbershop, laundering towels and tending to other details.

The Meijers may have lived outside of town, but they felt a strong sense of connection to Greenville. On weekends Hendrik would often go to the Greenville Hospital to give haircuts to patients who were not able to leave their beds. That hospital, like many similar institutions throughout the Midwest, had been a private home and was constructed of wood. Hendrik told his son, Fred, later that he never trusted the safety of the building; it struck him as flimsy and prone to fire. In the Netherlands, as in much of Europe, local laws had prohibited the use of wooden buildings as hospitals for more than a century.

Fred on the hay wagon

For the young boy Fred, life on the farm was relentlessly busy, keeping him active with forms of work that often seemed indistinguishable from play as far as he was concerned. He especially enjoyed working with horses, and there was plenty of opportunity for that in an era before tractors were widespread. Horses still powered most of the plowing, hayraking, harvesting, and transport of goods from one place to another. On one occasion, when Fred was nine or ten years old, Hendrik arranged for him to drive a loaded hay wagon the half dozen miles from Gowen to Greenville. Fred's mother was worried about entrusting the job to such a young boy.

"All that way — alone?" she asked.

"Don't worry," replied Hendrik. "He can do it." Gezina was pleased enough with the completion of the task that she took a photo of the diminutive Fred standing atop a mountain of hay, the horse's reins in his hand.

The young farm boy was a diligent student in school, where his quick mind and willingness to work always kept him in good standing. His penchant for raising difficult questions was a strong part of his identity in the classroom. One of his schoolteachers remembers him this way:

Helen Sellers

After receiving my teaching certificate in 1934, I got my first job teaching ninth-grade English in Greenville, Michigan. It was in the midst of the depression, and Hendrik Meijer had just opened a small grocery store on Main Street. One of my students that year was Fred Meijer. I remember he was a good student, cooperative and respectful. The only real hint, however, of things to come was that he was very inquisitive. His questions usually made you think.

Mr. Francis Garter was a history teacher at the high school in Greenville, a teacher Fred remembers very fondly. Mr. Garter had been born in China, and his wife was the daughter of a White Russian in those early years after the Communist Revolution, so he brought an international perspective to the classroom. One day he was talking to the students about anarchists. He described them as lawless hooligans who threw bombs, shot innocent people, and burned down buildings — all in an attempt to overthrow governments. Fred raised his hand and expressed his opinion.

"Mr. Garter," he said, "as far as I know, anarchists are peace-loving people who don't like unjust governments and who try to bring them down." Mr. Garter would not have known that Fred's father had been a member of an anarchist organization in the Netherlands, and had tried to found a similar group in Holland, Michigan, in 1907.

American notions about anarchists were often based on the trial of Nicola Sacco and Bartolomeo Vanzetti, who were convicted of a deadly bombing and executed in 1927. Mr. Garter and his class may also have heard something about the Dutch anarchist Marinus Vander Lubbe, whom Hitler accused of burning down the German Reichstag. Hitler then used that accusation as an excuse to expand his political power in 1933. Vander Lubbe was beheaded in a prison in Leipzig in January 1934, and Americans had widely divergent opinions about him. Mr. Garter would not have known that Vander

Lubbe's brother had visited Fred's grandparents, the Mantels, in Hengelo on his way back from the Berlin show trial where Marinus was sentenced to death.

At any rate, Francis Garter treated Fred's interruption with the utmost respect.

"Class," he said, "we have an interesting opinion here. I want you to know that Fred is absolutely right — when it comes to the original beliefs of the anarchists. But as the movement has developed, and as people now understand it, they won't understand what Fred is talking about if he praises anarchists. And therefore he's right, in the true sense, but wrong if he wants to be understood by others."

"I thought that was great of him," says Fred, "because he had the type of knowledge of the world that most young teachers didn't have. What he said was, to me, a remarkable example of the best way to teach, to bring out the best in your students."

> *Ik ben dom geboren, en heb niet veel bijgelernt.*
> ("I was born dumb, and haven't learned much since.")
> — Fred Meijer, joking in Dutch

Fred remembers another example of teaching that was not quite so felicitous. A teacher he declines to name was talking about the Huns, and how before the dawn of written history they had swept through southern Belgium into northern France. Fred raised his hand and asked, "Are you sure they didn't come through Holland?"

"Why do you ask that?" she replied.

"Because there are cemeteries in Holland that are called 'Huns' cemeteries.'"

"Oh, they called the Germans Huns in World War I," she said, "and that's what you're thinking."

"Well," says Fred, "when somebody tells me what I'm thinking, I'm half angry already. She got one step right, but the second step she got wrong. If she had asked in a different way, I would have brought picture postcards to class to show the *hunnebedden* in Drenthe [the prehistoric burial grounds of the ancient Huns along the northeast border of the Netherlands], and maybe she and the class would have learned something. It's so important how you teach. But the teacher didn't understand that either. And I wasn't that tolerant as a kid, I guess. I just got angry. It's too bad. I don't think I ever participated in that class with a question like that again.

"I had a teacher in high school," Fred goes on, "who wanted us to memorize a bunch of dates. And students got good grades for that. I suppose they deserved those grades because they knew the dates. But they didn't know what the issues were; they just knew the dates. They got A's, while I got B's and C's in that class. But when I got to Mr. Garter's class I got straight A's. Those grades meant something to me, because he saw the importance of understanding the background, of thinking it through."

Fred was always busy with work outside of school — milking cows, helping his father with milk deliveries for the dairy business. He has many pleasant memories of that time in his life, plus a few that were not so pleasant. It seems that there was often a horse and a cart involved in his stories.

Bob Rasmussen

My cousin remembers riding with Fred in his cart pulled by a pony. He would have to hang on for dear life, because Fred would drive fast and hit the bumps on purpose.

Fred with the reins

Fred remembers being bawled out on occasion by Hendrik for his rambunctiousness. He always took these chastenings to heart. But he couldn't stop being who he was: he did things fully, with his whole being, whether it was work or play. And often he didn't see much difference between the two.

Of course, the requirements of the farm usually soaked up any spare time anyone might have. Fred's life in Greenville was in many ways not so different from the way Lena Rader was living, just outside the village of Amble, twenty-three miles away. They were both developing a sense of interdependence with their families, an understanding that even as children they made important contributions to the family's livelihood. They both shouldered responsibilities beyond their years and worked extremely hard, understanding the rewards that came with hard-won accomplishments. They were both exposed to two languages at home: German and English for Lena, and Dutch and English for Fred. And they both exhibited talents in music: Fred as a clarinetist, violinist, and singer; Lena as trumpet player, pianist, and organist. It is quite clear that their lifelong curiosity, flexibility, intelligence, and determination were in large part formed in the fertile soil of those early farm years.

"Lena worked hard on the farm," says Fred responding to a question about whether the two had any resentment about that hard early life. Lena nods in agreement. "She would milk cows in the morning, wash up after she milked the cows, change clothes, go to school, come home, change clothes, milk the cows again. If she had a social function, or a date, or anything like that, she had to get the chores done first. And that's how we lived from seven years old through high school. So while she was hard at work on the farm, but not resenting her dad for it, I was doing the same thing for my family, and not resenting my dad for it."

Suburban Americans of the twenty-first century may think of immigrants as somehow defective — people with funny accents who don't understand our ways. However, they generally bring to our society a rich range of experience and understanding of the world, along with a work ethic that is unknown to most contemporary Americans. That was certainly true of the Dutch, German, and Danish immigrants in the Greenville area when Fred and Lena came of age.

Although he had little time for extracurricular activities in high school, Fred was able to play the violin in the Belding Ensemble for fifteen years, and he was a clarinetist in the Greenville City Band for a few years as well. This was a time when most small towns boasted musical organizations, and musical literacy was widespread, though the level of talent might not always have been high. On one occasion, when the Greenville City Band played a benefit at the fairgrounds to earn money for uniforms, Fred asked his father how the band had sounded. Hendrik replied, "Do you really want to know?"

Niet ik, niet jij, maar wij
("Not I, not you, but we")

— a Dutch slogan that Fred heard
frequently while growing up

By the early 1930s, the Great Depression was securely lodged in America, though it didn't yet have that name. Money was getting ever tighter, and though the farm still helped supplement the Meijer family income, both it and the barbershop were in some trouble. Fred was an extremely dutiful child, and his parents never sheltered him from discussions about money. So he knew the value of a dollar, and he knew they were scarce. A farm family was in some ways a perfect example of the Marxist maxim "From each according to his ability, to each according to his need." As a farm boy, Fred was aware that everyone in the family was expected to do what he or she could to contribute to the general welfare.

But things didn't always go smoothly. One day Fred was helping in one of the family services at that time, milk delivery. His father, sitting on the wagon with Thorville MacFarland, a teenager from the neighborhood, decided to play a trick on Fred. In a calculated fashion, he gradually urged the horse to go faster, forcing Fred to run as he brought milk from the wagon to the steps of each house and then back for the next order. First it was a brisk jog he needed to maintain; then it was a hard run; finally, it turned into a mad dash. After a while, Fred had had enough of this joke, which didn't seem at all funny anymore. He ran to a porch with a couple of quarts of milk, dropped them off, and just kept running — all the way home. His father and

Thorville had to take care of the remaining deliveries. Such behavior was extremely out of character for Fred, and perhaps for that reason his father finished up the route, came back home, and didn't say a word of rebuke.

Fred vividly remembers an incident, when he was about thirteen years old, that took place on a Thursday, the day of the week when the barbershop was closed and Hendrik was at home. They had just bought a new horse, a spirited animal, part Arabian. That day it was Fred's job to take the horse and the milk wagon to the blacksmith for some work. The family was hard up, but they had spent the handsome sum of ten dollars building the wagon, which was a significant investment for them. It had rubber tires, just like a car, and was in nearly perfect condition. The dutiful young boy had a strong sense of adult responsibility, something his parents had always encouraged in him, as he proudly walked the horse down the street and around the corner.

When he got to the blacksmith shop, however, he somehow neglected to tie the animal securely to the rail, and while the blacksmith was preparing for his work, it broke loose. Still attached to the wagon, which was slamming against telephone poles, the horse set out across fields and backyards, picking up clotheslines, and paying no attention to the road — just heading for the farm. The wagon hit a couple of other obstacles and broke loose; the whiffletree gave way and dangled off to one side; the harness was ripped and hanging. Yet the horse kept twisting and struggling in the direction of the farm. And not far behind was Fred, trying to catch up to the horse, knowing that he had made a big mistake, knowing there was at least ten dollars — maybe more — getting wasted before his eyes. And it was his fault. He should have known better than to tie a new horse carelessly.

He got back home just a minute or two behind the horse, panting and red-faced. It couldn't have been more than a half mile or so, and a horse impeded by a wagon isn't that much faster than a speedy thirteen-year-old runner.

"There are some parents," he says, "who get angry out of all proportion to what their child has done. One of the nicest things my dad ever did for me I didn't really realize until thirty or forty years later. I was running after that horse, and my dad came running out toward me. There was all that damage to the harness and the wagon and, for all we knew, the horse. And all my dad said to me was, "Are you okay?" Just that — nothing else. Nothing about the trouble I had caused. He didn't criticize me. He knew I tried to do what was right most of the time. I think that was wonderful."

Telling the story more than seventy-five years later, Fred's eyes fill with tears as he shakes his head, smiling at the memory of his father's kindness and love.

"You know," he says, "all in all, during those years when we were poor in terms of money, I often think what rich parents I had in giving me an understanding of the world."

ROOSEVELT PROMISES WAR ON DEPRESSION

But the barbershop and the dairy were bringing in less and less income as the national financial crisis deepened. The local refrigerator factory, owned by the family of Hendrik's friend Ellis Ranney, had laid off many workers, and everyone became more nervous about spending money. Haircuts were, in some sense, a luxury. It was easy enough, after all, to have someone in your family cut your hair at the kitchen table, and save two bits in the process. Your hair might not look as good, but who would notice? Who would criticize you for it? So the receipts at the barbershop dwindled as the Depression spread.

DEPRESSION DEEPENS; 12 MILLION UNEMPLOYED

The dairy continued to function: Fred's mother milked the cows and maintained the milkhouse, while Hendrik, Johanna, and Fred delivered to customers. But there was a cloud on the horizon: pasteurization. The largest dairy in town, Blanding's, had bought the neces-

Johanna and Fred

sary equipment to offer pasteurized milk, while the Model Dairy could only counter with the claim that its unpasteurized product was creamier and tasted better. "In Greenville the price of a quart of milk dropped from twelve cents in 1929 to a nickel in 1932. With milk at twelve cents a quart, Hendrik's dairy had not been a paying proposition. Now the bottles cost as much as the milk did, and he was running out of bottles." (*TY*, p. 122)

In many agricultural states the crisis in milk prices caused farmers to organize. The famous Sioux City Milk War of 1932 saw farmers dumping milk into gutters rather than bringing it into the city. They were irate because farmers were paid two cents a quart, while retailers charged eight cents a quart to their customers. In Wisconsin, Minnesota, New York, and elsewhere, groups of farmers created unions, cooperatives, syndicates, and granges, often with a leftist or populist slant. One might have thought Hendrik would look to such groups for help in his predicament. But with the help of his hard-working family — Fred and Johanna had long been his partners along with his wife, Zien — he had become an independent entrepreneur, and he was not at all tempted by the pressures of his peers. Hendrik was perfectly willing to go it on his own. When a group of Greenville barbers put pressure on him to double the price of a twenty-five-cent haircut, he refused to go along. When the other barbers threatened to put him out of business, he stormed out of the meeting, shouting, "I wouldn't have you SOB's for pallbearers." (*TY*, p. 120)

Hendrik owed about $7,000 on the building he'd put up. The renters couldn't always pay, the dairy was losing money, and still the bills had to be paid. When he tried to sell his building for the amount of the remaining mortgage, the prospective buyer laughed and said he'd buy it for half that amount when Hendrik went bust. The building was not worth what it had cost to put it up several years earlier.

Maybe, he thought, he could start up a grocery store. People might not need a barber to cut their hair during a depression, but they would always need to eat. A trip to Grand Rapids, to the wholesale grocery suppliers Lee & Cady, showed just how little Hendrik understood about the business. He had thought that perhaps the wholesalers would rent his building and set up shop for themselves. No, they told him, but you can do it yourself.

There were already twenty-two grocery stores in Greenville, most of them barely getting by. Kipp's, the busiest of them, was right across the street. Hendrik's friend Ellis Ranney thought he would be crazy to try such a thing, and he said so. When Lee & Cady asked for a credit reference, though, Ranney said they would surely get their money back, no matter how badly the business went. "You won't lose money on Meijer," he assured them. That was enough for the wholesalers, who needed new business in this terrible economic climate and were willing to take a risk.

Mijn ja is ja, mijn nee is nee.
("My yes means yes, my no means no.")
— Fred Meijer, remembering an expression
his parents often used

Hendrik sold the barbershop business to his former apprentice, Leo Swartz, for $350, to be paid in small installments over the next five years. Swartz agreed to hire his erstwhile boss on weekends, which Hendrik saw as a way to keep at least some money coming in.

"On June 20, 1934, a truck from Lee & Cady delivered the first load of groceries to the little store that Hendrik named the North Side Grocery. Zien saved the invoice: it was for $338.76. . . . Ten days later, on June 30, 1934, unaccompanied by advertising save the word of mouth that went out through the barbershop and along the milk route, the North Side Grocery opened its door." (*TY*, p. 127) Fred, fourteen years old and still waiting for his teenage growth spurt, stood behind the counter. He managed to sell, among other things, a package of gum to Mr. Ranney, who wished the family well despite his private doubts about their chances.

That first day, a Saturday, the store took in seven dollars in cash and credit. It was not an auspicious beginning, and the summer trade continued to be slow. Hendrik often worked downstairs in the barbershop while Johanna, now eighteen, ran the store, and Fred filled out customer orders and painted the latest special prices in large letters on the front windows: "Bread, 10 cents a double loaf. Coffee, 16 ½ cents a pound."

Fred painting the weekly specials, 1934

Bob Rasmussen

My mother started trading with Meijer shortly after they opened in 1934, because they had the best prices. We drove in from Sheridan, twelve miles away, every Friday night. My first memory of Fred is as a teenager, wearing a white apron that almost touched the floor. He would always ask, "Can I help you?"

Chapter Two

Coming of Age

> I admit that a grocer's shop is one of the most romantic
> and thrilling things I have ever happened on. . . . The citron
> and spices and nuts and dates, the barreled anchovies and
> Dutch cheeses, the jars of caviar and the chests of tea, they
> carry the mind away to Levantine coast towns and tropic
> shores, to the Old World wharves and quays of the Low
> Countries, to dusty Astrachan and far Cathay.
>
> — H. H. Munro (Saki)

For the next year, until August 1935, this pattern of livelihood
continued. Johanna continued to run the store; Hendrik cut
hair and dealt with finances. Gezina, a committed vegetarian,
wondered whether they should be selling meat in their establishment, but she overcame her doubts and worked hard at managing the
farm and the family. Meijer stores have always sold things the family
itself never used, and in some cases did not approve of. Not only did
they sell meat, but alcohol and tobacco also became available, two
things Fred himself has never used.

"My father drank a lot of coffee," he recalls. "He gave me a taste
when I was nine years old. I didn't like it and haven't used it since.
Later my father told me he would buy cigarettes for me if I wanted
them, but he thought I'd be wrong to smoke. Dad psyched me out, I
guess. I never tried them. And the fellows in high school who drank

quite a bit, or said, 'You don't know what you're missing by not smoking,' all of them are now dead or in nursing homes."

Muriel Wise

Mrs. Meijer never let anything go to waste. She would take home all the dented and unlabeled cans, and the meat and produce that wouldn't sell. I never saw her take the choice cuts of meat or the best produce. It must have been interesting, with all those unlabeled cans, to see what you were going to have for dinner.

Fred, who was called "Brother," did all sorts of odd jobs in the earliest days. But this arrangement was about to change. Johanna, who had graduated from Greenville High School as the valedictorian of the class of 1934, had always nurtured a dream of going to the university. During the summer of 1935, that dream became a reality. Ellis Ranney's brother Roy, a University of Michigan alumnus, helped her apply for a scholarship, and she was chosen. There wasn't much money to send her off with: Hendrik took twenty-five dollars from the till of the fledgling grocery, and Ellis Ranney insisted on giving her another seventy-five dollars. At the end of that summer, Johanna left for Ann Arbor.

With Johanna's departure, Hendrik quit working as a barber; Gezina also began working full-time at the store. And Fred became more and more a fixture in the business, though he was still only fifteen years old. Although he sometimes thought about going to college himself — history was his favorite subject — it was never to be. His higher learning would have to take place in the grocery business.

"I remember one time," says Fred, "when Bill Gordon told my dad, 'You're working these kids too hard.' And my dad came home to me and asked, 'Am I working you too hard?' In other words, he told me what Bill Gordon had said, and wanted my reaction. Now, I never went to a baseball game or a basketball game or a football game — all through high school. I went to the pep rallies that were during school hours. At 3:00 I got out of school, and by 3:30 I was in the store. But I never thought my dad worked me too hard. It was an exciting experience, and also hard work. I probably put in forty hours a week all through high school, but I enjoyed it."

Russ Cole

Fred tells a story about a customer who brought a ham bone back to him for a refund, stating the ham wasn't any good. The ham was gone; all the customer had was the bone. Fred cheerfully gave her a refund, believing that the long-term value of the customer was worth more than the ham.

As Fred remembers it, however, that wasn't the end of the exchange. Once she had the money in her purse, the customer asked if she could have the bone back. She wanted to use it for soup. He gave it back to her. Things were rough all over. Asked about this incident seventy-five years later, he still remembers the name of the family, and he still keeps it private.

Muriel Wise

Times were hard during the Depression, and many families were on relief. These families were very self-conscious, and would have been embarrassed if they were seen paying for their groceries with welfare scrip. Meijer did a lot of welfare business, and I think the biggest reason for it was that we were taught to be discreet, so the person behind the welfare customers never knew how they paid. At some stores in town you had to check out through the Welfare Lane. After people started getting back on their feet and off welfare, they never forgot how they were treated at Meijer.

"As a matter of fact," says Fred, "at one time we did 60 percent of all the welfare business in Montcalm County — and there were twenty-two stores in Greenville alone when we started, plus the stores in Carson City, Howard City, Stanton, Sheridan, Sidney, and many others in Montcalm County. But we in our store did 60 percent of the whole county, and we were proud of that, because we must have given value, and also treated people with dignity." (*IHOW*, p. 46)

Many of the local customers brought eggs along with them when they came to the store, which they exchanged for groceries. In the 1930s it was common for people to use the old-fashioned word "trading" instead of the more modern "shopping." They still recalled — and often practiced — the barter system. Eggs were an especially common currency in rural areas such as Greenville, while exchanging homemade butter became less common as churns disappeared from many farmhouses. But almost every farm family, and many in the towns, had a few chickens. They would gather whatever eggs they could not eat, wash them carefully, and hold them up to a light in a darkened room. Candling, as this procedure was called, was a way to check the eggs for blood clots. If you saw a dark spot inside the egg, easily visible through the thin shell, it meant a chick had begun to form inside, so you would discard it.

Bringing your eggs to trade at the grocery store meant you were giving your word that they had been properly washed, sorted, and candled. There was an atmosphere of community trust behind this practice, as well as a recognition that everyone was in a tight spot financially. The Meijer store routinely took in more eggs than it could sell, so Fred spent part of his time going around the city trying to find other stores that could use their product. In addition to the competitive spirit, which was strong, there was also a sense of cooperation among the merchants, who tried to help each other out when they could.

Many of the items for sale in the store were carried only in bulk, and were measured out to each customer's specifications. Tea, coffee, butter, crackers, sugar, salt, cheese, sauerkraut, vinegar, and black pepper were then packaged at the counter and added to the order. It was a time-consuming process. The idea of serving yourself in a grocery store had not yet reached into small towns. Chicken feed, block salt, and veterinary preparations for animals were also big sellers in a well-stocked rural grocery store.

Bob Rasmussen

To stretch the dollar during those Depression years, my mother would shop the Meijer fire sales whenever they had them. Hendrik and Fred would buy out the stock of a store that had a fire and sell it very cheaply. However, you never knew what would be in the cans without labels.

"I think I'm very *zuinig* ('thrifty')," says Fred. "I always turn out lights in the house, and so forth. I must have been schooled by my mother. One time we borrowed a hundred dollars from the bank in Greenville. The banker's name was Browne, with an *e*. Now the general rule was that everybody in north Greenville was poor, and everybody in south Greenville was rich. Not quite true, but that was the stereotype. When you're hard up, you make fun of the people you think are wealthy. So we always called him Mr. Browne-with-an-*e*.

"At any rate, we borrowed a hundred dollars from the First State Bank, where Mr. Browne-with-an-*e* was president. It was not our usual bank, but for some reason I went there. We wanted to borrow a hundred dollars at 6 percent per annum.

"When I came in, Mr. Browne asked me, 'How's the weather out there today?' I told him it was invigorating.

"'Invigorating?' he laughed. 'Why don't you use Thrift Market language?' Well, I may have been only fifteen years old, but I didn't like that. I thought it was a putdown. I remembered it. But what are you going to say to the head of a bank?

"So, a half year later, I came back there to pay off the loan. Mr. Browne was there to collect the money. 'That'll be a hundred and six dollars,' he said. Well, my mother must have prepared me for this, because I said, 'Shouldn't it be a hundred and three? *Per annum,* after all, means "per year," and we've only had the money for six months.'

"'Well, okay,' he grumbled, "if that's how you feel about it.'

"So I paid him a hundred and three dollars, and I feel good about that extra three dollars to this day. That's seventy years ago. It's not the money. I don't know if I'd had the guts to do that if it hadn't been for the word 'invigorating' and the putdown. It's the lack of respect that I remember."

Muriel Wise

I still remember how it happened like it was yesterday. I was standing on the corner by the old stone fountain just outside the Meijer store and thinking how badly I needed a job. My father was gone, and I lived with my mother, grandmother, and two aunts.

Just then, Mr. Meijer came out, walked over to me, and asked me if I wanted a job. I was only fifteen, but he knew that there was no wage earner in our home. I started the next day. Fred taught me how to be a cashier. I was so short I had to stand on a stool to run the cash register, but how excited I was to have my first job. Since I was still in school, state regulations required that I could only work so many hours. Mr. Meijer called the school principal to coordinate my work with my classes. I worked for them for the next forty-five years. I will always be thankful that they thought about a little fifteen-year-old girl and made her part of their family.

Against all odds, the store continued to flourish. It wasn't always very profitable, but there was stability, along with a steadily growing trade. They kept the store open late on Friday and Saturday nights to let farmers buy their groceries after the movies were finished. They were open on Sundays, something of a rarity in Montcalm County. Fred's workday often stretched to fourteen hours or more when he was not in school.

Max Guernsey

During the Depression, Fred and his father couldn't afford to pay my father in cash, so they made an arrangement to pay some of his wages in cash and some in groceries. A friend once asked my dad if he thought he'd get all of his money.

"I'm paying my bills and I have food on the table," he replied, "which is more than most folks have right now." As soon as things started to get better, they gave my father his regular pay plus ten dollars a week and a little extra until everything was paid up. If they gave you their word on something, you could take it to the bank.

Victor Spaniolo

The *Greenville Daily News* normally carried a three-by-ten ad from Meijer's Market, and during our friendship I was able to convince Mr. Meijer to increase his lineage, to the point where he finally bought a full-page ad once a week, for $75. This was fine, except that it was perhaps more than the family could afford. At one of our sessions with the publisher and the accountant, it was discovered that the Meijers owed the *Daily News* more than a thousand dollars. It was the largest receivable on our books.

The publisher wanted to know who was responsible for this huge bill. I had to answer that it was my responsibility. I went to Mr. Meijer with my problem, and with the admonition that we could not accept any more ads until this bill was cleared. Mr. Meijer understood my position, and said he would do the best he could. Business had been increasing. He could see the advantage of the full-page ads. Within six months the bill had been cleaned up, and I was a happy person.

Slowly the store's volume grew, though its profits were still agonizingly low. Fred remembers times when his mother would sleep with enough cash under her head that she almost didn't need a pillow, because they didn't own a safe. Within a couple of years of their opening, by early 1936, Fred and his father had visited a few grocery stores that were trying something new. They were selling their products for cash only, not on credit, and they were able to offer prices that were on the order of 15 percent lower than their competitors' prices. These stores cut back on deliveries, or stopped them altogether, and they became self-serve by shelving their products so customers could get their own rather than have a clerk bustle around the store putting together an order. By the midsummer of 1936, the Meijer Market, now renamed the Thrift Market, stopped making deliveries and began selling groceries on a cash-only basis. There were a few complaints, but people saw significant savings, and the store's traffic continued to expand.

The Meijers began the self-serve revolution in Greenville, a trend that was happening all over the country, by placing a stack of wicker baskets near the front of the store with signs encouraging the customers to pick one up and begin shopping. It worked very well, except that many of the customers walked off with the baskets as well as their order of groceries. Eventually, they put wheeled baskets in the front, and customers caught on. Many Saturdays, after the Friday payday at Ranney's Refrigerator factory, the store did more than $300 in business.

A few entries from Fred's diaries during that period illustrate just how intensely focused he was on the world of business, though there are occasional hints of how he kept his eye on the world beyond Montcalm County as well.

SATURDAY, OCTOBER 31, 1936

J. D. Rockefeller, H. Ford, and J. P. Morgan are all for Landon. We had a good day in the store yesterday. We heard both Roosevelt and Landon give their final speeches tonight. Roosevelt said he hated war and would continue to keep the country safe from war. He also said that the "money class" hated him, but that he welcomed their hate. Landon gave a weak speech. Landon sure is no orator, but Roosevelt is an excellent one.

WEDNESDAY, NOVEMBER 4, 1936

12:30 a.m. Pa and Ma's 24th wedding anniversary. We had a speech by the new Methodist minister today. I thought the speech was a very narrow-minded one. He said all foreigners who tried to stir up trouble or were radical should be sent back, and that he hoped the ship would sink with them on the way back. Pa was fined $10 yesterday by a federal man because he forgot to scratch a wine stamp. That sure is justice, isn't it?

TUESDAY, SEPTEMBER 28, 1937

I took my music lesson today and we had ensemble. I was promoted into the 1st violin section. The clerks had a meeting and went to see Fred Richmond and by talking very plain, persuaded him to close Thursday afternoons. The Social Security man was at the store. I have to fill out 27 blanks. We had never sent in our Social Security before.

[Roosevelt's 1937 plan for Social Security had been challenged in the courts. Many merchants, including the Meijers, thought it would be declared unconstitutional, and did not make provisions for paying the tax. Now they had to begin the process.]

FRIDAY, NOVEMBER 19, 1937

I made more price tags today and painted some signs. Pa and I went to a pancake supper tonight given by Cass St. PTA at Masonic Hall. We are selling Swift milk 64 cents a case below cost. We put on a 4 can limit (5 cents per can). It is sure funny to see how the people try to sneak two batches.

TUESDAY, DECEMBER 14, 1937

I worked in the store on the ad this morning. We are advertising 160 articles in grocery and produce. We are running a 5-column ad in the *Daily News* and a one-page ad in the *Buyers Guide.* Pa and I went to Grand Rapids today to the Veltman Cookie Co. and to Ionia to a flour mill.

SATURDAY, MARCH 12, 1938

Worked in store all day. We took in $448 today. It was an all-time record. Hitler went to Austria today. He now has complete control.

For Fred it was a busy life, focused on the intricacies of maintaining a business where a price difference of a penny could make a significant dent in the family's fortunes for the week. One can see the emergence of his lifelong habit of paying meticulous attention to details while not losing sight of the big picture.

The grocery enterprise encouraged spontaneity and creativity. One day, for example, a peddler came through Greenville with his truck and offered to sell a load of Gold Drop peaches to the store for the excellent price of 45 cents a bushel. He didn't have the peaches with him, but he promised that he would be there on Friday afternoon so that they could sell the fruit on Saturday morning. Taking him at his

Thrift Market, 1937

word, they placed an ad in the Friday night paper offering "Gold Drop peaches in your own container" for 50 cents a bushel.

On Friday night they waited . . . and they waited. No trucker. They waited longer. Still no peach truck. So early that Saturday morning, Fred and Hendrik drove to the market in Grand Rapids to get a load of peaches. By the time they returned to Greenville, well before the store was to open, there stood the peach peddler with his load of Gold Drops.

"By golly," says Fred, "we sold out both those loads between 8 a.m. and noon. That showed us that we could sell peaches, and from then on, our objective was to beat the A&P price on peaches — have them a little riper, ready to can — and we used to sell a hundred bushels to the A&P store's five or ten bushels, once we got rolling. For a while, we were the peach kings of Montcalm County." (*IHOW*, p. 35)

Within two years the business had expanded into another building, becoming an early version of a supermarket in the process. In 1939, while still nineteen years old, Fred became a full partner in the business, an arrangement that formalized what had been happening for some years already: now he shared not only in the work but also in the decision-making process. "My father never did anything without consulting me," he remembers, "and I never did anything without talking to him." It was the beginning of an intense working partnership that was to last another quarter-century.

Marv Peterson

I had just turned sixteen, and had asked Fred for a job after school. My hourly wage was ten cents, which doesn't sound like much, but this was during the Depression, so I was thankful for even that. I reported for work promptly after school, and Fred introduced me to everyone working in the store. After that, he showed me around, which didn't take long because the store was so small. He said he would get me started washing windows.

Fred returned with a bucket of water, a ladder, some rags, and a gallon of ammonia. He showed me where to start. I climbed the ladder and began washing the windows, but soon decided I needed more ammonia. I left the bucket and carefully climbed down the ladder, retrieved the ammonia, and started back up. Halfway up the ladder I slid, and in a split second I was on the floor along with a lot of ammonia, the fumes of which quickly spread throughout the store.

In minutes everyone was outside except for me. I wasn't about to leave and was mopping and wringing vigorously when I felt a hand on my shoulder. It was Fred.

"Marv," he said kindly, "I think we should go outside, open all the doors, and clear out the ammonia fumes." This we did.

I recall worrying about how I would tell my father I got fired in the first hour of the first day of my first job. But I wasn't fired. Neither Fred nor his father said a word about it, except that I could go back in there and finish the job once the fumes had cleared. It was a lesson I've never forgotten. Over the years — after serving in the army, going through college, being in business, and having people work for me — I've tried to hold true to the principle that preserving the dignity of others is the best thing you can do.

What Fred remembers of the incident is that maybe the ladder was a bit shaky, contributing to Marv's unsteadiness. Marv had thought he'd get a serious dressing down for the incident from a family that knew his family socially, and what stuck with him was that there was no criticism. "I've never believed in bawling people out," says Fred. "If they make an honest mistake, you correct it and move on. If they're sincere, and can't do the job, then it's your fault for hiring them."

With their growing enterprise, the Meijer family finally began to experience something approaching prosperity, despite the continuing Depression. They had begun their business in 1934 with an inventory of $338.76. By 1941, Fred and his father counted their inventory at more than $13,000, an increase on the order of 3300 percent in seven years. The profits for that year were a very respectable $7,000. The little family business, it appeared, might be able to add another store to its "one-store chain."

Chapter Three

Lena Rader

Thirty-five miles northeast of Grand Rapids lies the small farming community of Amble. Though some city folks might have called it a dot on the map rather than a bonafide town, it boasted three grocery stores, three churches, a big creamery known throughout the county, and a one-room country school. On one particular day in 1932, the teacher, Miss Willison, had entrusted two of her most dependable students, Lena and Arlene, with going to the creamery four blocks away to fetch the usual two pails of milk for the noon lunch.

It wasn't that two strong seventh-graders couldn't easily carry the pails, but there were railroad tracks to cross. Already this morning two

Amble Creamery, around 1930

freight trains had rumbled through, one headed east to Saginaw, the other west and around Lake Michigan to Chicago. Sometimes the trains hauled lumber, though Michigan's timber industry had pretty much finished off the state's forests by the late 1920s. More often they carried agricultural products: wheat, corn, flour, potatoes, chickens, or livestock being shuttled between farms and cities.

Someone had to get the milk, and sending boys on this unusually warm February day could result in a delay involving snowball fights; or, heaven forbid, they might hop a slow-moving freight car for a ride to the feed mill on the other side of town. In this school there was a general sharing of duties, but usually the boys brought in the firewood and the girls carried the milk.

So Lena and Arlene had been chosen, and they were hurrying back, each one carrying her precious payload of fresh milk, not wanting their classmates to have to wait for lunch on account of them. But there was a problem: a line of freight cars blocked their way. They could hear the big locomotive far up the tracks and see the black smoke billowing from the smokestack, but the train wasn't moving. Shifting their pails nervously from one hand to the other, they contemplated their choices: wait, walk around, or . . . what? Without a word, they both came to the same conclusion. With Lena leading the way, they got down on their knees in the coal-blackened slush, and half pulling and half pushing the milk pails, they crawled underneath the big box car.

When the girls got back to the school, they had not spilled a drop of milk. Miss Willison smiled and announced, "Lunch time," oblivious to the fact that her student count could very well have been diminished by two for the afternoon class.

Lena Elizabeth Selma Rader was born in the family homestead one mile east of Amble on May 14, 1919. She was introduced to the world by Dr. Kelsey, a country doctor and pillar of that community, where a hospital and school still bear his name. Lena's father, George Rader, had come to America from Germany in 1893 at the age of sixteen. He and his older brother, Henry, passed through Ellis Island and headed for Michigan, where an uncle had a job waiting for them in the then-booming lumber business.

Eventually, George was able to buy forty acres in Winfield Town-

Lena's father, George Rader

ship. He cleared the land and built the house where Lena was born, a tall box structure surrounded by a neatly pillared porch. By the time George had built the house, he decided to leave the lumberjack trade and become a farmer. While attending the Emmanuel Lutheran Church in Amble, he met Mary Lutterloh, also of German ancestry, and they were married in 1915.

Winfield was a bustling township, a good place to raise a family in a community that folks were proud of, where neighbors could be counted on. Mary Rader was a hearty example of the strong and determined immigrants who made up the populace, mostly Danish, Norwegian, and German. She kept busy planting her spring garden right up to the time she gave birth because, she said, she was feeling so good.

Lena was the second and final addition to the Rader household; Herman, her brother, preceded her by two years. They got electricity in the home the year Lena was born, and, as Herman recalls, "our telephone was the old wooden wall hand-crank model and we were on a party line, where everyone could listen in on everyone's conversations, and generally did." In fact, Amble had the distinction of being served by the smallest telephone company in the state of Michigan. Hertha Koeppe started it in 1934, and she didn't sell it until 1967, transferring her 97 customers to the Drummond Island telephone company.

Lena (fourth from left) with Amble School classmates

German was the only language spoken in the Rader home, and that presented a challenge when Herman and Lena went to school. Miss Willison did not understand *Guten morgen, Lehrer* ("Good morning, Teacher"). But children learn quickly, and they were not the only ones to show up at school without any knowledge of English. This was a world of immigrants, where children regularly helped their parents negotiate the English-speaking world, and where children were expected to make their way in the language of the New World.

Herman and Lena usually walked the mile to school with neighbor kids. On bad winter days their father would hitch one of the horses to the sleigh and take them in that way. Snowplows were still far in the future for this part of the country.

Lena's birthplace

Lena and her three-legged stool
(Photo courtesy of Bob Strodtbeck)

Life was good growing up on the farm, as Lena remembered it years later. The work was hard but rewarding. There were cows to milk twice a day, starting at five in the morning, with only a kerosene lantern lighting the barn. Lena would often rouse the rooster, who would then make his announcement to the world from his favorite fence post.

"By nine or ten, I was pretty good at milking cows," she recalls. "I had my own three-legged stool, and the minute I sat down, Mutsy, one of the barn cats, would be right there. I got so I could squirt the milk into his mouth from six to eight feet away. Daisy was my favorite cow, and she could always be counted on for giving a full pail. Sometimes one of the cows would put a foot in the bucket, and the milk would then be given to the cats. I remember once, when I was fourteen, my folks had an emergency and I had to milk all fifteen cows by myself."

After breakfast there were animals to feed, eggs to gather, washing, cooking, cleaning, gardening, or canning by mother and daughter. One of the jobs for the day might include washing empty, lily-white 25-pound flour sacks, which they then cut and sewed into curtains, tablecloths, or aprons, a necessary commodity in busy kitchens during that era. Meanwhile, the father and son headed for the fields. There was a fairly common division of labor into men's work and women's work, as on most American farms. But, in fact, they all understood that they were working together toward the same goals. And in a pinch they could all do what was needed.

Herman Rader

My dad and I did the field work. We had two teams of horses: Prince and Barney, and Colonel and Topsy. We never mixed the two teams. Dad was very proud of his horses. He put brass rings on their harnesses, and always kept balm ointment and liniment handy for whenever a cut or a sore needed attention. We didn't get a tractor until I was in high school. It was a sad time for our dad when he had to trade in his horses.

The house was heated by a coal furnace in the basement and a wood stove in the kitchen, on which all the cooking was done. This made it quite uncomfortable during hot summer days. The yard was filled with a riot of flowers: lilacs, goldenrod, iris, corn lilies, peonies, pansies, phlox, sweet Williams, poppies, sunflowers, daffodils, moonflowers, and morning glories.

Lena

In addition to the barn, there was an array of outbuildings: corncrib, granary, chicken coop, pigpen, woodshed, and outside privy. A windmill supplied drinking and cooking water, while a rain barrel provided for the washing needs. The women washed clothes by hand, and this meant heating water in the washtub on top of the stove. Then they rubbed the clothes repeatedly over a ribbed washboard, with suds provided by homemade soap. They wrung the clothes out by hand and hung them outdoors on the clothesline, using the time-honored methods that prevailed all across America before the advent of the washing machine and dryer. In the winter, the long, heavy underwear — "long johns" — would freeze stiff on the outside lines and would bounce up and down like dancers doing a comic ballet. The women ironed the clothes with a heavy metal triangle, a "sad iron," which they heated on top of the stove.

Mother Rader had a large garden, one of the finest in the neighborhood, in which she took great pride. When Lena was eight years old, she asked if she could have her own garden. "Dad prepared a plot next to Mother's," says Lena, "and from then on I had my own garden to take care of."

The family orchard produced Red Haven peaches and a variety of apples, including McIntosh, Northern Spy, and Red Astrachan. While most farmers' wives took their eggs to town to trade with the local grocer, Mom Rader's prized Rhode Island Reds had their own special customers, who would come to the house to buy their eggs. Each year, for two weeks in October, country schools would close for potato harvest, "a potato vacation," since all the harvesting was done by hand. Stewart Myers, who grew up in Grand Rapids but whose aunt was the Amble postmaster, remembers coming up on weekends to pick up potatoes for two cents a bushel.

The coming of cold weather meant it was time to slaughter cattle

Mary Rader

and hogs; the family would then do the butchering by hand. They smoked and salted hams and bacon, and they rendered the lard. The fall harvest from the gardens and orchard filled the cellar to capacity. Besides canned fruits and vegetables, there were bins of potatoes, squash, carrots, cabbage, turnips, beets, and onions. They packed apples in barrels and buried those barrels in straw outside; when dug up in the spring, those apples were delicious. These farmers were thus practicing a cold-storage method now commonly in use (with modern variations) throughout the food industry.

Lena's parents never believed in going into debt. One day in 1929, George Rader called a family meeting to discuss an important matter: there was enough money for either indoor plumbing or a new car, but not for both. Three hands quickly shot up for indoor plumbing. Father got his new car three years later, a new 1932 Model T Ford.

Even with all the farm work, Herman and Lena found plenty of time to play with the neighborhood kids. They would build tunnels in the hay, swim in the creek, and play "Red Rover" or "Kick the Can" after chores in the evening. Lena's friend Connie lived in Muskegon, but she would stay with Lena during the summer and never wanted to go home, even though there were chores to do every day.

Herman Rader
Tamarack Creek ran through the back of our farm and had a couple of good swimming holes. This is where Lena learned to swim. I would hold the back of her overalls and she would dog paddle.

The windmill in the yard was about thirty-five feet high, with a small platform near the top. On lazy summer days the girls would take their lunch to the platform and have a picnic. Another favorite pastime was climbing into the pigpen to ride the pigs, many times ending up in the pig trough or the mud. The highlight of the summer was always the Sand Lake fair and the annual Amble ox-roast celebration. One year Lena won first place in the rolling-pin-throwing contest, though she broke one of her mother's favorite rolling pins in the process.

A bronze statue of Lena riding a pig, in the farm garden of the Meijer Gardens. The actual Rader family windmill is in the background, with the platform near the top. *(Photo courtesy of Bob Strodtbeck)*

When Lena was seven, her parents asked her if she wanted to take piano lessons. The cost was twenty-five cents for half an hour. Her dad promised to buy her a new piano for Christmas if she could learn to play by then. Spurred on by the challenge, she proved to be an apt student and received the piano, which even today graces a spot in her living room. It was probably from this experience that one day her sons, Hank, Doug, and Mark, would be given the same opportunity, though their enthusiasm may have fallen short of their mother's.

The holidays were an especially exciting time. Two weeks before Christmas, Lena's dad would hitch a horse to the stone boat and head for the woods to chop down the Christmas tree he had had his eye on all summer. After he set it up in the parlor, mother, brother, and sister would decorate it with popcorn strings, tinsel, and homemade ornaments. Relatives would come over for Christmas dinner, and there would be nuts, candy canes, homemade fudge, and other gifts to be exchanged.

**Lena playing
her original piano**
*(Photo courtesy of
Bob Strodtbeck)*

Herman Rader

We always had a lot of company, especially on Sunday, because everyone knew Mother always baked pies on Saturday. One summer day a
storm came up while we had company and hailstones the size of mar-
bles filled the yard. Dad said, "If you kids go out and pick up these
hailstones we'll have ice cream." We all ran outside with pots and pans
while Dad got out the hand-cranked ice-cream maker.

When Lena was in the fifth grade she spelled her way up to the fi-
nals, which were held at the county seat in Stanton. There, in front of
the judges and her proud parents, the competition came down to her
and her cousin Ilah. She stumbled on the word "believe," putting the
lone *i* in the wrong place among the three *e*'s. Lena graciously con-
ceded first place to her cousin.

Where she didn't come in second very often was on the playing
field. At school recess and lunchtime there was always a ball game.
The boys would rush outside to choose sides, and by the time Lena got
out there, she was usually already chosen. She was only one of two
girls that the boys allowed to play on their team; she pitched and
played second base. When her school played other schools, she would
often embarrass the boys on the opposing team by striking out the

Lena in 5th grade

side. In high school she played basketball as well, having practiced diligently at the hoop her dad put up inside the barn.

Baseball was the great American pastime, and Amble was known far and wide for its team, the Amble Independents, who played teams as far away as Grand Rapids, and usually won. Stubby Overmire, one of their own, went on to pitch for the Detroit Tigers. With her natural talent — and in another time and place — Lena might have played professional baseball for the Grand Rapids Chicks, whom she went to see every time she had a chance, and whose achievements were portrayed in the movie *A League of Their Own.*

By the time Lena was a teenager, the Rader homestead consisted of 160 acres. The train track ran through their north field, and the train whistle could be heard several times a day. An occasional car would go by on M-46, the main artery between Lakeview to the east and Howard City to the west. But things were normally peaceful — except for one Saturday afternoon. That day bank robbers tried to knock over the Amble bank. The teller, Viola Beckley, however, had other ideas: she threw an inkwell through the front plate-glass window, shattering it and alerting the townspeople. The would-be robbers dashed out the front door into their waiting car and sped away, only to be apprehended a few miles down the road.

Amble School, 1926. Lena is in the second row, third from left (with bow); Herman is in the front row, fourth from left; Miss Willison is in the center of the third row (with glasses).

Growing up on a farm was the American dream personified. Teenagers always had something to look forward to: ball games during the week, square dances at the Grange Hall in Six Lakes, a double-feature movie at the Roxy Theater in Howard City on Saturday nights, and church functions on Sunday. The Raders attended the Lutheran Church in Amble, where Lena played the piano and organ.

Even as the Depression began to tighten its grip on the country, there was still an abundance on the table in the Rader household. But the family did lose its savings at a bank in Lakeview when it was forced to close. George Rader was on the bank board at the time and refused to withdraw his money, even though he knew there was a good possibility that the bank could fail.

Meanwhile, just twenty miles away, the Meijer family was on the verge of losing everything. This was the point at which Hendrik Meijer, in desperation, had decided to go into the grocery business.

Lena graduated in 1937 from Lakeview High School, having left behind her beloved country school and Miss Willison after the eighth

Lena's Lakeview High School graduation picture, 1937

grade. Since there were no buses, she rode to Lakeview with a neighbor who worked in town. After graduation, she contemplated becoming a kindergarten teacher and did, in fact, enroll at Central Michigan College in Mount Pleasant. But she changed her mind at the last minute to accept an offer from a Lakeview bank, where she worked for the next few years as a bookkeeper and teller. These were the years when America was being entertained by Glen Miller and Benny Goodman. For ten cents, you could watch Cary Grant, Katharine Hepburn, Ginger Rogers, Fred Astaire, and Humphrey Bogart on the silver screen. The average yearly income was $1,725; life expectancy was 62.9 years; and Hitler was overrunning Europe.

Then came a phone call that would change everything for Lena. "It was a Friday night," she recalls, "and we had just finished supper. The day had been unusually hot. I was helping Mother bake some huckleberry pies for Sunday dinner when the phone rang.

"I picked up the phone and said hello. A voice with a heavy Dutch accent answered: 'Dis is Henry Meijer and I vould like to talk to Lena Rader.' 'This is she,' I replied. 'Hi, Lena, ve own a grocery store in Greenville, the Thrift Market, and vould like to hire you to verk for us,' he said. 'Mr. Meijer,' I replied, 'I have never met you. How did you get my name?' 'Vell, two of your friends verk here, and they said you are a good verker. Could you start Monday?' 'Monday! That's April Fool's day!' I said. 'Vell, I never tought about dat, but dis is no April Fool's joke. See you Monday?' "

Even though they had never met, and though the terms of employment were never discussed during that brief initial phone conversa-

Lena, her father, mother, and brother

tion, Lena accepted. She would be leaving the farm and moving to the city and a whole new way of life.

Lena reported for work the following Monday. Hendrik introduced her to Gezina and Fred and the other store employees, Max Guernsey, Fred Bond, Al Waldorf, Edna Klifford, Einer Jorgensen, Muriel Wise, and the two friends who had recommended her, Mary Mulick and Phyllis Kraft. She learned that her pay was to be twelve dollars a week.

Muriel Wise

When I started working for Meijer, the normal workweek was 54 hours and no one thought of taking breaks. Over the years, the workweek hours kept getting lowered, 52, 50, 48, 44, and finally 40. I remember Lena's first day on the job, and we hit it right off. She has always been like a sister to me. Success never changed her.

Because of her experience at the bank, Lena's first assignment was to help straighten out the books, a necessary but unwelcome task in a business where customers were the first priority, and buying and merchandising were more exciting. The first week on the job, she also learned to run one of the three cash registers during busy times, especially on Friday and Saturday, when all the farmers came to town to do their weekly shopping and trading of farm goods.

Lena made the transition from country mouse to city mouse easily. Since she didn't have a car, she roomed at Lampson's boarding house during the week, within walking distance of the store. The daily price for the room and three meals a day was one dollar. "The meals were as good as I had at home," she recalls. "Fresh bread was baked every day." On Saturday after work, Herman would pick her up so she could spend Sundays with the family, and then he would return her to the store on Monday.

Lena enjoyed the companionship of her fellow employees, as well as the other female boarders at Lampson's, who, like her, had found employment in town. During hot summer days after work, they would sometimes go down to the lake for a swim. One New Year's Eve she went with a bunch of friends to a party out of town. It rained and the road was a glare of ice when they started out. "We had to crawl all the way back to town," she recalls. "I got back to Lampson's at 5:00 a.m., and had to be at the store for inventory at 7:00. It was a long day."

Fred Meijer

Lena was a good worker and popular with the customers. We had one customer who was really hard on everyone in the store — rough, gruff, demanding, and always complaining. He would come in, get his cart full of groceries, and wait until Lena was about to take her lunch break. Then he would want her to reopen her lane for him. He would then become Mr. Nice Guy. She was the only one who could handle this particular customer.

After six months, her wages were increased to thirteen dollars a week. But the owner of one of the local hardware stores was offering her fifteen. Fred heard about it and went to his father, who suggested that they match it.

"We can't do that," Fred protested. "If we give her a raise, we'll have to give the other five cashiers one too, and that's twelve dollars more a week."

"So, what's the problem?" asked Hendrik.

"Well, I don't think she's worth it," answered Fred.

"We had just survived the Depression by the skin of our teeth," Fred now recalls, "and were still having a hard time paying our bills. I was making what I thought was a sound business decision. My dad didn't see it that way, and he was right."

Lena worked at the store for four and a half years before she and Fred became engaged. Because the owners didn't take wages, they simply got in touch with the head bookkeeper, Harry Hoy, when they needed money. One day, Fred took out an amount that Harry thought was suspiciously large. When Lena came in to work the next day, Harry asked to see her finger. "I knew it!" he said, smiling at the diamond he saw there.

Chapter Four

An Unlikely Leader

Creativity is a learning process where the teacher and pupil
are located in the same person.

— Arthur Koestler

There was a quality of grace and humanity, within which
the relentless determination to succeed found a dignifying
frame, and which inspired love in others.

— Adam Nicolson, writing about Lord Nelson
(*Seize the Fire*, p. 153)

The Meijer family bought property, a closed-down automobile
showroom, for a second store in nearby Cedar Springs, together with an adjacent lot, which would provide ample room
for parking. It was to be run by Johanna, who had graduated from the
University of Michigan and was teaching school up north in Mount
Pleasant. Now, though, she was excited by the prospect of rejoining
the family business and helping to expand it. They were planning to
take possession in November, and open the store soon thereafter. It
was a time of optimism for the family, despite ominous signs of a wid-
ening war in Europe.

"My mother was radical as heck," says Fred. "She carried it too far.
Because Stalin's name was associated with the Union of Soviet Social-

ist Republics, and she admired Socialists, she believed their slogans and propaganda, and she couldn't see what a terrible man Stalin was." It was a blind spot shared by many people on the political left in America, including the American writers Richard Wright and Arthur Koestler, together with Frenchman Andre Gide, Briton Stephen Spender, and Italian Ignazio Silone, all of whom recounted their political journeys in *The God That Failed.*

"She could certainly understand how bad Hitler was," Fred went on, "partly because he threw three of her brothers and a nephew into the prison at s'Hertogenbosch. But in those years she couldn't see what a murderer Stalin was."

Fred's twenty-second birthday came on a Sunday, December 7, 1941. "I was lying on my stomach in the sitting room. It was a nice warm day in December. The sun was coming in the plate-glass windows that my dad had put into the house, and I was listening to music when the news came." (*IHOW,* p. 50) It marked the end of pleasant birthday thoughts, and shattered the Sunday calm.

JAPAN BOMBS PEARL HARBOR, OTHER PACIFIC BASES; CONGRESS DECLARES WAR

2000 Dead, Many Wounded; 20 Warships Knocked Out

Japanese planes had attacked Pearl Harbor in a deadly morning raid. Two waves of bombers, more than 300 planes that had been launched from distant aircraft carriers, attacked the sleeping Pacific Fleet. The firestorm wrecked battleships and destroyers beyond repair, and destroyed nearly all of the available planes. More than two thousand soldiers lost their lives. Since Japan was allied with Hitler's forces in Europe, it meant that all of America's attempts to stay out of this European war were now at an end.

It looked as if the family plans would also have to be put on hold. Despite his parents' earlier pacifism, despite his own doubts about what a war could accomplish, Fred was determined to join the army and fight with the Allies. His parents' homeland was occupied by Nazis, a couple of his uncles had been imprisoned for their resistance, and the family was by now convinced of the war's necessity. The Meijer Thrift Market expansion would have to wait.

It was a scene enacted all across America in the months after Pearl Harbor. Draft buses would come through small towns gathering potential conscripts from every walk of life. Packed together in pursuit of a common purpose, these boys and men would be driven to an induction center in a large city, and thus would begin their military life. Dozens of World War II movies begin with just such a scene. There's always confusion; there's always the loud trombone voice of a sergeant seeking to straighten out the stragglers; and there's always the swearing in at the end of the long day, with a line of recruits joining the U.S. Army.

But that's not quite how it turned out for Fred. He took the bus out of Greenville all right, heading out on the long ride to Detroit. But once he arrived, things did not go smoothly. Although he had always considered himself perfectly healthy, he had long suffered the mild inconvenience of a small hernia. In fact, he had tried to enlist in the Army, the Navy, and the Army Air Corps earlier that year — before Pearl Harbor — and was rejected because of the hernia on those occasions. Now, though, he figured that the rules might have changed, because now there was a full-scale war. There was talk about the danger of further bombing raids by the Japanese on the U.S. mainland, even on Michigan (because of the auto industry). Surely the Army needed everyone it could get.

Furthermore, Fred spent his days driving a truck all over the Grand Rapids area, rolling large barrels of vinegar onto the truck, lifting hundred-pound sacks of sugar, handling bushels of fruit. Anyone who saw him would have thought he was perfectly fit to serve in the military, and that's certainly how he saw himself. But Fred was turned down in Detroit and sent home. After that first attempt, he was drafted for another bus trip; but the second journey to Detroit was no more effective than the first. Yet another doctor sent him home on account of the hernia.

The first Meijer truck, with Fred, an unidentified employee, and Marv Peterson

Fred kept getting draft notices. Now there were rumors that the army was willing to arrange for corrective surgery. The fourth time he got on the G.I. bus, the driver recognized him and put him in charge of orienting the newcomers. It was a job that involved keeping the rowdiness to a minimum. There had been occasional trouble with drinking, but Fred managed to keep the bus reasonably quiet on the trip across the state. And this time when he got to the induction center, he thought he was in for sure. For a few minutes, at least, it looked that way; no one said a thing about his hernia, and he was told to go stand with the inductees in another room. He had just a few extra minutes to call home and tell the family that he was finally in the Army. And then a familiar face showed up, a former Diamond Crystal salt salesman named Walt Barr, by this time an officer, who knew Fred from the store in Greenville. He also knew about the previous visits to the center — and about the hernia.

"What are you doing here?" he asked. "You've been turned down quite a few times already, because of that hernia, haven't you?"

"They didn't find the hernia this time," said Fred. Walt was having none of it. He marched Fred over to another doctor and showed him the papers already on file for this seven-time-rejected recruit. The new doctor never even bothered to examine him. He told Fred in no uncertain terms that he was out.

And that was the end of Fred's military service. He had been in the U.S. Army for about an hour. In one sense his rejection was a relief, making his options for the future clearer than they had been. But it

Fred at his desk preparing a weekly ad

was not an easy rejection for him to endure. His friend Dan Meed had been killed in action, and Fred felt some twinges of regret that, even though he looked and felt able-bodied, he was not going to be able to join in the great military enterprise of his generation. He called home again and told his father about the new turn of events. Now it was one more trip on the bus, this time to rejoin the family business and see where it might lead him.

Fred often says that he would probably have been a history teacher if he had not gone into the grocery business. When he graduated from high school, his sister, Johanna, was still studying at the University of Michigan, and he might have considered going there as well. But that year was 1937, the Great Depression had not lifted, and he was needed in the family business. So he did not go to college. Always inquisitive, with a nearly flawless memory and a tireless determination to learn with or without a classroom, he educated himself in the ways of business and the world at the same time. The years he spent building the business with his father provided invaluable lessons for him.

Harvey Lemmen, *Former Meijer president*
Maybe he didn't go to college, but Fred always had a professor right by his elbow.

More than forty years after his father's death, Fred seldom went a day without talking about Hendrik with reverence and admiration, while fully recognizing that life with Hendrik was not always easy. Once, complaining to his father about an aching stomach, Fred said he was worried that he might be getting ulcers. Hendrik had an instant comeback: "You're supposed to give ulcers, not get them." Yeah, thought Fred, you give them — I get them. Yet, despite the occasional disagreements, they were not only father and son, they were full partners for the thirty years they worked together, and they were best friends. "My father and I would argue and fight," he says, "but when we got done, we always had a meeting of the minds."

Roger Horling

I was loading trucks one day when Fred and his father dropped by. Mr. Meijer started talking to me while I kept on working. Finally he looked at me, and in his Dutch accent said, "Roger, who pays your vages?"

"You do, Mr. Meijer," I replied. "Vell den, ven I vant you to stop and talk, it's okay to stop and talk."

Fred remembers an occasion, early in the history of their first store, when he came home from work to find his father in a huff. "Brother," he told his son, "I just threw out the minister." As it happened, it was the Methodist minister who fell afoul of his father's wrath, and the occasion was fairly straightforward. The Meijers were not church members, but they gave a yearly donation, an equal amount, to both the Congregational and the Methodist churches in Greenville. That particular year, though, the Congregational church had suffered a fire that destroyed much of its sanctuary, and under those circumstances Hendrik gave a larger sum of money to that church. The minute the Methodist minister heard about it, he came over to the house, hoping to get the same amount for his flock.

"You said you were going to treat us both equally," said this pastor, in a smooth voice with years of oratorical experience behind it. "Are you going back on your word?"

At that, Hendrik showed him the door. He took his word seriously, and he didn't appreciate having someone act as if he had gone back on it.

Hendrik was somewhat self-conscious about his Dutch accent as well as his occasional outbursts of frustration, so from an early age he encouraged the even-tempered Fred to serve as spokesman for the business. This practice gave the young man a maturity beyond his years, but he nonetheless learned constantly from his father.

Harvey Lemmen

Fred and his dad shared an office, visited the stores together, and were with one another all the time, or so it seemed. Hendrik's title was president and Fred was general manager, but Hendrik had for years empowered Fred to make most of the big decisions. Their relationship was almost seamless. Hendrik's experiences in life covered two continents, and he had a great understanding of business and people. I think Fred inherited some of his teaching and coaching skills from his father.

Max Guernsey

Whenever Fred wanted to try something new or different — which was often — he would talk it over with his dad. Sometimes Hendrik wouldn't be too keen on an idea, at which times he would counsel Fred and then let him do it anyway. "How else is he going to learn?" I heard him say more than once. "If it doesn't work, he won't make that mistake again." Even though Hendrik had only a third-grade education on paper, he had a Ph.D. when it came to real-world smarts.

Pam Kleibusch

The relationship between Fred and his father was phenomenal. Whenever you saw one, you saw the other. They even shared the same office. Fred had more respect for his parents than anyone I've ever known.

Pam Kleibusch has worked with four generations of the Meijer family. She started her career as a teenager, as assistant to Fred and his father, and celebrated her fiftieth anniversary at Meijer in 2008.

While Fred had been riding the bus back and forth to Detroit, trying vainly to get himself into uniform, his father continued to work on plans to open a second store. And he didn't give up easily. But if Fred was determined to join the Army, they'd need to make some changes. During her college years, Johanna had continued to work with the business whenever she could. Now Hendrik thought it might be wise to ask her to quit her teaching job in Mount Pleasant and come back to Greenville. Hendrik wrote a description of the property to his daughter: "The building is 60 by 90 feet and we have to make some changes and buy a house in back of it for $1200 and that solves the parking problem. . . . We looked it over again yesterday and it does not look bad. . . . Should you come home a week from tomorrow, we shall show you what it is all about. . . . Providing we go through with it."

She could then run the new store in Cedar Springs when it opened, while Fred went off to war. Johanna agreed, and she came back home at the end of the school year. But Johanna had more trouble than Fred did getting along with her sometimes hot-tempered father, so it was in some ways appropriate that she was going to manage the new store in Cedar Springs, where she would not be working daily in close contact with Hendrik.

But the Cedar Springs store seemed to be taking forever to complete. The store in Greenville, newly named "Meijer's Thrift Super Market," was doing quite well now, drawing customers from nearby towns and regularly selling more than a thousand dollars' worth of groceries on Saturdays. Its operations had been expanded and streamlined several times.

Lena Rader was a new employee in Greenville. She spent most of her fifty-four-hour workweek at the cash register, and she remembers, for example, that the Mexican migrant workers came in very late on Friday or Saturday evening. They had worked all week and had no other time to shop. The crowds were large, and the store was busy. Employees did not have any morning or afternoon breaks, just an hour at lunch.

Later Lena became the company bookkeeper, a person the company desperately needed. Until Lena took over the function, Fred or Hendrik would simply drive a nail in the wall behind the cash register, and they would impale a bill on the nail. If they owed money to twenty suppliers, there would be twenty nails with bills hanging on them; when they paid the bill, they threw the piece of paper away. It was a jury-rigged system, and it was greatly improved when Lena brought her orderly mind, together with her high-school training, into the process.

Meanwhile Fred, despite his youth, was gaining in stature, though he may not have been quite aware of it. He recalls with some embarrassment an example of a lost opportunity for growth. There were three black families living in Greenville, all customers at the Thrift Market. The men in the families had earlier been customers of Hendrik's barbershop; they knew him as a man who treated people well, regardless of race or social class, and they knew that a barber who welcomed black customers would behave the same way when he

Lena at her bookkeeping

became a grocer. One day one of the black customers asked Fred if he would be a pallbearer at a family funeral. Stymied by this request — not quite knowing what to think of it — he declined. Later he told his father about it.

"That was a sign of respect for you, Fred," said Hendrik. "You should have accepted the honor." It was a lesson Fred kept with him in the years that followed.

Rob Ver Heulen

I've observed that when Fred meets someone for the first time, he usually begins the conversation with a question about that person. Eventually, this leads him to asking the question, "What can Meijer do better?" Given that people like to be asked for their opinions, folks quickly become comfortable and talkative with him. I've often wondered if he does this consciously or if it's just because of his genuine interest in people.

The Meijer store was the biggest grocery store in Greenville now, and they were constantly tinkering with new ideas. They had expanded and remodeled their store several times, and they employed a full-time carpenter to help with their projects. Fred remembers that his father gave him the responsibility of overseeing Mr. Guernsey's work, even though Fred was not quite twenty years old, and Mr. Guernsey had been a working man for longer than that. The first time Fred gave the carpenter an assignment, his father listened carefully. When Fred was done, Hendrik took him aside.

"Fred," he said, "you told Mr. Guernsey how to do it, and how long it would take. Then you laid out three other jobs for him to do later. Now let me tell you this: In the first place, you told him how to do it. He's forgotten more about carpentry than you will ever learn. Don't tell him how to do it! Ask him if he knows how to do what you agree on, and if he understands it, that's good enough.

"Number two: you told him it will take three hours. What if it takes four? Then he feels he's disappointed you. What if he's done in two hours? Then you look silly. Don't tell him how long it takes. He's a conscientious man: he will do it well and as fast as he can. Trust him.

"Number three: You gave him three jobs to do beyond this one. Don't do that. If you do that all the time, Mr. Guernsey will think he's never caught up on his work. He will be frustrated. Give him one extra job, so that when he's done he knows what to do next without asking you. Then, when you know he's on that second job, you can go see him and give him another one."

This was a lesson Fred never forgot. You can call it human psychology or management by objective, but the real meat of the lesson was to understand and respect those who work for you, and to treat them with dignity. It may have been easier to retain these lessons because of

Dennis and Max Guernsey

the close community ties felt by everyone who worked for the growing but still small Meijer Super Market in Greenville.

The family had planned to open its second store in December 1941. The coming of war slowed down the process, along with complications in obtaining construction materials and doing some of the work necessary to open a new supermarket. But the war also brought a new sense of purpose and prosperity to the region. Factories were retooling for the war effort, property values were rising, and, because so many young men were in the military, jobs were easier to come by. There was a palpable energy in the atmosphere. But there were also shortages, with price controls soon to come. The Cedar Springs store finally opened its doors in the spring of 1942.

"During the war," Fred recalls, "there was very little male help. Johanna ran the Cedar Springs store for four years, and worked very hard at it, doing a lot of the manual labor herself. She had almost no manpower. She had men in the meat department, and I think she had a man in produce, but she ran the rest of the store with part-timers." It was a time when employers had to show a great deal of creativity in their relationships with employees. In a small town, of course, your employees were also your neighbors and friends, so the relationships often resembled those in an extended family, a feeling the corporation tried strenuously to keep alive as it grew in size and complexity. The sense of camaraderie and family loyalty remained with many of these employees for years afterward.

Max Guernsey

I started working for Meijer in May 1940. I was thirteen at the time, and my job was helping my dad, who did all of the carpentry and handyman work. I made fifteen cents an hour, but Fred had to give my wages to my father until I turned fourteen in October of that year. I was making fifty cents an hour by the time I left for the service in 1944.

Hendrik gave me a five-dollar bill for a going-away present, which was a lot of money back then. After my discharge, I returned to Meijer and remained there until I retired forty-two years later. . . . In all those years, I never had to ask for a raise. Hendrik and Fred were always more than fair when it came to paying an honest wage.

It was the right time, in many ways, to extend the cost-cutting Thrift Market approach to selling food. And by now Hendrik and Fred were very accomplished at finding the best deals available, at cutting a few pennies from the cost of everything from sugar to meat to peaches to vinegar. Having a second outlet meant that they could buy groceries in greater volume and thus get better prices. That meant they could offer better prices to the public, further expanding their customer base. Without being entirely conscious of the fact until years later, Fred and Hendrik were pioneers in a new way of selling and distributing food that was sweeping the nation in the years during and just after World War II. No longer was it possible or practical for every small neighborhood to have its own mom-and-pop store just down the street. The newly emerging supermarkets, with their persistent emphasis on low prices without sacrificing quality, were the beginning of a powerful revolution in the way Americans bought and consumed their food.

"I'll accept credit for being a pioneer," says Fred, "as long as everyone understands that being a pioneer is simply having the courage and willingness to learn as you go."

For the rest of the war years, the two small supermarkets continued to thrive, though Cedar Springs did not have quite the population base of Greenville, and hence had a correspondingly smaller trade. When he wasn't working long hours in the store — often as much as twelve hours a day for seven days a week — Fred occupied himself with community activities. He continued to play violin and sing in community musical groups, and he joined the Rotary Club.

"The first thing I did with the Cedar Springs Rotary Club," he says, "was to go around with Carl Denton and sell war bonds." The ravages of war were being felt everywhere, and those men who were not serving in uniform felt a special determination to help in whatever way they could.

Despite his busy schedule, Fred also enjoyed dancing. His early experiences in high school had been embarrassing, and he was convinced that he had no natural talent for it. But he kept trying, to the point where he became comfortable if not proficient on the dance floor. Often, when he wanted to ask a girl for a date, he'd suggest that they go to a dance. "Now this may not have been fair of me," he says, "but if a girl said she didn't dance, I figured she was probably too religious for me anyway. I never thought that she might have felt as awkward as I did about it." He did not pursue the nondancers.

Fred was engaged for several years to a young woman from Belding; but he got the distinct impression that her parents didn't think a mere grocer with a high school education would fit into her professional family. On the principle that you don't just marry a wife, you also marry her family, he eventually broke off the relationship and began dating again. One evening there was going to be a dance in Edmore, sponsored by the Junior Farm Bureau. A couple of the cashiers at the Meijer store were planning to go, and they suggested to Lena that she should ask Fred. "It wasn't my idea," Lena says, but she did ask him if he'd be interested.

Fred initially turned her down, thinking it might not be a good idea to go dancing with an employee. Then he thought about it for a few minutes. He'd known and liked Lena for quite a while. In addition, she was asking him to a dance, a pretty clear sign of compatibility, as he saw it. And she had a winning smile into the bargain. He went back to her a few minutes later and said, "I think I'd like to go to that dance" (*Greenville Daily News,* Dec. 10, 2007). Before going, he also decided in his own mind that if things went well, if the two of them got along, he'd ask her to marry him. Not right away, but eventually.

As Fred and Lena remember it more than sixty years later, the dance went well, and their courtship continued under the watchful eyes and frequent grins of their fellow workers.

First, though, Fred had a relatively minor personal hurdle to negotiate. He decided that it was time to get his hernia repaired. It had been a minor irritant for years now, a slight impediment to his otherwise robust approach to life. He made arrangements with a Dr. Bird, a prominent local surgeon, and trundled himself off to the rambling old mansion that was the Greenville Hospital. The surgery went well, but that night, while Fred was still recuperating in his hospital bed, Hendrik had a vivid dream. He dreamt that there was a huge fire in the hospital, with lurid flames bursting upward into the night sky, and that Fred had died in the conflagration. Although there was no fire, and Fred was fine, the dream re-energized Hendrik in one of his earlier concerns.

As a prominent local merchant, Hendrik now sat on the board of directors of the hospital, and he brought up the issue of fireproofing at the next meeting. The general consensus on the board was that the hospital could not afford it.

"No," said Hendrik, "you can't afford what you have now." He never mentioned his nightmare at the board meeting, but it was a dream that was to bear significant fruit for the hospital in the years to come.

Fred recovered quickly and was soon back to work, to courtship — and to plans for a third Meijer Supermarket. The new one was to be built on land the family had recently purchased in Ionia, a few miles south of Greenville. World War II had come to an end in August 1945, with the dropping of atomic bombs on Hiroshima and Nagasaki. The troops were returning home in large numbers, and the nation now began to enjoy the delicious prospect of peace and plenty. It was a time of new beginnings all over America.

On January 5, 1946, Fred and Lena were married in a modest ceremony at her parents' house in Amble. Members of the two families assembled, the minister from Lena's Lutheran church officiated, and everyone enjoyed the simple yet beautiful wedding. The couple planned to spend their honeymoon in Florida, a respite from the frigid Michigan winter.

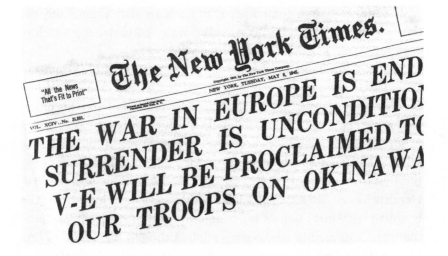

Chapter Five

Lena Meijer

F red and Lena were married during the first postwar year, a
time when GIs were returning home, marrying in record numbers, and incubating a new generation of children, soon to be
known as "Baby Boomers." The two honeymooners headed south,
with planned stops in Lansing, Michigan; Findlay and Cincinnati,
Ohio; and Memphis, Tennessee. Fred had a list of stores he just knew
Lena would want to see along the way.

In 1947, baseball's color barrier was broken when Jackie Robinson
became the first African-American to play in the major leagues. In
1948, Truman defeated Dewey for the presidency. Meanwhile, the
Meijer family was busier than ever, running a chain of three stores,
two of which were new. While Hendrik and Gezina were visiting her
parents in Europe, Lena got to make the decision on what color to
paint the front of the Greenville store.

SUNDAY, JUNE 30, 1948

Dad! Lena wanted the front all red and you weren't here to defend
your yellow, so it's all red now. It looks good, too. Lena says so.
(Excerpt from a letter by Fred to Hendrik)

Greenville had been and was their home, and it was just assumed
that it would always be. However, they couldn't help but notice that

exciting things were happening in Grand Rapids. All of their suppliers were there, as well as a lot of potential customers. After talking it over, the family decided that Grand Rapids would be where they would have to expand in the future.

In the fall of 1951, the whole Meijer clan — Fred and Lena, Hendrik and Gezina, sister Johanna and husband Don, now both active in the business — began moving to Grand Rapids. Eventually, they all built homes on Meadowfield, a quiet street in the northeast part of the city. During this time the minimum wage was increased to seventy-five cents per hour; frozen TV dinners became a hot new item; Dr. Jonas Salk discovered the polio vaccine; Elvis appeared on the Ed Sullivan show. The Civil Rights Act was passed. Alaska and Hawaii became the forty-ninth and fiftieth states, and the Soviets put the first man in space.

By now Lena was a busy wife, mother, and homemaker. The long hours, hard work, and family values she learned from her parents during those impressionable years on the farm laid the foundation and provided the underpinning for her to help run a thriving grocery enterprise. This changed with the birth of little Hendrik (Hank). She passed the ad layout sheets, paste, and pencils along to others, and replaced them with bottles, diapers, and the joys of parenting.

With resourcefulness and efficiency, she set about organizing the household so that meal times were family times. She patched skinned knees and dried teary eyes, all with the calming reassurance that tomorrow would be another day. Then came Little League, band recitals, and numerous school functions characteristic of three growing, energetic boys. This now silent business partner also found time to attend an ever-growing number of store openings, company events, and business functions.

The Meijer place was where all the neighborhood kids gravitated and were always welcome. As a result, there was never a knock on the door from a policeman, a call from a teacher, or a complaint from a neighbor. It was probably one of the few homes where no one thought of running away, which was commonplace with many adolescents during their growing up years.

There were disappointments and crises to be sure, both from the business side as well as in the family. Several times the financial security of both business and family would be threatened. Over the years, Lena's parents both died, as well as Hendrik and Gezina, whom she had worked with for many years. With the passing of Gezina, the invisible mantle of matriarch of the Meijer family was quietly bestowed on Lena.

Whether it be a CEO from a Fortune 500 company, the President of the United States (she has met five), European royalty, or everyday folks, she treats everyone the same. Her unpretentious manner and infectious smile make a positive lasting impression. Like Will Rogers, she has never met a person she didn't like. Lena's sense of purpose and patience, with no hint of self-importance, were clear to everyone who knew her. Although able to afford being waited on, she did her own shopping, gardening, and housework, all the while driving used cars and personally signing each ice-cream card she gave away.

Rick Zehr

I was managing the Plainfield store. One Saturday, Fred and Lena came into the store so Lena could do her weekly shopping. An hour later I received a call from the service manager informing me that Lena was sitting on a bench in the front of the store with her groceries. I quickly went out there and asked if I could help in any way. "No thanks, Rick," she replied very calmly. "I'm just waiting for Fred."

I waited a few minutes, and it became evident that we had lost Fred. I called my Loss Prevention manager and team leaders and instructed them to start looking for Fred. In a panic, I called the corporate Loss Prevention office and told them our plight. A few minutes later, I received a call from the corporate office. They had found Fred. He had decided on the spur of the moment to go to the office to have a meeting with Hank and Doug, and forgot about the time. The next Saturday, when they came in, Lena said to me, "I want to make sure Fred doesn't leave the store today. Could you put him in your office and lock the door?"

For many years, just before Christmas, Carol Alexander has driven Fred and Lena around to visit special friends: most are elderly and some are shut-ins. They start in Amble and work their way toward Greenville. "It's an all-day affair," she says. "We start filling the car with fruit baskets. We spend about an hour at each home. They are usually waiting to serve us tea, punch and homemade cookies. I'm sure, for some of these folks, the visit is the highlight of the season. Even though this is the busiest time of the year for the company, Fred and Lena have never failed to make these visits."

Earl Holton, *Former Meijer president*
It was a tough decision when we decided the first time to stay open for Thanksgiving. Some of our competitors had already started, and we were getting requests from customers to do the same. This meant, however, that someone had to stock the shelves and run the cash registers. The ads were all set, and people were scheduled to work. Lena told Fred that she wished all the employees could be home with their families. Fred came in and discussed her concerns with me and asked what we should do. I reminded him that this was his company. He then quickly made the decision to remain closed for that year. Even though it was a costly decision, it was more important to Fred to honor Lena's wishes.

Someone once observed that water seeks its own level and that oil and water don't mix. Because of their background, beliefs, and outlook on life in general, the relationship between husband and wife meshed so well that criticism was seldom heard and praise was commonplace, creating a strong family structure that remains today.

Bill Smith

During one of our conversations, I asked Lena if there was anything she was afraid of. Obviously not farm animals, heights, water, moving trains, or all-terrain vehicles, which she rode for the first time when she was in her seventies. No answer, but I could see she was pondering the question. I probed a little further. "What about the time you and Fred had to sign over all your personal possessions as collateral to the bank for a business loan? Weren't you afraid of going broke?" Still no sign of consternation. I wasn't about to give up. "Well, what about the dark, airplanes, black cats, or . . . ?" "Oh yes," she said. "When I was young, we had a mean rooster. He would attack me whenever he got a chance. I used to walk all the way around the house to get to the barn. Yes, I was afraid of that rooster. Until I got older."

Fred, Lena, and friends riding four-wheelers

Chapter Six

Raising a Family

"I had a very profitable honeymoon," says Fred. "How many people on their honeymoon would stop in and see people in the business world that way?" The newlyweds took their time driving south, while stopping at a half dozen places to visit grocery stores and glean new ideas about doing business from what they saw. One of the people they visited on their way south was Bill Albers, a founder of the organization that became the Food Marketing Institute. Albers had been the president of Kroger's, and he had more recently founded his own thriving chain in Cincinnati. He was an example of the kind of merchant Fred wanted to become: he had a vision of his own success, but he also had a strong civic presence and a sense of how to help and encourage others in the business.

More specifically, Albers convinced Fred that if he was going to make a success of the business, especially if the company was thinking of further expansion, they needed to hire only the best people, those who had experience in the business, to run their departments for them. Fred explained what they were doing at the time, but Albers insisted that it was not enough. The apt student caught on very quickly, and as he continued driving south, he started making plans for how the company could develop itself further.

When the newlyweds finally made it to Florida, unfortunately, their knowledge of the Sunshine State was limited. They had arranged to stay on the beach at a resort in Pensacola, on the northern panhandle. By their estimation, it should have been the high season there; instead, they found a cold and rainy beach, a half-deserted resort, and precious little sunshine. They spent their beach time huddled together for warmth, never entering the chilly waters of the Gulf of Mexico.

Upon their return to Greenville, they moved in with Hendrik and Gezina and returned to work in the main store. The only material change in Lena's life was that, like other members of the family, she stopped getting a paycheck: she was now one of the owners, though the rewards must initially have seemed meager, and though she continued to work as before.

In those early years, just after the end of the war, housing was something of a challenge. And it must have seemed a bit cramped living with the older couple. But they didn't stay for long. Before getting married, they had purchased an older house that was in need of renovation. That process took several months, but before too long they had settled into their own place, the former Tucker house on Van Deins Street in Greenville, and they began living life in a more independent setting.

Victor Spaniolo

Fred and Lena became good friends of ours after their marriage, and on occasion we would drive to the Grand Rapids Civic Auditorium to dance to Lawrence Welk. He was not a famous bandleader then, just one of many big bands. But we did have fun.

The newlyweds returned to the ever-changing world of the stores, with a special emphasis on the new store they were to open in Ionia, their third. Construction was well under way on the Ionia store when, in the spring of 1946, a fire broke out in the middle of the night in their first store, lighting up the skies above Greenville and drawing a crowd of gawkers out of their early-morning sleep. "Awakened by a policeman, Hendrik hurried to join the growing crowd of onlookers. It was the wrong time — as if there is ever a right time — for a fire. The back room, which doubled as a warehouse, was piled high with merchandise, including cases that had already been delivered for the new

After the fire

store in Ionia." (*TY,* p. 186) Fred got there as quickly as his father did, and seeing the chance to rescue something from the disaster, he helped break through a brick wall in the rear of the building to save the company's ledgers and account books.

Fortunately their inventory had been insured, though they lost a good deal of money on the building. But the Meijers quickly took steps to repair the damage. No one was killed or injured: the upstairs tenants had all gotten out safely. "It could have been worse," said Hendrik. He may have been thinking of his nightmare about the hospital, but he may also have simply been focusing on what could be done, not what couldn't be undone.

For both Fred and Hendrik, this setback, like many others they were to encounter over the years, seems to have given them extra energy. Rather than pulling their wagons into a circle, which might be the most common response, they kept moving forward. They knew, from experience, that there was a future for them in well-managed grocery stores. A day after the fire, they opened "Meijer's Produce Market," a makeshift structure on property they owned across the street. From there they could see the burnt-out shell of the building Hendrik had built in 1923, together with the five or six additions they had put on in the intervening years. It must have been a sad spectacle. On the day after the fire, they already had a war-surplus Quonset hut delivered to their site. The *Daily News* described activities at the site, and said that Hendrik "would run a close race with army and navy reconstruction battalions famed for their genius at rebuilding bombed out bridges and command posts." (*TY*, p. 188) Fourteen weeks later, the Meijer Super Market was back in business.

That summer the family celebrated its second marriage. Johanna's fiancé was Don Magoon, a former business instructor she had met in Ann Arbor during her college days. Now a captain in the army, he had just returned from his service in occupied Japan. Don and Johanna were married in June 1946. The family was now made up of three couples — all equal partners — who were hoping to live off the proceeds of the family business. It was a risky proposition in some ways, but the local economy was thriving, and by the fall of 1946, the Ionia store opened its doors for business. The site wasn't quite ready, especially the parking lot, which had not yet been paved. Unfortunately, opening day was rainy, and Johanna's new husband, Don, spent nearly the entire day pushing cars out of the mud.

But things were beginning to go well with the three-store chain. Fred made what he saw as necessary changes in the management of the three meat departments, putting to use the advice he had received while on his honeymoon. And now there was at least symmetry between family and business: three stores and three couples, together with the prosperity of an American Midwest coming back to life after a long war. A sense of growth and development was in the air.

After years of dealing with suppliers in Grand Rapids, the family began discussing the possibility of opening stores there. In 1948 the first Meijer Thrift Market went up at 4242 South Division Avenue. The skills the business had honed in a small town transferred very effectively to the city, and the new store prospered. Within four years, two more stores followed, and the company made the decision to move its headquarters to Grand Rapids. A short time later, Fred and Lena made the same move, and by 1956 they had settled into a house on Meadowfield Street, designed by Fred Veltman, an architect cousin of Fred, where they were to live for forty-six years.

In February 1952, Fred was hard at work preparing for the opening of the company's sixth store, its third in Grand Rapids, on the corner of Michigan and Fuller. Lena was at home, expecting their first baby; she had just been told by her doctors that the delivery might have complications, and it should therefore be scheduled as a cesarean section. She was told to show up at the hospital at four o'clock in the afternoon, to prepare for delivery the following day. Just then, Fred ran into a problem at the office. The employee who had been working on the Grand Opening ads suddenly quit her job, with the ads unfinished. Remembering that Lena had helped with ad layouts for many years, he took the project home around three in the afternoon, thinking that they could do it together again, just like in the old days.

"Well, that really didn't go over so well," he recalls. "Lena burst into tears, and her tears were dripping down on the ad paper. I saw that wasn't going to work, so I took all the ads back to the office," where a supervisor named Jack Van Overloop finished them up (*IHOW*, p. 78). Then Fred took Lena to the hospital.

"This supermarket," says Hank, writing about it many years later, "was my exact contemporary — opened the week I was born. I could be melodramatic and call it a large and rather demanding sibling, but my father never neglected me, or my younger brothers, in his passion to nurture the business. My mother had been laying out the week's grocery ad for the *Grand Rapids Press* at a card table in the living room when she felt the first labor pains. Tears streamed down her cheeks as she put aside her pencil, called to my father, and packed for the hospital. (I was born cesarean — two grand openings the same week.)" (*Thin Ice*, p. 286)

If there was any thought that life in Greenville had been busy, it would be nothing like the next ten years leading up to the opening of

The Michigan and Fuller store grand opening, 1952

WE'RE WORKING FOR YOU!!

1. To bring you fine quality food to nourish your family.
2. To bring you the lowest every-day low prices to help you balance your budget.

BIRDSEYE, FROZEN PEAS 2 pkgs. 49c

PHILADELPHIA CREAM CHEESE 3-oz. pkg. 15c

CALIF. GRATED TUNA can 25c

PINK SALMON tall can 55c

"Thrifty" Says:
MEIJER'S ALONE Do This to Help You Save More

↓ ↓ ↓ ↓

Only new merchandise is marked at new price.

MI-CHOICE Oleo 2 lbs. 47c

TREESWEET ORANGE JUICE 46-oz. can 29c

MEIJER'S will NOT scratch out or cover over a lower price, and remark items at a higher price even if costs go up.

Freshness and Flavor for a Dime at MEIJER'S Produce Department

MEATS

ARMOUR'S STAR READY-TO-EAT
SMOKED PICNICS Entirely Cooked 41c lb.

FOX DELUXE TABLE READY
FRYERS lb. 69c
Legs and Thighs 98c lb.

ARMOUR'S DEXTER BRAND
SLICED BACON 1-lb. Tra-Pak 45c

SPARE-RIBS, LEAN, MEATY, lb. 43c

PORK HOCKS lb. 35c
Just the Lean Meaty Portion

PORK LIVER Sliced or Piece 37c

PORK LOIN ROAST Rib End lb. 39c

ARMOUR'S STAR
SLICED DRIED BEEF ¼-lb. pkg. 39c

FOR EXAMPLE
When our buying price goes down 2c we drop our price at once, as always.

BUT
When our buying price goes up 2c we leave the price of the merchandise on the shelves marked to sell at the same old price.

LOOK FOR THESE SAVINGS MARKED WITH RED PRICE TAGS ON SHELVES

SUMMER SQUASH	lb.		10c
BEET GREENS	lb.		10c
RADISHES	3	bunches	10c
GRAPEFRUIT Large	ea.		10c
SPANISH ONIONS	lb.		10c
GREEN PEPPERS	2	for	10c

MIRACLE WHIP Salad Dressing qt. 59c

MEIJER'S BREAKFAST BLEND COFFEE lb. 71c

GULLIVER'S PEAS 2 cans 23c

KOOL-AID 6 PKGS. 25c

JOPPES MILK 3 Qts. 56c

ICE CREAM Qt. 45c

ICE CREAM SMOCKER'S TOPPING 2 for 27c

MULLER'S OVEN-GLO BREAD 20-oz. loaf 16c
A Real Economy Loaf

MULLER'S Home-Made COOKIES 27c pkg. or 30c pkg.

MULLER'S LAYER CAKES LGE. SIZE 53c
Devil's Food With Cocoanut or Golden Layer Covered With Cherry Icing

MEIJER'S SUPER MARKET

STORE LOCATIONS
GREENVILLE 4242 S. DIVISION
IONIA 1645
CEDAR SPRINGS EASTERN

STORE HOURS
GREENVILLE IONIA CEDAR SPRINGS
MONDAY-THURSDAY 8:30 A. M. to 6 P. M.
Fri.-Sat. 8:30 A. M. to 9 P. M.
GRAND RAPIDS EASTERN-DIVISION
9 A. M. to 9 P. M.
SAT.—9 A. M. to 7 P. M.

LILY WHITE FLOUR	KREMEL	THREE LITTLE KITTENS CAT FOOD It's All Fish!	Lipton Tea Bags	ARMOUR'S CORNED BEEF HASH
5 lb. bag 51c	pkg. 7c	8-oz. can 8c	48-Count 55c	43c

the first Thrifty Acres store in 1962. Fred and Lena's second son, Douglas Frederik, was born in 1954, followed by Mark Donald in 1957. During those years, eleven new Meijer supermarkets opened, six in Grand Rapids, two in Muskegon, and one each in Battle Creek, Holland, and Grand Haven. Both families, commercial and biological, were making their way in the world.

The three boys grew up in a lively residential neighborhood that was being rapidly populated with other children about the same age. They were part of the Baby Boom generation, a demographic spike that changed forever the way America saw itself — politically, culturally, and in the world of business. The anecdotes related by the sons and their longtime neighbors, taken together, form a quintessentially middle-American set of family memories.

Bob and Jody Hamilton, *Neighbors*

We were the first to build on Meadowfield in 1953. It was a middle-class neighborhood on the northeast side of Grand Rapids. Fred and Lena built and moved there in 1956. Shortly thereafter, Fred's sister and family and Fred's parents, Hendrik and Gezina Meijer, moved to the same street, all living a few houses from each other. At that time it was almost all young families. The street is only two blocks long, ending in a cul de sac. With no through traffic, there was usually a street game of ball going on all summer. At one time, twenty-one kids lived on the street. It was a busy neighborhood.

Hank and Doug

Halloween on Meadowfield Street: Doug on Fred's lap, top center; Mark on Lena's lap; Hank, left, behind Popeye mask.

The family (from left): Louise, Don, and Johanna Magoon; Hank and Hendrik Meijer; Carol Magoon, Gezina Meijer, and Elbert Magoon; Doug, Fred, Mark, and Lena Meijer.

Jack DeKorne

We moved into our home in 1956, around the same time the Meijer family moved in down the street. Our kids were about the same age as Hank, Doug, and Mark, so they quickly became friends. Almost every evening the boys would be playing ball in the cul de sac in front of our house, with the ball sailing into all the neighbors' yards.

One evening I noticed there was no ball game going on. I asked my sons, and they said, "Mr. Meijer says we can play in their back yard." The next night I went over to investigate, and sure enough, the kids had developed a ball diamond on Fred and Lena's new lawn. The grass was all torn up on the pitching mound and home plate, and well-worn paths were developing on the baselines.

About that time Fred came out of the house. I said, "Fred, I'm sorry for this mess. I'll get the other fathers, and we'll come back and get the lawn repaired."

"That's not necessary," he replied. "I can always get another lawn put in, but we can never replace these kids."

The Meijers' back yard shared a fence with the Kent Country Club. In the summertime, there was the consistent sound of balls clicking off the heads of drivers, along with the shouts of glee or dismay that accompany the game. Now and then a stray golf ball would make its way onto what remained of the lawn/baseball field. On occasion, a baseball would fly the other way, too.

Since Fred was not at all interested in golf, he never made use of the fairways, though he was a member of the Country Club by virtue of owning a home in that location. In wintertime, however, his sons made regular use of the now-deserted open spaces on the other side of their fence. With Fred's help, they built a big triangular stile, a series of steps leading up to the top of their fence and down again onto the snow-covered golf course. They spent many weekend hours sledding down the empty hills and broad curving white expanses. As a teenager, Doug took up golf in a rather serious way; but until that time, the main attraction of the country club was on wintry days.

Jody Hamilton

One day I heard a knock on the door. There stood Hank with a somber look on his face and his piggy bank in his hand. He was about eight or nine years old at the time. He said, "Mrs. Hamilton, I broke your window and I'm here to pay for it." He went on to say that he didn't know why everything happened to him. It was all I could do to keep from laughing. This was a typical action of the Meijer boys. They always took responsibility, even at that age.

Jack DeKorne

In the neighborhood, the three Meijer boys and our four DeKorne sons were part of a group of eleven that were always playing together in their spare time — usually baseball. Our young daughter was the only girl, and she felt like she was being left on the fringe of all the activity. She even asked her mother one time, "When will I become a boy?" But she hung in there.

Fred noticed her outside status, and one time, returning from a trip, called and said he had something for her. It was a brand new genuine leather baseball glove. He said it was just for her, not the boys. She was now accepted as a team player with some stature and importance. That was Fred, thoughtful and considerate regardless of your age or gender.

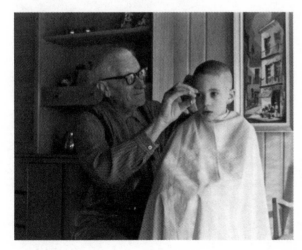

Hendrik cutting
Doug's hair

Doug Meijer

One time, while playing ball in the back yard, I got too close to the person at bat and ended up getting stitches around my eye.

Another time we were at a motel in Petoskey, and I was jumping on the bed. I was warned not to do that, but didn't listen. I fell off, cutting my head open on the radiator. Luckily there was a hospital next door. Maybe I'm the reason my brother Mark went into the ambulance business.

Doug Meijer

Our Grandpa and Grandma Meijer lived a few houses from us. Grandpa, being a former barber, always cut our hair every other Sunday afternoon. Afterwards, Grandma Meijer would give us ice cream, so we usually looked forward to haircut time. Grandpa had just cut our hair the Sunday he passed away. Our dad took it very hard, as he and Grandpa were so close for so many years. It was one of the few times I saw him cry.

Gezina eating an ice-cream cone

After Hendrik's death, Fred's mother, Gezina, became president of the company, and she was later named chairman of the board. Although her positions were largely ceremonial, she continued an active interest in the business, often visiting stores with Fred. She attended board meetings right up until her death in 1978 at the age of 91.

Bob Fields

Even after Fred's mother became confined to a wheelchair, she still liked to visit the stores. I was managing the Kalamazoo Westnedge store, the fifth Thrifty Acres store built. The cafeteria was located on the balcony. Mrs. Meijer liked to go there to eat and to visit with the employees. Since this was before we had an elevator, two of us would carry her up the narrow stairway in her wheelchair. This was not easy, since the stairs had a switchback halfway up. Needless to say, I was always pretty nervous.

Hank Meijer

We were taught early on to respect people of all ages and ethnic backgrounds. The same was true of those with handicaps or special challenges. There were never any ethnic jokes told in our family.

Weekend trips for the growing family were invariably related to the expanding business as well. Hank remembers several occasions when the entire family, out for a Sunday drive, would find themselves at lunchtime inside the very successful Thrifty Acres on Westnedge Avenue in Kalamazoo, getting food for their repast from the vending machines along the west wall of the upstairs cafeteria. "I'm sometimes surprised at how natural it seemed to have lunch that way," he says.

Mark Muller, a Grand Rapids realtor, once told Fred that when his father, Ben, came home from work, and the family was eating dinner together, the one rule was that no business could be discussed. Fred thought such an arrangement very strange: business was often the central topic at Meijer family meals. It was built into every nook and cranny of their life together.

Although business conversations at home sometimes included stories of the hurdles they faced — the competition, the headaches with construction, the increasing costs, the hectic pace — Fred always emphasized the positive side of it as well, saying he thought it was important to "sprinkle in the joy along with the problems. My gosh, we never thought we would have it so good. This is a good business we're in, and we're enjoying it."

In the collective memory of the three sons, the vicissitudes of the commercial world did not intrude much on their sense of play; in fact, they remember their childhood as idyllic. They attended public schools, making friends across a broad cross section of society. In the neighborhood they got to play with a large group of other children, importantly including their Magoon cousins just down the street, and they felt at home wherever they wandered. If there were occasional tensions among the adult members of the family, living in such close proximity, the children never knew about it. It may have been a delicate balancing act for the adults at times, but for the children the world seemed to have been formed primarily for their growth and enjoyment.

Mark Meijer

Dad was usually in a hurry, but Mom had one steady speed that served her very well. Her style of nonverbal communication spoke volumes and kept things toned down in a bustling household with three boys.

Bob Hamilton

Fred used to bring home boxes of unlabeled cans that couldn't be sold at the stores. Lena laughingly remarked one time that it's kind of hard to plan a meal when you don't know what's inside the can. They didn't believe in wasting a thing.

Muriel Wise

Hank, Doug, and Mark have always called their elders Mr. or Mrs. regardless of how well they knew the person. Fred and Lena have always asked folks to call them by their first names. Respect on one hand, humility on the other.

Doug Meijer

Mom was a great cook, making many things from scratch. We ate together as a family almost every night. She ironed our clothes and was always at our school functions, whether it was band, rocket football, or Little League baseball.

Mark Meijer

I believe that my parents' reluctance to spank their children and their ability to administer positive discipline without threats or spankings were methods they acquired from their own parents. In fact, I don't recall Hank, Doug, or myself ever getting spanked. There may have been times we deserved them, but they were never an option in our house. We knew the rules, the consequences, and what was expected of us, and we pretty much respected that.

Doug Meijer

We never got a spanking growing up. It's not that we were perfect, but neither were we rebellious, except one time I for some reason decided to test the limits. I said something I shouldn't have, and Dad said, "If you say that again I'll wash your mouth out with soap." That should have given me an indication it was something serious, but the temptation was just too great, and I said it again.

Hank and Mark just sat there with their mouths open. Dad looked at me and I could see the wheels turning, like he's asking himself, What do I do now? But the challenge had been made and I gave him no choice. Off we went to the bathroom. By now I wished I hadn't said what I did, and knew he was wishing something similar.

I think all I really got was the smell of Lava soap as it passed beneath my nose, but that was enough. I never tried that again.

Doug Meijer

One afternoon Hank, Mark, and I came into the house, and Mom was standing in the kitchen next to a half-eaten package of Oreo cookies. "Who ate the cookies?" she asked. We all looked at each other. I knew I hadn't, so it must have been Hank or Mark, but they too proclaimed their innocence. "If you won't tell me who got in the cookies," said Mom, "you can all go sit until someone confesses." I was not happy with whatever brother was the guilty party, having to sit while the neighbor kids were out playing ball. There we all sat, staring at each other.

Finally, Dad got home, and Mom told him about the cookies. He started to laugh. "I stopped home at noon. I'm the one who ate them."

Larry Levin

Doug Meijer and I are the same age and grew up together. His house was the only one of our group that always had plenty of food in the fridge, and we would all head there after school. We'd walk in, greet Lena — and Fred if he was home — and head straight for the kitchen. It was always bonus time around the holidays. Since Fred and Lena had lots of friends who had come from other countries, there were always plenty of homemade treats from around the world that had to be eaten up. We were happy to accept that responsibility.

Bob Hamilton

We always had a key to Fred and Lena's house in case something happened while they were gone. One time, in the middle of the night while they were away, their alarm went off. I went over there and it wasn't long before the police arrived. After determining it was a false alarm, one of the officers said to me, "The people living here spell their name the same way as the ones who own the stores." I told him they were one and the same. Surprised, he declared, "They live in this neighborhood?"

I tried not to laugh, and I asked, "What's wrong with this neighborhood? I live here." He was embarrassed because he had assumed, like most people, that Fred and Lena lived in a big house in an affluent suburb or gated community.

Hank Meijer

Most people today wouldn't even consider driving without wearing their seat belts, but that wasn't always the case. When the first cars

The Meijer family in 1964

with seat belts arrived on the market, many people thought the belts were cumbersome nuisances, and they only buckled them around the waist, if at all. You can bet our parents embraced them the moment they arrived, and we all wore them at all times. The only exceptions were when Mark, Doug, and I would lie down in the back of the station wagon to sleep as we traveled through the night. Even that's a little scary when I think about it now.

One summer vacation that Fred especially loved was a week they spent on a dude ranch in Colorado. He loved riding the horses, those lively muscular reminders of his farming childhood, and watching the rest of the family try them out as well. He also loved the stunning scenery, the crisp bright mountaintops and endless shadowy valleys. He often describes such a landscape using the Dutch word for something intensely beautiful, *skitterend*. But most of all he loved the opportunity to meet one of the summertime ranch hands: their guide that summer turned out to be the son of Ezio Pinza, the famous Italian singer. Fred had long admired Pinza the elder, one of the most illustrious operatic basses

Fred on a Colorado dude ranch

Mark, Doug, and Hank

of the early twentieth century, who, after his retirement from opera, went on to a glamorous career on Broadway and in films. Fred thought it was delightful to meet the son on a dude ranch some years after the well-known father had died.

Mark Meijer

Mom and Dad always had an appreciation for music, and encouraged and exposed us to a wide variety, including opera. Mom played the piano, organ, trumpet, and cornet. Dad sang in the Schubert Choir for many years, and learned to play the violin at an early age.

Hank, Doug, and I took piano lessons for two years, which was tough when there was a ballgame going on outside. Doug and I played in the high school band. He played the trumpet, trombone, and French horn, while I was a drummer. I'm surprised no one in the family ever complained during our jam sessions in the basement.

Mark Meijer

Dad always stopped at a new store or a potential supplier when we took our family trips, and we'd often make these visits with him. We visited strawberry farms in California, meat-packing plants in Iowa, and canning and potato-chip factories in Ohio, among other destinations. We all received quite an education when we made these stops.

Once, on our way to California, we had a four-hour stopover in Las Vegas. Dad wanted to visit a new store there, so he rented the cheapest car he could find: a Corvair with no air conditioning. Suffice it to say it was hot in Las Vegas that day, and all five of us were packed into that little Corvair and sweating up a storm going who-knows-where.

On our return to the airport, he bought all of us ice-cream cones. That proved to be the second mistake. The ice cream melted faster than we could eat it, and we were a sorry sight when we finally boarded the next flight. Nevertheless, we were glad to get into that air-conditioned plane.

Mark Meijer

I began working at the store on Alpine Avenue after school and on Saturdays when I was about twelve years old. Dad started me at fifty cents an hour. I was assigned to the sporting goods department, an awkward fit for me because hunting, fishing, and organized sports in general were not my thing. George Boyer, the department manager at the time, eased the transition for me. George was a great teacher who had a very special way with people, and many customers shopped at the Alpine store because of him.

Hank, Mark, and Doug as teenagers, with their grandmother and parents

Dad stopped by one day, as he often did, to see how things were going. George told him that I was learning fast and doing the same things as the other employees, and that I should be paid the same. That huge increase in pay, up to what the others were making, was the largest percentage pay raise I ever received.

As the boys grew older, they all developed a keen interest in skiing, perhaps an outgrowth of their sledding adventures at the Kent Country Club. Up to that point, Fred had not tried skiing. But when his sons started doing it well, he also took it up, quickly becoming quite good at it. He even went so far as to install his own bindings in a makeshift basement workshop. Most casual skiers had their bindings installed by a professional, but Fred saw a chance to develop a new skill, and he took to it energetically. He continued the sport long after his sons had grown and gone, and it became one of his most avid athletic pursuits. For years he went on annual trips to resorts in Colorado with a group of local friends, until advancing age, with its accompanying brittle bones, made it unwise to continue.

Doug Meijer

As we got older we would take family trips skiing up north on the weekends. Dad would get home from work, and Mom would have everything packed. We always looked forward to these mini-getaways. Dad was a good skier, and kept doing it into his eighties.

Larry Levin

During our high school years, 1855 Meadowfield was the place to go after a high-school basketball or football game. There was an indoor pool, a big basement complete with Ping-Pong and a pool table, and an entertainment center. I remember one night, after a football game, word got out that there was a party at Doug's house, and 125 kids from seven different schools showed up. There were cars parked all over with kids coming and going all night. Fred and Lena were gone for the evening.

Finally, after everyone had left, which was after midnight, we went down both sides of the street with garbage bags to clean up. We all knew Fred and Lena trusted us, and we wanted to protect that trust.

Dr. Mark Posthumus

Doug Meijer and I went to the same high school. One day he told me that he had a tandem bicycle, and that my girlfriend (now my wife) and I could borrow it. The next day, Deb and I went to the Meijer house and knocked on the door. Fred answered it and said Doug wasn't home. We told him Doug said we could borrow his bicycle. "Let's go see if we can find it," he replied. It was in a back corner of the garage and had a flat tire. Together, we moved things around to get to the bike, and Fred proceeded to fix the tire. As we rode away, he told us to have a good time, and went back into the house. The surprising part of it all is that we had never met Fred, and he had no idea who we were.

Larry Levin

After graduation, I was sharing an apartment with Doug and another friend. One day Fred called and, thinking I was Doug, proceeded to share some confidential information about happenings within the company. I tried to break in and tell him I wasn't Doug, but he was on a roll. After he finished and I had heard more than I needed to know, he finally understood that he was talking to me. "That's okay," he said. "You're one of the family. Have Doug call me so I can fill him in too."

Mark Meijer

The examples set for me by both my father and grandfather helped me to gauge my risks when I was considering starting my own ambulance business. My father and grandfather shared the gift of being able to balance a great imagination with a generous dose of realism, and both were able to consistently take risks that proved to be good decisions.

My ego was on the line when I was debating whether to start my own business, and like most budding entrepreneurs, I was unsure if I would succeed. I'll always remember what Dad told me when I asked him for advice. He didn't say "Do it" or "Don't do it." Instead, he told me, "If no one gets hurt and no one loses his or her money, then no one will fault you for trying." His words gave me the confidence I needed to move forward.

Over the years Doug and Hank decided to work at the Meijer Company, where they are co-chairs of the board. Mark founded the Life EMS Ambulance service, and he continues to serve on the board of the Meijer Corporation, among his other activities. The sons and their wives are actively involved throughout the community. Seven grandchildren have come along as well, born between 1986 and 2007, bringing yet another generation into the embrace of the family's traditions.

Bob and Jody Hamilton

Fred and Lena were just ordinary people. Their name was in the phone book and they mowed their own lawn. Most of the neighbors drove better cars than they did. Three of our children were the same ages as Hank, Doug, and Mark. The entire family was involved in all the normal school activities, usually contributing more than their fair share.

Fred and Mark, 2008 *(Photo courtesy of Bob Strodtbeck)*

They were the perfect neighbors, but more importantly, wonderful friends. It was a sad day when we watched the moving van at their house almost a half-century later, moving them to their retirement home. Thankfully, we still get to spend time with each other.

Chapter Seven

A Family Business

Civility and humanity are ever the companions of trade.
The man of trade is a man of liberal sentiment. A barba-
rous and commercial people is a contradiction.

— William Hutton, 1781

H utton's optimism about what he calls "the man of trade" is
not widely shared today, but examples still abound, especially in those enterprises run by families. Family-owned
businesses have always formed the backbone of the sprawling American economy: they make up about four-fifths of all registered corporations in the nation. Consider the following statistics reported by the
University of Southern Maine's Institute for Family-Owned Business:
some 35 percent of Fortune 500 companies are family-controlled.
Family businesses, by that definition, account for half of the U.S.
gross domestic product (GDP), generating 60 percent of the country's
employment and creating more than two-thirds of all new jobs.

Indeed, some of the world's largest corporations — including
Wal-Mart and Ford Motor Company — are family businesses,
though those two also offer stock to the general public and are in
many ways not quite what comes to mind with the term. Other well-
known examples include Hallmark, Smucker's, Levi Strauss, and
Marriott Hotels. For all of these companies, which are identified by
the founding family's name, there is a strong sense that a family's

reputation is inextricably tied to the company's fortunes and its public image.

To complicate matters, according to a variety of studies, only one in three family businesses succeeds in moving from the first to the second generation: this makes it clear that moving forward is not an automatic process. Each new generation has its own ideas about taking the company forward, and each new generation faces challenges that didn't exist for its forebears. Going forward is a precarious business. If matters are not handled well, the business that a founder has worked diligently to maintain can come crashing down in a firestorm. In the American experience, this has often included lawsuits, bankruptcies, scandalizing headlines, broken families, and destroyed careers.

The Meijer Company, in the course of its seventy-five years in existence, has moved into the third generation, defying the odds and overcoming whatever hurdles it has encountered along the way while continuing to grow and prosper. Careful planning, open communication, and honest confrontation with difficulties have all played a part in the process.

In the case of the Meijer Company, a number of disagreements surfaced as the chain was expanding in the late 1950s. Don and Johanna Magoon, who as partners controlled 40 percent of the business (the same percentage that Fred and Lena controlled; Hendrik and Gezina controlled about 20 percent), were not comfortable with the direction of the company. As early as 1946, only weeks after he married Johanna and joined the company, Don Magoon had spoken of returning to his academic career. When, a decade later, the company was heading into deeper waters financially, he and his wife were again having second thoughts. It was not simply a matter of business disagreements, though there were plenty of those as well.

"Fred was unduly sensitive about not having gone to college. He regarded Don's learning almost with awe, and took it for granted that his brother-in-law belonged in the family council of decision-making. 'Fred did more to involve Don than anybody I ever saw,' Harvey Lemmen noted years later. 'Don was not the type to walk in. Fred had to pull him into things.' However, Hendrik's admiration for Don was never so unalloyed. Said Lemmen, 'They were oil and water.'" (*TY,* p. 213)

Fred, Hendrik,
and Don
Magoon

Those earlier tensions came to a head in the decisions surrounding the creation of the then-unheard-of combination store that would eventually be named Thrifty Acres. This new project would put the Meijer enterprise seriously in debt, and it would use a format entirely unproven in the market. It was, indeed, a risky proposition. Things came to a head in the late 1950s: the Magoons decided that they would rather pursue other paths in their life, and they tried to persuade Fred and Hendrik to pay out dividends that would allow them to do so while earning a reasonable income from the business.

Fred argued vigorously — and successfully — against paying dividends, reasoning that the company needed all of its meager profits to be able to finance the new direction he desired. A proposed merger with the Plumb supermarkets in Muskegon had recently fallen through, in part because of Don's misgivings about it. Fred and Hendrik were contemplating an entirely new kind of store, and there was no room for dividends in their plans. Instead, the three couples decided that the best way to continue was for Fred and Lena to buy out Don and Johanna's share of the business.

At that time the store chain consisted of a dozen small supermarkets and two party stores; its book value was $1.6 million. However, after extensive negotiations, which exacerbated the ruptures in family relations, the Magoons decided to sell their share to Fred for $1.25 million, an amount that was to be paid over the course of the next fifteen years, with interest. Hendrik thought Fred was paying far too much money, and he told him that he'd be working the rest of his life to pay off the debt. But Fred insisted on going ahead with it.

Don Magoon then left the company and worked for a while as a business consultant. Several years later, he and his family moved to Ypsilanti, Michigan, where he resumed working in a university environment. "Johanna, who raised three children, became active in social causes — from civil rights to arms control — that reflected the progressive values of the Mantels." (*TY*, p. 214)

As things turned out, Fred completed the payments to the Magoons earlier than scheduled. Over the course of the next few years the new stores succeeded beyond anyone's wildest dreams. By the time Fred had paid off his debt to his sister and brother-in-law, the company was worth well over $100 million, and it had profits more than ten times the amount he had paid for his sister's share of ownership.

As one can imagine, the changed face of the corporation caused many problems in the family: it was a rupture that continued for many years, long after Hendrik's death. Fred and Johanna both had strong personalities, and they looked at the world in very different ways. In the years after the buyout, the two siblings had little contact. It was not until the late 1980s that they really came together again. Talking on the phone one day, they decided to meet at a restaurant, just the two of them, and confront the decades of trouble in their past. The conversation lasted for several hours, and it was wrenchingly emotional for both of them. "At the end of it," says Fred, "she told me that she loved me, and I told her the same thing. It was the last time I saw her alive."

In 1963, in the wake of the buyout, Fred laid out his ideas about succession in a two-page handwritten letter to his wife and his parents. He had just been through a set of experiences that were both emotionally and fiscally unsettling, yet the tone of his letter is calm, thoughtful, and realistic. In the event of his death, he outlined three options for the future of the corporation. It could go public, it could be sold, or it could be maintained under a form of collective management. He then explained carefully which of those options he favored, and why. He went on to spell out detailed plans for the salaries and compensation levels of Harvey Lemmen and Earl Holton, the two highest executive officers at the time. He also included a list of people he thought should be on the board of directors.

Because the new format of Thrifty Acres stores was still in its infancy, he was not entirely confident of its success. In case the business could not continue profitably, he also outlined principles and conditions under which the board might wish to sell the company. Finally, he said that if none of his sons, by the age of twenty-one, showed an interest in joining the company, it should then sell shares of stock and become a public corporation. Every few years, when he thought conditions warranted it, Fred drew up similar scenarios, always looking to maintain the vitality and growth of the company, but recognizing that circumstances could change and that the future was never guaranteed.

This meticulous approach to planning for the future is not as common in family corporations as one might expect. A notorious counterexample is that of Henry Ford, who appointed his son Edsel to lead the auto manufacturer, and then worked to undercut virtually everything his son accomplished. In fact, says Thomas Goldwasser, "founders-entrepreneurs often feel that they will guide their businesses forever. Obviously, they know better but will not admit it to anybody, especially to themselves. Consequently, they avoid the essential ingredient for future success — training somebody to take their place. In most cases, they assume that leadership will remain in the family, which historically has meant a son, but they refuse to pass the baton gracefully to the person coming along behind them. Even if an attempt is made to groom a successor, he is considered at best an ersatz leader and administrator." (*Family Pride,* p. 209)

Clearly, such behavior was not Hendrik's approach, at least not where his son was concerned. It is quite possible that some of the tension with Johanna followed a pattern described by Goldwasser; but Hendrik had felt no qualms about Fred. He had made him a full partner at an early age, and he felt increasingly comfortable with his son's decisions. When the two of them were in the final stages of preparation for the first Thrifty Acres, Fred says,

"I asked my dad one last time, 'Do you think we should do it?'"
There followed a long pause. They were sitting in Fred's car
. . . outside the office on Michigan Street, having just come from

a tour of the stores. He looked across the seat at Hendrik, and the older man said no.

"I was really surprised," Fred recalled. "I asked, 'Why would you say no?' . . . I knew he was in favor of it. And he said, 'Because I'm too old to see it through. . . . If we go broke in this deal, I don't want you to tell yourself, "I did it because my dad wanted it."'" Then Fred, who was forty-one years old, asked Hendrik, "Well, what would you do if you were my age?" To that the old man answered decisively, "I'd jump in with both feet." That was all Fred needed to hear. (*TY*, p. 224)

Years later, when Doug and Hank became co-chairmen of the company, there was no such watershed moment. They had both worked at Meijer for years by then. Doug had begun working in the Alpine Avenue store in 1965, when he was eleven. Over the years he has held twenty-three different positions in five stores, offices, and the warehouse. He has worked in fifteen different departments, including real estate, personnel, and distribution — all before the age of thirty-three. He entered the business on a full-time basis directly after he graduated from the University of Michigan.

Hank took a brief detour into the newspaper business, where he was a reporter, editor, and publisher of newspapers in Michigan and Ohio before coming back to Meijer in the late 1970s. Both Hank and Doug had garnered experience in every nook and cranny of the enterprise. This gave them a sense of the business that Fred felt very comfortable with; and though he continued to serve as the company's leader for a decade or so after the usual retirement age of sixty-five, he felt very confident about passing the baton to the third generation. Neither Hank nor Doug aspired to play a role in the hands-on management of the business, as Fred had done for so many years. So they have left plenty of room for nonfamily executives within the corporate structure to grow and advance their careers without the fear that someone in the family might be competing with them for a position.

It has not always gone smoothly, but for most of its life the company has grown at a steady pace, allowing its employees many opportunities for advancement and mobility, along with a stable work environment. Because most of the company's promotions come from within the organization, spurred by an increase in the number of stores and the new jobs that result, there are many ways for employees to develop their talents. They can move from one market to another, and they can work in a wide variety of departments within the business. It is entirely possible for someone to begin as a grocery bagger, to develop expertise in shoes, sporting goods, hardware, and produce, and over time to become a senior executive officer, all within the same corporate family.

For decades there has been speculation in the financial press and elsewhere about whether the Meijer Company might go public or be sold to another chain. Such actions would raise a great deal of cash, and they might allow for much quicker expansion, or create other opportunities for the family. Fred has generally opposed any such move, but he always held a family meeting when the subject came up, and he asked all members what they thought. The family is in complete agreement with him on the subject, particularly on the idea of going public. "Stockholders demand profit statements every three months that are made public," he says. "We are involved in a lot of things that are, I think, respectable, but are sometimes not considered to be good business." (*Toledo Blade,* October 4, 1992)

Much of the company's charitable giving falls into this category. The company donates far more — as a percentage of its profits — than do its largest competitors, Wal-Mart and Target. Those corporations cannot spend shareholders' money without approval, and their corporate generosity must necessarily be geared to self-serving interests as well as community concerns.

In 1975, for example, the company made a painful decision: they decided to close Store #21 on the north side of Kalamazoo. They had just finished building a new store in nearby Battle Creek, and they had already staffed it. Since it would be impossible to offer the employees of Store #21 any jobs in Battle Creek, it looked as though they might have to lay off the entire crew. With that realization, they did something that would probably have been impossible for a publicly held company to do: they built a new store on Gull Road in Kalamazoo, which they knew would not be profitable for years, but which would keep everyone at Store #21 in a job. "This was the only time," says Fred, "that we have ever built a brand-new store just to keep from laying off a crew." (*IHOW,* p. 173)

A sense of charity, of caring for the community, is built into the value system to the point where it's often difficult to separate personal from corporate kindness. This approach works very well in a family business, in part because it allows all the people who work there to get the feeling that they are part of an organization devoted to more than just profits. It becomes more difficult, however, as the business reaches gargantuan proportions in a very competitive environment. Running an organization with something like 70,000 *associates,* the word Meijer uses for its employees, can put severe strains on the sense of family.

There are myriad ways to work at maintaining cohesiveness within a large company, and Meijer develops as many of them as it can. There are meetings and seminars, training sessions and social events. One of the mainstays of cohesion, however, is for corporate executives to make regular visits to the far-flung stores and distribution centers. Fred has always made a point of visiting stores regularly, a tradition he began with his father as the fledgling chain grew from two to three to six to more than twenty outlets by the time of Hendrik's death in

Hendrik and Fred

1964. Such visits helped them keep their fingers on the pulse of the business: to become familiar not only with the personnel and the products being sold but also with the unique challenges faced by each store within its community.

The same reasons still prevail, but the ability of the family to carry on with these visits has become more difficult with each addition to the chain, which now comprises nearly 200 supercenters and six distribution centers. Though they may be more spaced out in time than previously, the visits continue, a tradition carried forward by Doug and Hank, as well as their father. During these visits there is always business to be discussed with the store's management, of course; but there is a persistent emphasis on the personal side of life as well, which extends far beyond profit-and-loss entries in the ledgers. The owner-visitors typically spend much more time greeting associates who are not in management than with their bosses. With everyone, Fred and his family try to make clear that they are fellow human beings, not simply owners of a financial enterprise. It's a quality that the longtime employees take for granted, though it often comes as a surprise to newcomers. It's a quality that goes back to the very beginning of the company, and is the enduring legacy of Hendrik.

Although he can be formidable in backstage corporate dramas, Fred always comes across with his employees as the friendly, talkative father figure, showing by example rather than by fiat, seeing to things on the ground floor of retailing rather than from the back office.

The following quotes are just a few examples of how the corporate sense of family has been experienced by employees and customers over the years.

Al Waldorf

After World War II, I came back and picked up where I had left off at the store. I wanted to build a house, but I had very little savings and no collateral, so the bank turned me down for a loan. Fred's father must have heard about it. He came over to me one day and said I should go back to the bank and try again.

Returning this time, I found the money was waiting. Hendrik had already cosigned for the loan.

Ken Pearson

In 1968 my wife gave birth to twin girls prematurely. At the time, the Meijer insurance didn't provide the coverage I thought it should have, and we were saddled with large hospital bills. Soon afterwards, I saw Fred in the warehouse where I worked, and I asked if he could have someone look at our insurance. He listened intently to my whole story, and took notes. I didn't give it another thought.

Two days later I received a personal check from him to cover our costs, and a couple of months later we all received a new health-insurance policy.

Ken Brondyke

I retired after forty-one years at Meijer. I knew Fred was out of town on my last day at work. When I got home, he was on my answering machine, thanking me for all my years with the company.

Don Koster

Back when I started, every Meijer employee received a turkey for Thanksgiving and a gift at Christmas. I remember one year receiving a cooler and a clothes brush; another time a blanket and a shaving kit. The Meijer family would have a Christmas party for the employees and their families in the basement of Finger's Restaurant. Hendrik would play the ocarina, which he called the sweet potato, and everyone would sing Christmas carols. During the summer they would close the stores for a day so we could have a company picnic at the lake. We always felt like part of the family because of the way we were treated.

Fred Welling

Fred never drank coffee, but his dad enjoyed his morning cup. We would be traveling somewhere with Fred driving, and his dad would hint that we should stop for coffee. Fred would just keep driving. Finally, Mr. Meijer would say, in his Dutch brogue, "Fred, next exit I vant a cup of coffee." And we would finally stop.

Ernie Escareno

In 1973 I was working in Kalamazoo at Store #21. The eating area was on the balcony, and consisted of vending machines. One day Fred was in the store, bought a sandwich out of one of the machines, and came over to sit with us. He was raving about how good the sandwich was. He asked me if I ever ate them. "Not often," I said, trying to be polite. All I could think was, if he thinks that's good food, I wonder what he eats at home. Hank later told me that his mom was a superb cook, but that his dad had never been fussy about food.

Bill Whittaker

I had forty-six wonderful years with Meijer, starting right out of high school. I was promoted to store manager in Grand Haven in 1961, and retired from that position in 2002. The first store was 18,000 square feet and had 45 employees. The store I retired from was 200,000 square feet, eleven times larger than the original store, with 900 team members. I still remember standing in the parking lot of that original store with Fred and his dad the day before Grand Opening. Hendrik said to me, "Bill, if we don't do $25,000 a week, we'll go broke." We always did more than that.

Zora Smith

I have often wondered how many jobs Meijer has provided to families over the years. In our family alone, and spanning four generations, fourteen out of eighteen adults have worked at Meijer. For some, it was a temporary summer job. For others, it became a training ground for other careers. For one, it was his only job from the time he was a teenager until the time he retired forty-two years later.

Don Koster

I was working after school one day, looking forward to my junior-senior banquet that evening. The store, however, was a mess, and a truck had just arrived, which needed to be unloaded by hand in those days. The district manager had come in, and after looking things over, said I would have to stay and work. So much for my banquet!

Fred was in the store at the time, and somehow heard about my situation. He found me working in the back, and said, "You go ahead to the banquet. I'll take care of everything." I will never forget that act of kindness.

Dave Nesman

I was conducting a management training class one day when Fred walked into the room. He started shaking hands with the students, and apologized for the interruption. Then, as he invariably did in these situations, he asked what we were talking about. My heart leaped into my throat. It happened that one of the managers was unhappy about a recent management decision that affected him, and was telling the class about the unfairness of the situation.

Fred listened patiently, expressing his interest and concern. He talked about several possible solutions. Then he went on to say that it helped him sometimes to remember that we are not perfect people. "We don't hire managers to make right decisions," he said. "We hire them to make decisions that we hope are right. Then, if we find out later that we're wrong, we admit it and try to do something about it." I felt that this chance encounter was the best lesson of the day.

Doug Meijer

While we were growing up in the retail business, my dad always felt that Hank, Mark, and I should experience as many areas of the company as possible. I started working on Saturdays, sorting bottles in the back room, to earn money for baseball cards.

On breaks while I was in college, I worked third shift in the warehouse. My first job was selecting health and beauty products for the stores. We had a selecting rate we were expected to achieve. Our loads were assembled upstairs, where they were price-marked by the pricing crew. If you mis-selected an item, a voice would come over the loudspeaker: "Doug Meijer, upstairs." You would then go up there and exchange the mis-selected item. Of course, everyone in the building knew you had goofed. Talk about peer pressure. You learned to become proficient real fast.

Alayne Olson

One summer while in high school, my sister and I worked at the Meijer office in Grand Rapids. We would drive from our home, forty-five miles away, on Monday, and stay during the week with Fred and Lena. It was more like a vacation than a job. Aunt Lena was always easygoing, and they were both fun to be around. I still remember the wonderful home-cooked meals and the interesting discussions around the dinner table.

Muriel Wise

When stores started being open on Sunday, Meijer decided to follow suit, because many customers were asking them to. Fred called my manager and told him I was not expected to work on Sunday. He knew my beliefs about working on Sunday. I always wondered how many phone calls he made like that.

Leonard Krampe

One day the district manager came into the store I was managing and asked if I would take over managing the Greenville store the following Monday. Since Greenville already had a manager, I asked what was happening to him. I was told that the store was in such poor condition that they were going to have to let him go, which they did.

The next Monday, Fred stopped in and we were standing in the main aisle talking. Fred was feeling bad because the former manager was such a nice guy. Then we looked up, and saw the man we were talking about, with a cart full of groceries. He came over, shook our hands, and congratulated me. Then he continued shopping.

After Fred left, I went back to [the former manager] and asked why he would still shop with us after he had just been fired. He said, "Meijer was always good to me, and they have the best prices. So why not?"

Jim Montgomery

Fred paid a routine visit to Store #24 in Lansing soon after Thanksgiving one year. We were walking together through the store when I received a phone call regarding a turkey return at the service desk. When I arrived there, a customer explained that she had bought a turkey for Thanksgiving and that it was spoiled. The turkey's wrinkled, lightly browned skin showed that the customer must have put it in the oven and then taken it out for some reason. She insisted that the bird was spoiled, though I could not smell anything of the sort. I agreed to give her a full refund. When I returned to Fred, I explained what had just happened.

"How many turkeys did you sell over the Thanksgiving holiday?" he asked. I told him several thousand, for sure. "You made the right decision," he said.

Terry Griffith

I recall one of our produce buyers being frustrated about truckloads of produce being delayed on their way from the West Coast because of unusually heavy snowfalls in the mountains. Fred happened to be there, and the produce director explained the situation to him.

"If you've done everything you can do," said Fred, "then let it go and move on to the next opportunity. You can't open those mountain passes, and you can't drive those trucks. Don't beat yourself up about something that you have no power to change."

Leon Ballast

When I was ten years old, I was injured in an accident, which resulted in an occasional stutter. One time at a luncheon meeting I was seated with Fred, and stuttered throughout the conversation. A few days later my boss called me to his office. He handed me an article about a new breakthrough for people who stuttered. There was a note attached from Fred, asking whether this might be of help to Leon. I was pleasantly surprised that he would take the time to think about me and pass on the information.

Carol Alexander

Fred is always thoughtful about inviting people to ride with him, or of-fering to have me drive them someplace. Many times it's on the spur of the moment. He never seems too busy. It doesn't matter if it's a top executive or an hourly employee — he treats everyone the same.

Rick Keyes

Whenever I recall my experiences with Fred, I'm always taken back to the very first time I met him back when I was a pharmacy intern. We had heard that Fred was in the store, and we were excited and hoping that he might visit us in the pharmacy. Fred did visit the pharmacy, but what really impressed me was how long he stayed and spoke with us. He greeted every one of us individually and spent time making sure everyone felt acknowledged and appreciated. We were all im-pressed by how genuinely interested Fred was in our team, and also by how he was willing to slow down and take time to get to know his team members.

One of our pharmacy technicians had a Dutch last name. Being in-trigued by this, Fred asked her some questions about her heritage. One thing led to another until they started talking about different Dutch recipes that both of their families enjoyed. Before we knew it, Fred had picked up the phone, called Lena, introduced her and put the team member on the phone with Lena. The threesome talked about Dutch cooking and other aspects of the Dutch culture.

A week later, a letter from Fred and Lena arrived at the pharmacy. Inside the envelope was the actual recipe that Lena, Fred, and the technician had discussed. You can imagine our surprise when we saw that Fred and Lena would take the time to send the recipe to the team member, and what an impression it made on all of us.

Chad Busk

When I started in the legal department in 1980, Fred showed me a photo of my grandfather, Sam Busk, taken outside the first Meijer store in Greenville shortly after it opened in 1934. He told me he had known my grandfather since he (Fred) was in grade school. Fred also knew my dad, and bought shoes from him when he owned a shoestore.

Fred recently met my daughter Arian when he visited the Equest Center where they came to see her ride. Equest is an organization that offers therapeutic horseback riding to persons with disabilities. It is one of the many organizations Fred and Lena support.

Fred is, I believe, the only person to have known four generations of the Busk family.

Ted Bedell

In 1982, I was promoted to district director in Ohio. Late one night, I received a phone call telling me that our Findlay store had burned to the ground, and that a team member had died in the fire. At daylight the next morning, I'm standing in the parking lot when Fred arrives. I'll never forget the look on his face. You would have thought he had just lost a close family member.

Nothing was ever said about the loss of the building and inventory. Fred's only concern was for the employees and for the family of the team member who had died in the fire. He wanted to be sure we were doing everything we could for them.

John Zimmerman

One of our store directors' sons died at the age of thirteen, the result of a snowboarding accident. I attended the funeral along with hundreds of others from the company. Fred was just ahead of me in the receiving line. When he reached the store director, Fred embraced him and they both stood there holding each other in support while the tears flowed. It was a very moving moment, and it told us a lot about the leader of our company. Fred believes in the family, and he has always treated us as though we are part of his family. Those tears were true and made me even fonder of him.

Bill Whittaker

I was managing the Grand Haven store in 1983 when I had a heart attack. They rushed me to the hospital, and it wasn't long before Fred was there. I had another one in 1998, and because of the number of visitors, they posted a "No Visitor" sign on my door. Pretty soon, the door opened just enough for Fred to stick his head in and wish me well. I was out of work for four months. On my first day back, guess who was sitting at my desk to welcome me?

Dear Mr. Meijer:

This letter is about the consideration the Benton Harbor store employees recently showed toward my husband Bill, who is terminally ill with lung cancer.

Recently, the store manager, John Spaulding, and grocery manager, Ron York, appeared at our door. These two gentlemen came with a large basket of fruit and my husband's favorite, Greek Rotella salad. They also brought two cards signed by most of the employees. Seeing the two of them lifted his spirits tremendously.

We were choked with emotion and gratitude at this display of good will. This store, the manager, and the employees, should be congratulated for their humanity.

Sincerely,
Bill and Shirley Smith 4/19/96

Roger Horling

In 1999, my wife suffered a brain aneurysm followed by an operation. Her right eye was swollen, and she had a pronounced scar across her scalp. She looked pretty rough, but she wanted to go to the store. As we were walking in, Fred was there, talking on a telephone. He looked over and immediately hung up the phone to come talk with us. "What happened?" he asked. "Did you have an accident?" He was very sympathetic, and asked if there was anything he could do. He must have told Lena about it, too, because a few days later I saw her, and she immediately asked how Bea was coming along.

Bob Summers

A number of years ago, I was on a produce-buying trip to South America. Somehow I ended up getting food poisoning. I managed to get home, but I was so sick I thought I was going to die, and was afraid maybe I wouldn't.

Immediately, I got a phone call from Fred. He was calling from an airport somewhere, and he wanted to know if I had been to a hospital. He told me to stay home and not to worry about the office. I was off work for several weeks, during which Fred made frequent calls to see how I was coming along.

Dear Mr. Meijer:

I'd like to let you know what a special group of associates you have. My mother, Mary Ann Broughman, was an associate in your Owosso store. She worked there until June of 1995, when she had to have surgery for cancer. She was not able to return to work, and we took care of her at home until she died on January 24, 1996.

From the time Mom went off work until the end, Meijer people were there for her. They sent cards, letters, flowers, and more. They visited her often, and a day didn't go by when at least one or more didn't call. We received food baskets, gifts, and hundreds of acts of kindness. This wasn't a one-time deal.

Another thing they gave her was the realization of how many people truly cared about her. They showed her more love in six months than most people get in a lifetime. It surely helped me to know that between the friends at Meijer and us here at home, she couldn't have been more loved and cared for. What a special group of friends!

When I think back to everything Store #113 did for us, I'm still overwhelmed. It must be nice to know that the people who represent your company to the public are such giving and caring people.

May God bless you all,

Crystal Johnson

Chapter Eight

No Textbook Answers

Everything now being done is going to be done differently
and it's going to be done better, and if we don't do it, our
competitors will.

— Fred Meijer

There is an ancient superstition of the sea holding that, in a series of waves, each one is roughly equal in size until one
comes along that is much bigger than the rest. This "Ninth
Wave" is a powerful culmination of wind and sea. To catch it at the
critical moment requires instinct, timing, and courage. The Ninth
Wave of retailing hit Grand Rapids, Michigan, in 1962.

America had just come through the 1950s, the final extension of
the postwar years. Fidel Castro's revolutionaries had taken over Cuba,
the microchip had been invented, Barbie dolls were replacing hula
hoops and coonskin caps. Eisenhower played presidential golf, gaso-
line was 29 cents a gallon, and the big band era had been replaced by
something called rock 'n' roll, led by a young singer with an energetic
delivery from Memphis, Tennessee.

Down south in the tiny town of Rogers, Arkansas, Mr. Sam, as he
was called, opened a 16,000-square-foot store and named it Wal-Mart.
Up north, in a suburb of Detroit, the SS Kresge Company was having
its grand opening of a new store that would one day replace its thriving "dime store" business. This new store was also called a "Mart" —

with the letter "K" in front. A couple of states to the west, in Minnesota, the Dayton Hudson Company was unveiling a new store whose logo was a bull's-eye. Of these three new discount store prototypes, K-Mart and Target were offshoots of their larger publicly traded parent companies; Sam Walton, with fourteen Ben Franklin stores as a foundation, would go public just eight years later. They would become known as the big three in the industry. All three stores opened within weeks of each other in the summer of 1962. They were a new breed of general-merchandise store run by astute businessmen already established in the dry-goods business.

Unless a person lived near one of these new ventures, happened to be a competitor, supplier, or inquisitive investor, there was no way the average American would know — or for that matter care — about another new store. There were, after all, historical events taking place to be concerned about: the Cuban missile crisis was coming to a climax, and President John F. Kennedy was about to send the first troops to Vietnam. Those who grew up during that generation will long remember some of the year's events: the pull-top can was introduced for soda pop; John Glenn became the first American to orbit the earth; NASA launched Telstar, the first communication satellite that would transmit the first worldwide TV show. Escorted by U.S. marshals, James Meredith became the first black student to register at the University of Mississippi.

In Grand Rapids, Michigan, a growing community surrounded by the Great Lakes, schools were just getting out for the summer. Those who had graduated were preparing to enter the work force, college, or the military. They planned weddings or careers or both, all with the trepidation that comes from being on one's own for the first time.

On the southeast side of the city, on the corner of 28th Street and Kalamazoo Avenue, Fred and Hendrik Meijer were about to use the key that would open a store unlike any ever seen before. It was larger than all the fourteen existing Meijer supermarkets combined, and inside it would have thirty different stores, including a full-size supermarket. With 100,000 square feet of retailing space, it could have fit seven of the first Wal-Mart stores inside it — with room left over.

In 1962, Americans were already going through a transition in the way they shopped in some of the bigger eastern cities. The traditional catalog department stores — Sears, Montgomery Ward, JC Penney, as well as the SS Kresge and F. W. Woolworth dime stores — were being challenged by a new hybrid of maverick "mass merchandisers," or "discounters," that were springing up.

Until the 1950s, there had been no stores selling nonfood merchandise in ways that were comparable to a supermarket. A person shopping for slacks or a lawnmower had three choices: the traditional department store, which was often located downtown without convenient parking; the smaller specialty store; or a catalog. Discounting changed all that. The movement's most prominent pioneers started stores in vacant factories and mills in New England. (Atlantic Mills was the name of one early chain in the region that became known as "the cradle of discounting.") These merchants dispensed with such niceties as service and décor. They were promotion-minded cousins of the old department-store bargain basements, with plain pipe racks for garments and rickety wooden display tables. They priced their inventory below the suggested retail price that traditional stores used to obtain higher markups. Like the supermarkets, discount houses compensated for narrower profit margins with higher sales volume.

Also similar to the early supermarkets, the first discount houses were spartan, unassuming establishments, but with their wide variety and low prices they made shopping efficient and exciting to the customer. It was only because complacent conventional merchants had stayed so long with "standard" or "fair-trade" prices (usually those set by the manufacturer) that discounters had a reason to exist. Wherever fair trade prices prevailed, the discounters had a ready-made, authentic yardstick by which to demonstrate to the consumer how much lower their prices were on items identical to those found in the department stores.

With prices that ranged from 15 to 25 percent below conventional retail, the word "discount" began to take on significance. Major manufacturers whose goods were being discounted, including General Electric, Westinghouse, and Sunbeam, spent millions of dollars seeking injunctions and trying other legal maneuvers to maintain their right to enforce fair trade pricing. Meanwhile, conventional retailers sneered at the discount houses. "Do you know what discounting is?"

asked one New York department-store executive. "It's nothing more than selling inferior merchandise on Sundays." Others condemned discounting as everything from "a malignant cancer" to "an unsound method of distribution."

But the armies of the status quo were fighting a losing battle, and by 1962 the fair trade law had been so successfully challenged that it had become unenforceable in half of the country — including Michigan. Fair trade had remained in force long enough not only to give discounting its original impetus but to enable it to pick up considerable momentum.

This momentum brought a westward expansion of the discount idea. Arlan's and Miracle Mart opened outlets in Grand Rapids. Every aspect of their approach was geared to selling goods cheaply — and frequently to selling cheap goods. Some discount houses were shoddy operations, and others were guilty by association. At some stores, items were never in stock when a customer wanted them. Yet shoppers liked the low prices, and the early discounters proved that, by eliminating frills, they could produce substantial savings.

Fred and Hendrik thought they had an even better idea. The idea of one-stop shopping had actually been conceived in a barbershop in Greenville decades earlier. Hendrik, the barber, had somehow gotten his hands on a book by Emile Zola entitled *Au Bonheur Des Dames.* Although the book was written as a novel, the background of the story took place in a large downtown store in Paris called the "Ladies' Paradise." The store had multiple floors and sold everything, including foodstuffs. Hendrik passed the book on to Fred, and it continues to occupy a place of prominence in his library. The seed that had lain dormant was finally germinating, and it was about to sprout in a new hybrid American store. It would be an extension of their first thrift market, and because of its size, the name "Thrifty Acres" seemed like a perfect fit.

When Hendrik, sitting in Fred's car, made it clear that the decision was Fred's alone, he had passed the mantle to Fred. They studied other discounters and discerned three alternatives for selling food and general merchandise under one roof. One option was to put a partition between the supermarket and the discount house and use two separate rows of cash registers. That approach appealed to grocers concerned about the typically higher wage rates commanded by food store cashiers, and it eliminated the potential housekeeping problem of a customer laying a sweater down on a checkout counter that was wet from a head of lettuce or a carton of ice cream.

A second solution was to put a concourse down the middle of the building with check lanes on one side for food and on the other side for nonfoods, thus achieving the same physical separation of merchandising categories. A third approach was to install a single long row of checkouts with all the departments grouped behind it. That way had its operational complications: Would customers feel comfortable buying a blouse or fruit along with their motor oil? Could cashiers cope with the volume of grocery traffic combined with the awkwardness of checking out garden supplies or a bicycle?

These were all questions that awaited answers, but with the convenience of a single row of checkouts, the third way seemed most efficient, and "one-stop shopping" would soon be the favored descriptive. Regardless of what they bought, customers would pay for everything in a single transaction.

Earl Holton

I was attending a food-marketing meeting. During the coffee break I walked up to a group that was listening to one of our speakers, a distinguished Harvard professor.

"We were just discussing your new store, Earl. I've been explaining to everyone that you should be admired for trying, but your new format will never work." He continued to explain to me the views shared by many of Fred's skeptics — that customers will never buy groceries and general merchandise at the same checkout. Who was I to argue with a college professor?

As construction progressed, it became a novelty. The town was beginning to talk. A *Grand Rapids Press* photo showed a construction foreman riding a bicycle through the open expanse of the store, holding a set of blueprints. Hendrik and Fred built in some insurance that hinted at the riskiness of the venture, for example, extra thick concrete floors that would be suitable for an auto dealership if they failed.

The naysayers, who were many, scoffed. Not only was Thrifty Acres a bad idea, but Meijer was too small, lacked experience, and was undercapitalized. Looking for some support, Hendrik and Fred hired a consultant. His advice was, "Don't do it." In a five-page report he explained that it would jeopardize the rest of the company. Cash flow would be an immediate problem. Supermarket inventory turned over quickly, but general merchandise did not. There were no systems in place, no trained buyers, and no credibility with general goods suppliers. In his opinion, the store would not survive. After reading the report, Hendrik turned to Fred and said with a chuckle, "Well, at least we built across from a cemetery."

Fortunately, Hendrik and Fred believed in their dream. The store that was an anomaly and destined to fail would ultimately become the granddaddy of one-stop shopping (today's supercenters) that future generations across America would take for granted.

In the beginning it was an arduous journey into the unknown by a father and son, two visionaries who would change the way America shopped. They had indeed found what others had overlooked or were afraid to try. It was a test of perseverance, patience, but most of all a belief in themselves, their people, and their vision. One-stop shopping was a trip they embarked on without road maps or textbooks. It was also to become the final act of Hendrik's business life, the innovation that became his legacy.

"For more than fifty years Hendrik maintained his barber's license. He called the trade his safety valve. Visiting a retired salesman or an old friend, he would take the barber tools he kept in a worn leather case. Sunday mornings were reserved for Fred and the grandsons. Hendrik spread newspapers under a stool in the middle of the kitchen floor, unfolded a faded cloth, and pinned it on his 'customer.'

"His gestures with scissors and clipper were meticulous. He stood over the stool in a plaid flannel shirt, pleated trousers and leather slippers. As he cut the boys' hair, Fred watched and talked, leaning back against the wall with his hands cushioning the small of his back while the sun streamed through the kitchen window. The barber was careful to consult his customers on questions of style. The Princeton

— short around the ears and neck, a little longer in front — was the standard choice for Fred. The boys always wanted theirs longer, and Hendrik at least pretended to oblige. At intervals he turned off the electric clipper to brush a few hairs from his grandsons' brow. When he was finished, they examined the results in a hand mirror. Then, loosening the cloth, he carefully gathered it up, carried it to the door, and shook the tufts of hair into the breeze.

"He cut the boys' hair on Sunday, May 31, 1964. It was a warm, sunny day, and that afternoon he took Gezina for a drive in the Buick. When they came home, Gezina started dinner while he walked to the cemetery. After dinner he read for a while, then told his wife, 'I guess I'll go to bed. I'm kind of tired.' That night, in his sleep, his heart failed for the last time. He had just turned 80." (*TY*, p. 29) Up in Greenville, Mrs. Emmett Green was expecting Hendrik to help celebrate her eighty-fifth birthday the next day. "Mr. Meijer will come — he always comes," she said. But this time he would not be there for her party.

Chapter Nine

Going Broke? Oh, No, Not Again!

We almost went broke a number of times in the past seventy-five years. In fact, we were broke to start with, but we never went bankrupt. I remember those times well, but we survived through the evolution of our business. We have built our company to stay in business. When you sign a lot of thirty-year mortgages, you're looking at the long haul.

— Fred Meijer

In 1934 the country had been in the midst of the Great Depression that started with the stock market crash on October 29, 1929, known as Black Tuesday. Massive layoffs resulted in unemployment for more than 25 percent of the workforce. During the decade of the 1930s, nine thousand banks failed. By 1938, people watched as 140 billion dollars of their deposits disappeared. In rural areas such as Greenville, crop prices fell by 50 percent by the early 1930s, in a steady decline that reached bottom in 1934. Shortly after President Roosevelt was inaugurated in 1933, drought and erosion combined to cause the dust bowl throughout the Midwest, causing many families to lose their farms to foreclosure.

Germany, like other European countries, had been hit hard by the Depression, as loans they were receiving from America to help rebuild the country after World War I ended. In 1934, that country ran out of money, primarily because of reparations it was forced to pay the victors in that war. Democracy was weakened as dictators Adolf Hitler, Benito Mussolini, and Joseph Stalin came to power, helping set the stage for World War II.

Also in 1934, Alcatraz became a federal prison, gangster John Dillinger was shot and killed outside a Chicago theater, Max Baer defeated Primo Carnera for the heavyweight boxing title, and the Dionne quintuplets were born. On the lighter side, it was the year Donald Duck made his debut and the first Flash Gordon comic strip appeared. Frank Capra's "It Happened One Night" was released, starring Clark Gable and Claudette Colbert. It became a smash hit and was the first film to win all five of the major academy awards. Cole Porter's musical "Anything Goes" opened in New York City. The golden age of radio featured Lionel Barrymore as Scrooge in Charles Dickens' "A Christmas Carol," a role he would play until 1954.

This was the backdrop as the tiny 21-foot by 70-foot North Side Grocery opened that Friday morning of June 29, 1934.

Lee and Cady had given the grocers fifteen days to pay their first bill, for $338.76, but future orders would come C.O.D. "The Kipp brothers, who owned the grocery store across the street, stood in the doorway and made a prediction as Hendrik and Fred unloaded their opening inventory. The new store would not last six weeks." (*TY*, p. 127)

Money was tight, and every penny counted. There would be worse financial times to come, but thankfully there was no way for the Meijer family to know that. The fact that they had survived the first few months surprised everyone, including their most staunch supporters.

Some time later, after finally obtaining a $300 line of credit from their supplier, a large order of more than $600 came in. They had exceeded their credit limit by $300 and the order was marked C.O.D. Fred was at the back door when it arrived. Observing the big C.O.D. printed across the invoice and knowing they didn't have that kind of money on hand, he went to Hendrik to ask what he should do. "Get it unloaded," Hendrik told his son. "We'll argue about it afterwards."

"The driver was at the end of his route. When all the cases were unloaded, he discovered to his irritation that the order was a case or two short. He was so upset that he jumped into the cab with the invoice and drove off. When he returned to Grand Rapids without a check, the credit manager called Greenville. 'The driver left before we could pay him,' Hendrik explained. Then he crossed his fingers and hoped for a busy weekend. The following Monday, Hendrik and Fred drove to Grand Rapids with a check. There still was not enough money in the bank to cover it, but the check had to make a four-day circuit from Grand Rapids to Chicago and back before clearing the bank in Greenville — time enough to sell more groceries and run to the bank with a new deposit." (*TY,* p. 157)

While tens of thousands of other small grocery stores across the country were closing, the North Side Grocery not only survived those first few crucial months, but began to grow. Those early birth pangs of their new venture represented a defining moment for the Meijer family. Looking back, Fred identifies other crucial periods where bankruptcy or liquidation seemed imminent, some due to unexpected disasters, some to overexpansion. The next big test came in 1946, the year he and Lena were married.

The first meeting of the United Nations occurred that year. That year radar waves were used to measure the distance between the earth and moon, paving the way for the space age. In the U.S. Senate, a vote was called to end discrimination in the workplace; the measure did not pass. On the world scene, leaders were appealing to U.S. and Soviet leaders to end nuclear testing to "save humanity from ultimate disaster." The election of Ho Chi Minh in Vietnam went unnoticed in America.

In 1946 the Meijer "chain" consisted of two stores, one in Greenville, another in Cedar Springs, and a third scheduled to open in Ionia. Early on the morning of May 22, 1946, when the Greenville store caught fire and burned to the ground, the largest supermarket in Montcalm County was a total loss. Damage was estimated at $125,000, but the building was only insured for $5,000, far below its value. Fortunately, the merchandise inside the store was covered. However, only weeks away from becoming a three-store chain, the business now had only one store, and that was the small Cedar Springs operation, which was still losing money. Undaunted, Hendrik and Fred borrowed from both Greenville banks to rebuild the company, and they staved off disaster once again.

Meijer Store #7 in Rogers Park, built during the postwar building boom

Expansion into the Grand Rapids market in 1949 with the fourth and fifth Meijer stores brought about the next financial crisis. It all happened with an unexpected opportunity that would increase the company's size by 40 percent.

By that time, America was in a postwar boom, and new supermarkets and small shopping centers were springing up everywhere. As the U.S. population passed 150 million, major events were shaping up that would have far-reaching consequences for the country. It was the beginning of the Korean War, as well as the cold war with Russia. Newly elected President Harry Truman ordered the development of the hydrogen bomb in response to Russian atomic bomb tests. Americans built bomb shelters, while Albert Einstein warned that a nuclear war would lead to world destruction.

David Ben-Gurion became the president of the world's newest country, Israel, which was admitted into the United Nations as the fifty-ninth member. Senator Estes Kefauver and his Senate committee began investigating organized crime. Rodgers and Hammerstein's *South Pacific* opened on Broadway with the title song "Some Enchanted Evening." *Peanuts* appeared in the comic strips for the first time, and child star Shirley Temple announced her retirement. The first Volkswagen was imported to the United States; only two sold, which convinced the German manufacturers that the car had no future in America. Several years later, Peter Cook, a longtime friend of Fred and Lena, became the Volkswagen distributor for Michigan and Indiana. His entrepreneurial spirit helped the Beetle eventually become an automotive phenomenon in American history.

"Hendrik and Fred wanted to put a supermarket in one of Grand Rapids' first shopping centers. But the developer had already committed that site to another grocer. Looking elsewhere, they found property on South Division Avenue, a main artery through the city's southern suburbs. As they completed negotiations for the site on South Division, the shopping center developer called them. His deal with the other grocer had fallen through, and he offered to lease Meijer the unfinished building. Hendrik had already borrowed $25,000 to buy the first site; yet the second one was equally tempting. However, he discovered that to open not one but two stores in the big city required more money than skeptical Greenville bankers were willing to lend. At the same time, Hendrik and Fred seemed to have few doubts that the risk was worth it. They agreed to a chattel mortgage of their merchan-

Peter Cook's Volkswagen dealership, Thrifty Motors, just down the street from Thrifty Acres, 1963 *(Photo courtesy of Peter Cook)*

dise — along with fixtures and other equity — to finance the second Grand Rapids store, a financial arrangement that gave the bank a lien on everything they owned. If the company's suppliers were to try to recover their merchandise because Meijer could not pay for it, they would discover that the bank had a prior claim to the goods." (*TY*, p. 195)

Even though they had an agreement with the bank to keep the arrangements confidential, word soon leaked out, and suppliers began putting them on C.O.D. Suppliers were not about to sell to anybody who had given a lien on their merchandise; this was a lesson well learned, something the company never did again.

Fred remembers this period as a time of getting a real education in financing and dealing with big-city bankers. The bankers in Greenville had been their customers, and their business was usually conducted on an informal basis, sometimes in the bread aisle. On more than one occasion, Fred would run to the bank just before closing on Friday to borrow enough cash for employee paychecks. Then, after a busy weekend at the store, he would return at 9 o'clock on Monday morning to repay the loan, owing only pennies in interest. This was not the kind of thing that could be done in Grand Rapids.

"Talk about working under pressure!" he says. "If you want time to pass quickly, just try signing a few sixty-day promissory notes."

With the first two Grand Rapids stores up and running in 1949, the Meijers decided to build a third, which was to be their biggest, on the corner of Michigan and Fuller. It would also contain the company's offices and serve as a warehouse. Old Kent Bank agreed to loan them $125,000. As construction began on that building, the Korean War broke out, and they were informed that, because the permits were not yet given for the supermarket, they would have to be put on hold. However, the permits had already been issued for the office and warehouse; so they proceeded on the basis that the whole building would be for that purpose, knowing they couldn't open the store until — or even if — approval could be obtained. The bank became apprehensive because, without an actual supermarket to generate profits, loan repayment would be more difficult. The building was all overhead.

"At the time," Fred remembers, "I was dealing with a man named Martin Lilly, a vice president of the bank, and he told me that I would have to see the president, Mr. Heber Curtis. Mr. Curtis was an old-style banker, and we were talking with him at the same time that he was having problems loaning money to Ben Duthler and to L. V. Eberhard. He said: 'You grocers are all alike. You get in over your head and expect the bank to help you out.'

"I tried to explain to him that we had made the deal with them, and they should stick with it. And he said, 'Well, you can't put in a supermarket now, and that's not our fault. We're only going to loan you $75,000.' That was $50,000 less than we expected. Mr. Curtis continued to say, 'You merchants always spend more than you expect, and you always make the bank bail you out.'

"I said, 'Mr. Curtis, we have never in our life done that. When we make a deal, we try to think it through well enough so we don't have to come back, and we've never come back to the bank for more money to complete a deal. When we've made a mistake, we've figured out a way to complete the project without going back to the bank.'

"He says, 'You did it on South Division. You didn't have enough money, and you borrowed $25,000 and then you came back for $10,000 more.'

"I said, 'Mr. Curtis, that's not true. We borrowed that money to open the Eastern store. We borrowed $25,000 to open Division, and we opened it. And then we came to you and said we would like to open the Eastern store. We asked you to help us finance that by putting in an additional $25,000 and taking an additional mortgage on the South Division store, which was well worth the money.'

"He told me that wasn't the way he remembered it, and I suppose I was a pretty young kid to be talking back to the banker that way. But to make my point more complete, I went back to the office, documented every one of our moves, and wrote him a letter explaining that I was right.

"Well, what I found out was that you can be ever so right with a stubborn banker, but you aren't going to get your money."

Abe Abraham

The first time I met Fred, he came to our warehouse on Division Avenue and bought three thousand dollars worth of merchandise. They had just opened their first store in Grand Rapids. Until then, I only knew Fred by reputation, which was of an upcoming merchant but short on capital. He paid me with a check, and as soon as he left, I headed for the bank. That was the beginning of a business relationship that has been going on for more than sixty years.

The next — and biggest — bump in the road for the Meijers came with the opening of the three Thrifty Acres outlets in 1962. The headlines of that year were not lost on Fred, but they were somewhat overshadowed by the long hours and worry he expended trying to make the new stores successful.

This was the beginning of the civil rights movement, which was an important issue for Fred, as he was able to catch only the headlines and newscasters in the flurry of the days' activities. President John F. Kennedy was playing a personal role in advancing civil rights, as was Dr. Martin Luther King, Jr., who gave his famous "I Have a Dream" speech in 1963. On the other side, George Wallace, the new governor of Alabama, declared: "Segregation now, segregation tomorrow, and segregation forever." That same year, President Kennedy was assassinated.

210,000 blacks, whites march for freedom

Harvey Lemmen

We opened our first Thrifty Acres combination store in the summer 1962. Since it was the first store of its kind, no one knew if the n' concept would work. There were no road maps or consultant' were in uncharted territory.

That first Thrifty Acres store was larger than all of th supermarkets combined, and two more were sched' fall. Unfortunately, things were steadily going fr' were losing money fast, including more than '

Going Broke? On.

alone, which was a fortune back then. Fred had said that it wasn't going to be easy, but I had no idea it would be so tough.

Fred started to make some radical changes midstream and we finally pulled through the crisis. I'm sure most any other person would have given up on the concept, but he believed in his vision and stuck with it.

Not knowing anything about the general merchandise side of the business, Fred and Hendrik had hired two executives from the Arlan's Company, which originated in the Northeast and was opening discount stores across the Midwest. They were to run the general merchandise side of the store, while Meijer executives would run the supermarket departments. The fit was not a good one. The Arlan's men were used to being addressed formally, whereas men and women at Meijer were on a first-name basis. Those differences in forms of address were superficial, but they indicated fundamental differences in outlook.

Things continued to decline. As everyone was scrambling to meet the Grand Opening deadline, one day Hendrik was disturbed to find Earl Holton, his young district manager responsible for the supermarket portion of the store, nonchalantly drinking a cup of coffee in the back room — while the general merchandise part of the store was a mess. Earl explained: "My supermarket is all set, but when I try to help them with the rest of the store, they tell me to mind my own business."

Finally, after several delays, the store opened on June 5, 1962. But the excitement quickly turned to disappointment: sales were drastically lower than expected. Not only that, but with an outside company leasing space in general merchandise, Fred had no power to correct problems with inventory, pricing, quality, and customer service in that area. It didn't take him long to realize that this wasn't going to work. The Meijer people, with their background strictly in food, would have to take over and quickly learn the general merchandise side of the business. With no money, no trained buyers, no managers, no systems, no general merchandise connections, and no credibility they had to place unschooled Meijer grocery people in key positions. It became a critical moment in the perfect storm.

Going Broke? Oh, No, Not Again!

To add to the problem, the company's flagship supermarket was gutted by a fire from a burglar's torch, and the desperately needed cash flow was interrupted. To get the money they needed to stay afloat, Fred and Lena had to personally endorse loans, and they had to put up everything they owned as collateral.

However, Meijer grocery people soon became successful merchants in a whole new field by applying the principles they had learned in the food business. They found that customers' expectations didn't change just because they were buying a dress or a toaster. They still wanted good quality at a fair price. Over the next five years, Meijer continued to fine-tune the Grand Rapids Thrifty Acres store as it added stores on Alpine Avenue and in Kalamazoo, Michigan.

When the next crisis arose, in 1967, it came as a surprise.

Earl Holton

We had just opened several new stores in which we'd included large home-and-garden centers. However, we hadn't run financial projections to determine what all of this new construction and inventory would do to our cash flow.

We discovered the bad news at a food-marketing meeting in Cleveland when someone from our TOPCO buying cooperative asked Fred when he was planning to pay his two million dollars in overdue debt. Fred was stunned. He immediately called our accountant, who confirmed that we had a serious cash-flow problem.

Being short of cash was one thing, but not paying our bills was never acceptable to Fred. But we were out of money. I recall Harvey and me sitting with Fred in his office the following Saturday; we were waiting for the phone to ring to see if the bank would give us another large loan. I realized that if they declined, I would be looking for work. Fred, on the other hand, would lose everything.

The company had now been given a slow-credit rating by the vendors. If an invoice was due in thirty days, it might not get paid for forty-five or sixty days. General merchandise suppliers took quick notice at a time when many other discounters were in trouble. When a company is slow in paying its bills, some suppliers — especially clothing manufacturers — will not ship goods. During this period, Meijer often had to wait for merchandise, and some manufacturers would not ship to them at all. So Fred got on a plane, and he headed for New York. He remembers the trip well:

"There were about a half dozen credit firms in New York that recommend whether or not suppliers should sell to you," he recalls. "The biggest one is Dunn and Bradstreet, and the second biggest is Credit Exchange.

"I went to Credit Exchange first, and talked to a Mr. Meyering. It was obvious from the start that he wasn't about to help me. In fact, he was quite abrupt: 'Based on your figures, we can't help you,' he said. I went away from his office feeling very bad. Then I went to Dunn and Bradstreet and talked to a Mr. Ackerbloom and explained our financial situation. He listened and said, 'We can't recommend your credit, and here's why.' He proceeded to show me in detail how our balance sheet was weak, highlighting the problems with our current ratio of assets to liabilities. He went on: 'But if you do such and so, then we can recommend your account again.' What a difference in the two meetings! One man treated me rather rudely, and the other treated me like a gentleman and helped me.

"I came back from New York vowing to take Mr. Ackerbloom's suggestions, and within a month our credit problem was straightened out."

Since his father and he started the business, Fred estimates that the company has dealt with over one hundred banks and lending institutions. During that time, only one has ever demanded its money back. "It came during one of our financial down times," he says. "We did talk them into letting us pay it back over a five-month period, but when the chips were down, they closed in. Sometimes this gives bankers a black eye, but for us it was only one out of a hundred. I think this speaks pretty well for the banking industry, as well as for Meijer's reputation."

Fred learned his lessons well: in 2008, Meijer's credit rating stood in the top 5 percent in the industry.

There would be more crunch times for the company over the years. No one ever starts out in a business with the idea of going broke. Yet, starting with the recession of 1975, eighty of the top one hundred discounters went out of business, well-known names such as E. J. Korvette, Hills, Arlan's, Gold Circle, Zayre, Miracle Mart, Ames, Venture, Yankee, King's, Woolco, Zody's, Turn Style, Witmark, Federal, Best, W. T. Grant, and many others. Thousands of stores were shuttered or sold, tens of thousands of jobs were lost, and many creditors went unpaid. These had all been bright lights in the retail business for a time, but they all ended up fading into oblivion.

The decade of the 1980s will be remembered as an era of bankruptcies, during which 230 companies disappeared from the Fortune 500 list, proving that size does not guarantee success.

Chapter Ten

Building the Brand

Bob Summers

In 1965, I was a new produce buyer, and one week I didn't order enough sweet corn, which was the feature item in our ad. I knew we would run out by Saturday; but when I called our supplier, the price had gone up and was now well above what we were selling it for. Even after serious negotiations, the supplier wouldn't budge. So I told him to keep his corn.

About that time, Fred dropped in — as he did quite often — and asked how things were going. I related what was happening with the sweet corn, knowing that he would appreciate my decision not to lose so much money. Fred smiled and told me that he appreciated my efforts, and then he asked me how I thought customers would feel when they came in to buy corn and we didn't have any. He explained that having the product to back up our promise was more important than the price.

He thanked me again for doing a good job and wished me a good day. He never made me feel stupid. However, I called the supplier back and ordered corn for Saturday's business.

Kevin Holt

My responsibilities in operations included overseeing the gas stations, which involved determining gas prices. The importance of never having gas prices higher than our competitors was impressed upon me by

Fred. This was no easy task with 140-plus Meijer gas stations, each occupying its own market with a dozen or so competitors nearby, and with gas prices fluctuating daily.

Though we had a system in place to be competitive, invariably another gas station would price its gas lower than ours. It was not unusual to get a call from Fred letting us know that a competitor was one or two cents lower per gallon. He always passed his information along in a positive way, but there was no mistaking that he meant business when he said we shouldn't be priced higher than our competitors, not even by a penny.

What do these two anecdotes have to do with building a brand? Actually, everything. The dictionary defines *brand* as something imprinted indelibly on the heart, mind, or memory. The lesson that was taught in these two experiences has been crucial to the success of the Meijer brand. Every company, every product — indeed every person — has its own unique identity. A brand is a combination of image, reputation, and personality — its own DNA. Ranchers in the old west used to brand their cattle; even though the cows all looked the same, the brand they carried was a reflection of the owner. Other ranchers, by recognizing a brand, could tell how prosperous that ranch was, how the owners treated their ranch hands, and whether they could be trusted.

Companies spend a large part of their budgets on packaging, advertising, promotions, and public relations in their efforts to build favorable brand recognition. When you hear the word "McDonald's," or see the golden arches, your mind subconsciously registers a series of associations based on what you have heard, seen, or experienced. The same thing happens when your mind encounters Disney, Starbucks, Goodyear, Sears, Enron, or Mother Teresa. Advertising constantly reminds us that Rice Krispies go snap, crackle, and pop, that our fingers can do the walking through the Yellow Pages, and that it takes two hands to handle a Whopper.

The marketing of the Meijer brand took a quantum leap forward when three Thrifty Acres combination stores debuted in 1962: overnight they went from selling 4,000 food items to offering 105,000 food and general-merchandise products. If necessity is the mother of invention, then Fred and his management team, out of necessity, had to figure out how to market this new concept of selling clothes, paint, toys, jewelry, electronics, appliances, shoes, prescriptions, plumbing supplies (including the kitchen sink), not to mention banking services, shoe repair, a barbershop, party stores, and other services. Alongside the growing pains accompanying a new venture of this magnitude, the expression that became synonymous with the new format was: one-stop shopping.

It was the first time in retail history that anyone could make this claim. From the beginning, Hendrik and the family emphasized what they wanted to be known for when they opened the doors to their North Side Grocery in 1934: low prices and good old-fashioned customer service would make the difference in a community already oversupplied with grocery stores.

Al Waldorf

Hendrik was a very astute businessman, and Fred was a fast learner. They built their business by listening to the customers. They were always looking for and negotiating for the best deals that went with their dedication to low prices.

I remember we sold bologna and bananas below cost and bread and milk at about cost. I wondered why they picked these items as loss leaders. Pretty soon I realized: these particular items were highly perishable, and you couldn't stock up on them. You had to keep coming back to buy these staples, and when you did, you would most likely get the rest of your groceries, too. It was a real lesson in merchandising.

One thing that has always bothered Fred is making customers wait.

Mike Stewart

In 1981, shortly after buying the Twin Fair chain in Ohio, Fred and Lena were visiting the stores. I was the manager at the Marion, Ohio, store, and had been with Twin Fair for several years. The Twin Fair stores sold general merchandise and were usually part of strip malls, so we didn't open until 9:30. I was conducting a meeting with the employees in the front of the store, telling them about Meijer, our new owner. My assistant manager, Bill, was at the front door to let employees in and keep any customers out until we opened.

At 9:35, Fred and Lena walked up to the front door. Not knowing who they were, Bill told them that the store was not open yet because we were having a meeting with the employees. Fred told Bill it was after 9:30. Bill assured him that the meeting was almost over and he would have to wait.

I heard Fred's voice and immediately ended the meeting, while poor Bill was doing his job of holding Fred at bay. That morning I learned a lesson about customers: 9:30 means 9:30. Fred has joked with me numerous times over the years that I wouldn't let him come into his own store.

John Stephenson

I had just joined the company in the real-estate division, and Fred asked me to join him and Harvey Lemmen, the company president, on a trip to Detroit, where we had just opened two stores. I packed my bags for an overnight trip, and we spent the first day looking at new store sites. The next morning, we were going to stop at the newest Detroit store, whose hours were 7:00 a.m. to 11:00 p.m. We pulled into the parking lot at ten minutes to seven. There were customers waiting at all three store entrances. Fred got out and approached one of the groups. He asked what was happening, but he didn't tell them who he was.

"Waiting for the store to open," someone replied. It was then four minutes to seven, and Fred was getting nervous. He started going from door to door, peering in and knocking, trying to get someone's attention. At 7:00, the doors were still locked. By 7:04, Fred was fit to be tied. Still, no one realized who he was, and one of the customers tried to calm him down: "It's okay, sir," she said. "They never open at 7:00."

One summer evening in 1987, Earl Holton, the company president, was leaving one of the Columbus stores after it had closed for the night. Looking across the street, he saw that all the lights from a new competitor in town, Cub Foods, were still on. They were still doing business.

Earl approached Fred the next morning about staying open twenty-four hours. Fred needed no encouraging; he immediately agreed. Now the stores began operating twenty-four hours a day seven days a week, adding even more convenience to the One-Stop Shopping/Why Pay More? brand.

Operators of the central switchboard, which handles incoming calls for all stores, immediately saw a 50 percent reduction in customer calls. The number-one question they had been asked every day was, "How late are you open?"

> *De kost gaet voor de baet uyt.*
> ("The bitter taste of poor quality remains long
> after the memory of a sweet price.")
> — Dutch proverb, remembered
> by Fred from his childhood

One very important attribute of any successful brand is quality. As the tag line from one well-known manufacturer puts it, "The quality

---

Since our family opened the first Meijer store in 1934, we have been driven by a simple goal–your satisfaction. Today we continue that commitment to you and your family by ensuring that only top-quality products carry the Meijer name.

I am proud to put my name on this product. Think of it as your guarantee that we've done our best to bring you the best.

Fred Meijer

QUALITY ASSURED

---

goes in before the name goes on." Since many of the products sold at Meijer stores are private label, including the Meijer brand itself, quality has always been one of Fred's fetishes.

Mike Major recalls Fred asking him about a certain brand of mouthwash and toothpaste the dentist had recommended. "Isn't ours just as good?" he wanted to know. In checking, they found that the ingredients of the national brand were exactly the same as in the Meijer brand; in fact, that manufacturer was supplying both products for the Meijer label.

On another occasion, a Meijer buyer remembers visiting the potato-chip plant of a well-known brand that was also packaging the Meijer label. After the production quota of the national brand had been reached, the Meijer packaging was put on the production line. They were the same potato chips, but the customer was paying 30 percent less.

Customer Satisfaction

Tim Van Ravenswaay

I was managing one of the Lansing stores when one afternoon Fred called me on the intercom and asked if I was available. He had just observed a customer being denied a refund on toothpaste that was a K-Mart brand. So as not to embarrass anyone, he hadn't said anything to the employee who, after all, was trying to protect his interest, but he had intercepted the customer and wanted to meet her.

After introductions, Fred was touting the quality and value of the Meijer brand and offered the customer one of every Meijer brand product she could use, from anywhere in the store. It took us an hour and two full grocery carts, but we ended up with one happy customer.

Hendrik and Fred knew that a few people would probably take advantage of their liberal refund policy, but that's the price they were willing to pay to satisfy legitimate complaints and honest returns.

"We developed our refund policy," Fred recalls, "as a result of an incident that happened shortly after we had gone into the grocery business.

"A customer brought back a ten-cent package of a Rice Krispie-type cereal. It came from A&P, and said so right across the bottom: 'The Great Atlantic and Pacific Tea Company.' He said, 'My wife got this here. It's the wrong thing, and we want our money back.' I started to point out to the man, 'Sir, you couldn't have bought that here. This says Atlantic and Pacific.' My dad spoke up and said to give the man his ten cents back for what he bought here. Afterward, he took me off to one side and said, 'Don't send him to A&P for a dime. *We* can eat the cereal.'"

Freshness

The word "fresh" describes an attribute that every store and product wants to be known for. Freshness is most often thought of in reference to perishables in departments such as produce, meat, deli, and bakery, but the adjective can also apply to new trends in fashion, seasonal products, flowers, and an enjoyable shopping experience.

In the beginning, having the freshest and best perishables was easy, because father, mother, son, and daughter inspected everything that came through the back door. They purchased produce at the farmers' market or from local farmers. They bought cattle and hogs at the nearby stock auction, and they inspected them before giving the nod to place a bid. They got fresh eggs in trade for other goods from farmers' wives who knew the hens by name.

"The only way to get it fresher is to catch it yourself"

City bus in Louisville, Kentucky, 1998

One week in the fall of 1985, the produce department was going to feature fresh peaches at a hot price, and they wanted to know what could be done in the marketing and advertising department to make an impression on the customer. They decided to try something new: they ordered special peach-scented printing ink and used it to print a full-page color ad in the weekly "One-Stop Shopper."

It must have made an impression, recalls one advertising executive, because the printers complained that their shops smelled like peaches. The paper delivery people smelled like peaches, and whatever room you laid the "One-Stop Shopper" down in smelled like peaches. But the produce department set a record for selling peaches.

Bob Summers

Squeezing fresh orange juice every day was a time-consuming job that required cleaning all the machine parts afterwards. I had recently been promoted to produce director, and decided to have enough juice made on Saturday for Sunday sales. At the time, employees were paid double on Sunday, so we could save a lot of money.

The following week, Fred stopped in my office and mentioned he had been to a store over the weekend and was informed that we didn't make fresh orange juice on Sunday anymore. "Wouldn't it be nice if we had fresh orange juice every day?" he asked. I explained how much we were saving in labor costs by having Sunday's juice made on Saturday.

He listened attentively to my entire spiel before he put his hand on my shoulder and with a smile said, "Bob, you're right, but wouldn't it be nice if we had fresh-squeezed orange juice every day?" He had taken the time to listen, and then simply repeated his question. Guess what my next decision was.

Don Eberhard

In the mid-1970s, the food industry got a scare when a major Michigan supplier of livestock had some polybrominated biphenyl (PBB) accidentally get mixed in the feed. Animals eating this contaminated feed could and in some cases did die. The concern was that it would be passed on for human consumption through the meat, milk, or eggs.

A number of state and federal agencies were scrambling to determine the extent of the problem in an effort to protect the public. Immediately upon hearing about the problem, the Meijers made the decision to have samples of all beef, chicken, eggs, and milk tested for PBBs. This involved having samples air-freighted to a laboratory in Wisconsin several times a day. The cost was over ten thousand dollars a week, and this went on for ten weeks. We were the only retail company to take this precautionary measure, and it was done behind the scenes without any fanfare.

Darrell Schmuker

As the vice president over the foods area, it was my responsibility to attend the monthly board meetings and report on the previous month's sales and profits. The board meeting that is most memorable is one where we reported an unusually large profit.

Feeling very good, I wasn't prepared for the concern Fred had about why the profits were so high. Were our prices too high? What about the competition? Perhaps we should lower prices or run some hotter specials.

Consumer Reports, in its August 1997 issue, reported on thirty-five major grocery companies. Based on 22,000 consumer responses,

Meijer received the highest rating for food prices. The consistent message that Fred has preached over the years showed up in the mind of the consumer.

Duke VanDenBerg

We hadn't been in the general merchandise side of the business very long after opening our first Thrifty Acre stores back in the '60s. I was the buyer for sporting goods, still trying to decide what items we should be selling.

Fred was into skiing at the time. This was a category we didn't have, thinking that was best left to sporting-goods stores. He could have said just do it, but that isn't the way he does things. Instead, he took me to the basement of his house, and showed me everything necessary — skis, boots, straps, hangers, wax, and so forth. He was a good teacher, and over the years we sold a lot of skiing equipment.

Sandi Wagenknecht

On April 4, 2000, we were about to open our new store in Richmond, Indiana. Fred and Lena were there with the mayor for a ribbon-cutting scheduled for 6:50 a.m. The store was scheduled to open at 7:00 a.m., and there were several hundred people lined up at the door waiting. As soon as Fred saw them, he said, "This can wait. Let those people in." We did, and after the initial rush was over — about an hour later — we had our ribbon-cutting.

Tim Zehr

At some point as a store director, you are going to encounter a customer you can't satisfy on the first go-round, despite your best efforts. This is the critical point when you either retain the customer or you lose their business plus the business of everyone they tell their story to. No one knows this better than Fred.

He called me one afternoon and asked me if I recalled a conversation I'd had with a customer regarding a refund I had refused. I explained to him why I had denied the refund. He listened to my story, told me that I was right, based on our refund policy, and then asked me if I would please drive to the customer's home and give her the refund anyway. He suggested I take along a nice fruit basket and tell her we appreciate her business. It was a good lesson: if you're going to make a mistake, make it in favor of the customer.

Like many great teachers, Fred often speaks in parables. One day he was talking to a group of buyers when he held up a three-legged stool he had brought with him. He asked if anyone knew what this particular stool was used for, and a few of them recognized it. He explained that three-legged stools had been used in the past for milking cows by hand, something every farmer did prior to the advent of automated machines. In fact, the stool he held in his hands was the one Lena had used in her childhood to milk cows.

Then he asked why milking stools had only three legs. No one knew, and by now everyone was curious. He explained that floors in old barns were often uneven, and that a stool with four legs would be unsteady.

"Our business is like this three-legged stool," he said. "Each leg stands for an important principle. First, you need a great format, which we have with one-stop shopping; second, you must have the right products; third, you need to have the right prices. Just like this stool, you need all three legs in business, and they all have to be solidly planted on the floor lest you risk spilling the milk. Or, in our case, losing customers."

Michael and Laura Panfil's experience of the Meijer brand

Dear Mr. Meijer,

As former residents of southwestern Michigan, we'd like to convey our appreciation to you and your team for bringing to us the wonderful Meijer shopping experience. We frequented the Mishawaka and South Bend, Indiana, stores and counted it a privilege to do business with a company such as yours.

We were married shortly after those two stores opened in 1994. As a young couple on a tight budget, we quickly learned that doing most or all of our shopping at Meijer was in our best interests. Not only are your stores clean, brightly lit, and well stocked, but we could always find the products we were looking for, no matter how unusual. In addition, there were courteous team members around to answer our questions or point us in the right direction.

The food court became one of our favorite places for "doughnut dates." We also enjoyed being able to stop for Chinese food at great prices, without having to leave the store. And the many conveniences of having groceries, health and beauty products, clothing, housewares, and much more all under one roof are too numerous to mention.

We could fill page after page with reasons that we fell in love with your establishment. However, let us get to our main purpose for writing.

Due to a job change, we moved in late January. Our biggest adjustment after moving was the lack of any Meijer stores in this state! Having heard a rumor that your plans are to expand in the west, we can only hope that you will soon make your way down to Arkansas.

Our shopping experience these last five months has not been pleasant. In fact, it took us seven hours one day to complete all of our purchases in order to get everything we needed. The reason? We first had to wait in line at the bank to cash a check, when all we needed before was a Meijer One Card. Second, we had to go to seven different stores to find all the items on our list and to get the best prices. Also, we had to stop at a fast food place to eat while we were in between stores. When we got home, we realized that every item on our list could have been purchased at Meijer for much lower prices and all under one roof, saving us time and money.

> *(signed)*
> *Michael and Laura Panfil*

Chapter Eleven

Light Years Ahead

If you fail, it's because you took a chance. If you *succeed,* it's because you grasped an opportunity.

— Fred Meijer

While the term "light years" literally refers to distance in space, in layman's language it can describe a big head start or a quantum leap forward — when a new idea, product, or invention outpaces everything else in its field. Einstein's theory of relativity, offering a new way to look at time and space, was such an example in physics. Such new paradigms are nurtured and molded by visionaries who, often with more determination than talent, overcome obstacles that others cannot imagine.

In grade-school history books we read about Eli Whitney, who had an idea for separating seeds from cotton. His cotton gin transformed Southern agriculture and the national economy at that time. Cyrus McCormick knew he had a better idea on how to harvest wheat and grain products. His invention was the forerunner of the International Harvester Corporation, founded in 1902. Others who were light years ahead included Thomas Edison, Alexander Graham Bell, and Wilbur and Orville Wright. Bell, a scientist, innovator, and inventor, was awarded the U.S. patent for the telephone in 1876, and he tried to sell his device to the folks at Western Union for $100,000. They said, "No thanks. We have the telegraph. Besides, your telephone is nothing more than a toy." Two years later they were willing to pay twenty-five million; by then, of course, Bell was no longer interested in selling.

The founder of General Electric, Thomas Alva Edison, changed life around the world with his invention of the electric light bulb. Unhampered by his deafness, he became one of the most prolific inventors in history, holding over 1,000 patents. Someone once told Wilbur and Orville Wright that, if man were meant to fly, God would have given him wings. Undaunted, they set about unlocking the secret of aerodynamics and went on to build the first fixed-wing aircraft, which effectively shrank the world we live in.

Chester Carlson knew he had a good idea and persisted in his quest for many years, encountering disappointment and failure as he tried to convince others of the value of his electrostatic photocopier, forerunner of the Xerox machine. Imagine any office, school, or hospital today trying to function without a copy machine.

With the arrival of a new paradigm, everything starts over. It does not matter how good you were at the old paradigm, how big you were, or how strong your reputation. Your past success guarantees you nothing when the rules change. Steven Jobs, Steve Wozniak, and Ronald Wayne built the first personal computers (PCs) in a garage and formed Apple Computer in 1976, taking the world from mainframes that cost millions of dollars to desktops that almost anyone could afford. It was a major paradigm shift for IBM, which had believed that its mainframes would always control the world of information.

In 1869, the transcontinental railroad was completed with the driving of a gold spike in Promontory, Utah. For the next hundred years railroads would dominate how goods would be transported across the nation. Then another paradigm shift in transportation came with the mass production of the automobile. More automobiles led to better roads, which allowed for bigger vehicles, which in turn increased flexibility and reduced travel time for shipping freight. The railroad owners, blinded by their success, realized too late that the rules for transporting goods and people had changed. New ideas cause change and disrupt the status quo, and they are often shot down by those who continue to view the future as an extension of the past. Thomas Kuhn has put it this way:

The person who embraces a new paradigm at the early stage must often do so in defiance of the evidence provided. He must have the faith that the new paradigm will succeed in spite of the many problems that confront it. A decision of that kind can only be made by faith.

Henry Ford used his idea of a mass-production assembly line to provide a lower-cost automobile that most people could afford, thus setting a new paradigm for how America shopped. With an automobile people could travel further, driving past their local neighborhood stores to the bigger stores with bigger parking lots, bigger selections, and lower prices.

Prior to World War II, most Americans lived in small towns or on family farms. They relied on the Sears, Roebuck and Montgomery Ward catalogs and the postal service for many of their goods. Travel was just too costly and time-consuming, and large stores in the cities were too far away. The catalogs of that era would rival the department and big-box stores of today. Clothes, wood stoves, medicine, windmills, horse liniment, farm implements, beds, bedding, sewing fabrics, Victrolas, even baby chicks were shipped through the mail. When the fall catalog arrived, the spring catalog would be moved to the outside privy, in a time when toilet tissue was considered a luxury.

Meanwhile, the components of the modern-day supermarket first came together following the stock market crash of 1929 in Jamaica, New York. There, in a vacant automobile garage, Michael Cullen, a former Kroger store manager, opened his "no frills" store. His location and the stark setting of the old garage kept the overhead low and reflected the bargain prices found inside the "King Cullen" store. Cullen's idea was to sell high volume at very low markup.

With the country in a depression, every housewife who was just trying to put food on the table thought only about getting more for less. In addition, Cullen's selection of groceries, meat, produce, dairy, and everyday household goods offered unprecedented variety. He built enormous displays and advertised heavily. It was a paradigm shift that would attract shoppers by the thousands. His competition called him the "world's greatest price wrecker," a distinction Cullen welcomed, and it only added to the public's affection for the store.

Ironically, it was while working at Kroger that Cullen had sent his idea in a letter to the president of Kroger. His letter was intercepted by another Kroger official who couldn't believe Cullen was serious. But Cullen's new approach had hit a nerve with the public and the supermarket was born, although the word "supermarket" would not be used until three years later, when Kroger's president himself resigned to open his own version of the "King Cullen" store in Cincinnati. The idea of piling it high and selling it cheap was light years ahead of traditional grocery stores of that era.

Although independent operators were the first grocers to gamble on the supermarket idea, the chains were quick to exploit its potential. The supermarket was a product not only of the Depression but of the automobile. From 1920 to 1930 the number of licensed autos in the United States jumped from eight million to twenty-three million. Until the automobile age, New Deal economist Adolph Berle noted, the same local merchants who had denounced chain-store practices had sometimes enjoyed neighborhood monopolies. But the car reduced the consumer's dependence on and loyalty to the neighborhood store or chain: now shoppers were able to seek out lower prices and greater variety. And the supermarket, with so much more space than a conventional grocery store, offered both.

By 1936, A&P, the biggest chain of all, had begun casting off its old stores to cash in on the new supermarket phenomenon. The theory was that "three quick nickels are better than one slow dime." So, recognizing the magnetic appeal of the King Cullen idea, the A&P chain experimented with formulas that would satisfy the new criteria of low price and wide variety. A&P stores opened in old warehouses, and they even tried selling groceries in dime stores. A&P tested stores of many sizes and designs until its management hit on a format of a 10,000-square-foot store. The new format, first introduced in Ypsilanti, Michigan, and then in Detroit, was five times the size of the normal grocery store of the day. Hendrik Meijer's Thrift Market in Greenville, by comparison, occupied little more than 1,400 square feet. In the spring of 1937, A&P announced plans for nineteen supermarkets in western Michigan.

Just twenty-five years later, another paradigm shift would occur, not on the east coast as had been the trend, but in a quiet city in the

Midwest surrounded by the Great Lakes. In his book *From Mind to Market*, R. D. Blackwell put it this way:

> Meijer is a thriving, pioneering company that was light years ahead of its time back in 1962, when it opened its first Thrifty Acres store, a marriage of the supermarket and a discount store all under one roof spanning two acres. It is a revolution in retailing that took Wal-Mart decades to master.
>
> When Meijer customers change, it changes with them. They were one of the first to open twenty-four hours, realizing that not everyone works a day shift and sleeps during the night. While competitors slept, Meijer learned to do business according to the customers' schedules.
>
> Throughout the years Meijer has continued to innovate, introducing new products and services well ahead of most competitors. (*From Mind to Market,* p. 401)

Without even realizing it, Meijer was on the verge of a twenty-five-year head start. During that time there were no other companies willing to gamble on stores of that size. Fred and his team rowed against the normal way of doing business. Competitors watched in shock as

The grand opening of Thrifty Acres, the country's first "one-stop shopping" store, at 28th Street and Kalamazoo Avenue, Grand Rapids, 1962

Former and current team members surround Fred (front row, center), July 2008. One thousand years of Meijer seniority is represented in this picture. *(Photo courtesy of Bob Strodtbeck)*

customers flocked to Thrifty Acres, which offered a cornucopia of merchandise and convenience.

Elsewhere in the country, retailers paid little attention to what was happening in western Michigan. Because none of its stores was located in a major metropolitan area, and because its stock was privately held, Meijer could expand dramatically while keeping a low profile in the industry. Thrifty Acres was an anomaly to conventional grocers, as it was to conventional discounters. That did not displease Fred, who did nothing to invite attention.

Jeffrey Feiner, *Retail Analyst, Solomon Bros.*

The supercenter format is a new retailing phenomenon that will be as important to the remainder of the 1990s and the next decade as shopping malls were to the 1960s, discount stores to the 1970s, and specialty outlets to the 1980s. A great deal of the growth potential of supercenters can be attributed to consumers' increasing lack of free time, and their appetite for low prices.

Sid Doolittle, *McMillen & Doolittle Assoc.*

Customers love Meijer. It becomes a destination of habit in every city it enters. People depend on it because they know they can go there and find whatever they're looking for.

George Rosenbaum, *Leo J. Shapiro Assoc.*

It is critical that a supercenter not have a weak side. Meijer knows the competition better than anyone. They have been practitioners longer and better, and they are way ahead of the competition.

At a convention in California, a man was telling about his travels and his visits to the Eiffel Tower, the pyramids of Egypt, and the Great Wall of China, among others, to which a lady from Grand Rapids asked, "Have you ever been in a Meijer store?" "No, I haven't," he responded. "I'd say we're even," she said.

After Meijer had been quietly building and operating combination stores for twenty-five years, a light suddenly went on in the retail world as everyone began to take notice. It is interesting that it was French companies who first saw the possibilities of putting these "hypermarkets" on American soil (*hypermarché* is a French word used to describe a combination supermarket and department store, the same as our supercenter). Like gold prospectors who had just discovered the mother lode, five of the largest French conglomerates, beginning in 1984, would each open a few of these stores from Maryland to Texas.

The first was Euromarché, which opened its first Biggs hypermarket in Cincinnati in 1984. The corporation eventually opened seven hypermarkets, but it continually lost money for several years before selling to SuperValu and the American Wholesale Company, which also operates grocery stores.

Undeterred — as well as afraid of being left behind — two more French companies opened stores in 1988. Auchan opened three stores, two in Texas and one in Chicago in 1989. None of these was successful; they were all closed by 2003. Carrefour tried its luck on the east coast, opening two hypermarkets, one near Philadelphia and the second in Voorhees Township, New Jersey. Carrefour's Philadelphia location was so large (330,000 square feet) that many employees used roller skates to get around. However, after being plagued from the beginning by poor sales and union troubles, the parent company closed this store in 1993 — after only one year of operation.

Finally, the E. Leclerc Group, a latecomer to the hypermarket wars, decided to put its toe in the rough American waters of retailing by opening its Leedmark hypermarket in Glen Bernie, Maryland, in 1991. That also proved unsuccessful and quickly closed. Within a few short years, all of these French companies had exited the U.S. market. Some would come back years later via the acquisition of traditional established supermarket chains, but never with hypermarkets.

Why was it that these great European companies failed in the United States? After all, Carrefour operates successfully in over thirty countries and is second in size worldwide only to Wal-Mart, the world's largest retailer. Similarly, Auchan operates large stores in twelve countries around the world. It has mystified business observers and analysts how a small, privately held company in Michigan could do it, while its larger and better financed peers were failing.

Here warehouse clubs could beat the European hypermarkets on price; "category killers" such as Toys R Us, Sports Authority, and Office Max could beat them on selection; and grocery stores had the best locations. However, these reasons don't seem valid to many observers, since thousands of Wal-Mart supercenters would spring up in the next two decades, succeeding in the same markets where the European hypermarkets had failed. The year 1988 will go down in history as the year companies opened, experimented, and generally failed in their quest for success with hypermarkets. Meanwhile, Meijer was busy opening new stores.

Nineteen eighty-eight was also the year that Wal-Mart opened "Hypermarket USA" in Garland, Texas, the first of four to open in the next twenty-four months. Being new to the perishable food side of the

business, they partnered with a successful regional grocery chain located there. But Wal-Mart could not get them to profitability, and it put its plans for expansion on hold.

Don Soderquist, *Retired Wal-Mart Executive*

David Glass and I hit the road again, this time up to Grand Rapids, Michigan, to visit a wonderful 'combination' — a commonplace today, but revolutionary in the early '80s, founded by Fred Meijer. He was a great merchant, particularly in food, a category in which he had a strong background. Meijer had been successfully operating combination stores in Michigan for some time. It was obvious that his stores were doing a great deal of business. We were also impressed with the many service shops they had at the front of the stores to serve a wide array of their customers' needs — from banking to family photos to hairstyling. It was on that trip that we decided that we should do the same thing in Wal-Mart. (*The Wal-Mart Way,* p. 16)

Stepping back and analyzing their future with combination stores and the success that Meijer was having, Wal-Mart executives decided that future stores needed to be smaller than their first hypermarkets, and that the name should be changed to Wal-Mart Supercenters. These new stores, the first of which opened in Washington, Missouri, became in many ways a mirror of the Meijer stores in Michigan, right down to layout, fixtures, and aisle signs. The new formats proved so successful that eventually Wal-Mart would have over 3,000 supercenters worldwide.

"A wise man learns from his mistakes. However, it's faster and less costly to learn from someone else's mistakes." (Fred Meijer)

In 1988, K-Mart was the nation's largest discounter in both sales and store count. Wishing to hold this position, it also went into the supercenter business and opened the first American Fare — a 220,000 square-foot store — twenty miles northeast of Atlanta. Like Wal-Mart, K-Mart partnered with a successful regional grocery chain, Bruno's, in hopes of gaining expertise in the food side of the business. But as with Wal-Mart, the new hybrid proved unsuccessful. Only three American Fares went into operation. Then the company began to build smaller stores, which they called Super K-Marts, beginning with a new prototype in Medina, Ohio, in 1991. A total of 104 Super K-Marts lost a lot of money over the next four years, until they finally turned a profit in 1993. But by that time it was too late. The luster had faded from the famous "blue light special," and before long the former number-one retailer found itself in Chapter 11 bankruptcy protection; it was forced to close or sell almost half of its supercenters.

Meanwhile, sitting on the sidelines watching all this activity, the last of the big three major retail companies in the United States — Target — decided the smoke had cleared enough for it to enter the grocery business. Founded with department-store roots, Target opened its first store in Roseville, Minnesota, a suburb of St. Paul in 1962. That was the same year that the first Wal-Mart store, the first K-Mart, and the first Thrifty Acres opened. A division of the Dayton-Hudson Company, Target was so successful that by 1979 its revenue had surpassed one billion dollars, making it Dayton-Hudson's most lucrative division. Its signature bulls'-eye icon, introduced in 1968, became synonymous with the company.

The parent company changed its corporate name to Target in 2000, reflecting that division's dominance. The nation's third largest retailer, Target did not grow by acquisition, unlike the giant Wal-Mart, and has not yet crossed the northern or southern U.S. borders. The first Super Target combination store opened in Omaha, Nebraska, in 1996. Target's learning curve with supercenters has not been as strenuous as all the others, nor has its success been as dramatic. By the spring of 2008, Target had opened fewer than seventy supercenters in the Midwest and Florida, and had not announced any significant growth plans for this sales format.

In its issue of August 21, 2006, *Progressive Grocer,* a leading voice of the grocery industry for more than eighty years, named Meijer Inc. its retailer of the year. In explaining the decision to honor the family-held Meijer chain with the magazine's highest annual award, *Progressive Grocer's* editor-in-chief, Stephen Dowdell, said: "The reasons for our selection are many, and include Meijer's reputation as an exemplary performer in the Midwest, even in the face of ferocious competition, and as an innovator in the supercenter format, with aggressive growth plans and demonstrated ability to continue to improve and build upon the concept that the Meijer family pioneered. Over its more than 70 years in business, Meijer has acquired entire generations' worth of loyal customers."

Dowdell further cited Meijer's exemplary status as "one of the nation's leading family-run grocery organizations that is well-loved by shoppers for its great selection and low prices." He also pointed to the chain's good corporate citizenship, evidenced by its "unswerving support to local education and community organizations."

Chapter Twelve

Handshakes and Contracts

In the old days, your word and a handshake were all that were necessary to cement the deal. Live up to your promises. If you can't deliver, don't promise.

— Fred Meijer

I n 1942, Hendrik and Fred had been itching to open a second store. The Thrift Market sales in Greenville were growing steadily. On Saturday, their busiest day, receipts were now over $1,000. The opportunity presented itself in the form of an abandoned car dealership in Cedar Springs, a small town fifteen miles west of Greenville. They talked it over with Gezina and Johanna, and decided to buy a 60-foot by 90-foot building on Main Street for $3,000. Seventy-five years later, you could put forty structures of that size inside a typical Meijer store.

No sooner was the ink dry on the contract than a rival grocer opened up across the street. And then Kroger announced that it would be replacing its small conventional store with a new supermarket. Hendrik and Fred were nervous. There would be more grocery stores than they thought a town of 1,104 could support. A wrong move could jeopardize all they had built up in Greenville.

They went to a lawyer to see if they could get out of the deal. They offered to forfeit their down payment and give back the building. "The contract is binding," he explained. "However, there is always some-

The Cedar Springs store, Store #2, ca. 1954

thing wrong with every contract, so we can claim that there is no clear title and we can probably find some other reasons." But Hendrik and Fred were adamant about the contract: "We're not going to do that. We bought it, and we'll live by our agreement." It turned out they were right: the town couldn't support all those grocery stores. Meijer was the last one in town when it finally closed its doors thirty-one years later.

This was the first contract Fred had ever signed for a building purchase, and it only required one signature. It would not be the last. There would be hundreds more, with some acquisitions requiring his signature ninety-nine times. Over seven decades and thousands of agreements, one thing that has never changed has been the promise: "We will live by our agreement."

"Twice in the last fifteen years," Fred says, "we have gone to the bank and told them that we would be agreeable to them raising our interest rates even though they were locked in. We said to them, 'Interest rates have gone up substantially, and we have a right to pay off. Had they gone down substantially, we'd have paid you off and requested or demanded a lower interest rate. Because they've gone up substantially, we would be agreeable to you raising your rate.' I think they were quite surprised that any of their customers would raise their own cost of money." (*IHOW*, p. 127)

"I guess no one had ever done that before," says Fred. "If a bank committed to what turned out to be too low an interest rate, that would be their loss." To him, fairness and long-term relationships outweigh the terms on the document.

"When we've negotiated leases, and been stuck on a single point, quite often I'd say, 'Okay, let's set this down on a piece of paper and go to the next one.' If you've got twenty issues you're working on in a lease, whatever the little points and big points are, by the time you get pretty near all of them resolved, then some of the other ones don't seem quite as important, and you end up being able to negotiate them out. I think I've used that approach when I've had parties in a dispute. I would say, 'Give me all your problems. Now, if we settle all of this, are you going to be happy?' 'Yeah.' 'Okay.' Then we'd try to settle it. And nobody raised their voice." (*IHOW*, p. 137)

John Stephenson

Being responsible for buying and selling Meijer real estate for many years, I learned a lot from Fred about negotiating. He always said, "Negotiate the best deal; the sellers know what they can afford to sell it for." On the other hand, his sense of fair play and his generous nature wasn't always in our best interest.

Bud Stehouwer

I started calling on Meijer as a supplier shortly after I was discharged from the army in 1945. They had three stores at the time. Back then, major companies like Standard Brands and Shedds, who I worked for, sold their products off delivery trucks. One of our items, Keyko margarine, had been rationed during the war. Now we had a surplus, and were offering a discount of five cents per pound. Fred was always looking for a deal. He bought two hundred cases. It was my biggest margarine order that year.

Things were tight for them back then. Their Greenville store burned to the ground in 1946, and they didn't have much insurance on the building, but we never worried about getting our money. All the vendors liked calling on Meijer because of the way they were treated. They never forgot those loyalties. When my wife and I celebrated our sixtieth wedding anniversary, we got a huge fruit basket and congratulations from Fred and Lena.

Fred Welling

In 1964, we were in the process of building our first two Thrifty Acre stores in Kalamazoo. We leased space to noncompeting businesses all along the concourse at the front of the store.

We had negotiated with a local bank to have a branch at one store, but the bank was reluctant to take a second smaller store. Fred wanted them in both stores, and he offered a deal whereby they could leave at any time if they weren't satisfied. They agreed. By now, construction was well under way, but we were obligated to have their area ready by the grand opening.

As we were nearing completion, the president of the bank called Fred, and in a very belligerent manner said we weren't doing enough to get their space ready. Fred called me to explain the situation. He asked me to meet with the banker even though I should expect to be given a rough time. I should just sit there and take it. That's exactly what happened. The bank president did a superb job of chewing me out. We did have the space ready on time, and they were happy tenants for many years. Fred knew no one would win if we both lost our tempers.

Tom Vilella

We had scheduled a meeting at the Frederik Meijer Gardens with executives of a large printing company that had been printing our weekly "One Stop Shopper" for more than twenty years. The reason for the meeting was to try to convince them to invest several million dollars into new equipment that would be needed to reformat the "Shopper." We both knew that this sizable investment would only benefit Meijer, because we would be the only company using the unique format.

Fred was recovering from hip surgery, so I had invited Hank to attend. A few minutes before the meeting, Pam called to say that Hank would be a few minutes late, but that Fred would also be there. I met Fred as he arrived and thanked him for coming. His response was, "We can't afford to lose a long-term relationship with our vendors."

While contracts are a necessary part of today's world, they are usually lengthy, repetitive documents spiked with nearly incomprehensible legal jargon. Handshakes over an agreement, usually done on the spur of the moment, seem to come from a simpler, more humane world.

Jim Montgomery

As far as I know, Fred has never smoked or consumed alcohol. About twenty-five years ago, he came into my store and made an offer to a couple of managers who were smokers. He told them that he would personally give them $50 apiece if they stopped for one year. In those days, our company was much smaller, and he was on his own antismoking campaign. I had heard that several managers in other stores took his challenge, and true to his word, he paid up when they reached their goal.

Dave McIntyre

I was waiting to board the Meijer plane, taking my last puffs on a cigarette. On the flight, I was seated next to Fred and Harvey Lemmen, the company president. Fred reminded me that smoking was not good for my health. Then he offered me a bet. If I quit smoking for one year, he'd give me $100. If I lost, I was to pay him one penny. I took the bet, we shook hands, and he called Pam to make a note of it.

Every time that year, when I ran into Harvey, he would pat my chest pocket for cigarettes and ask how I was doing. Later, at a store directors' meeting, Harvey reminded Fred that the year was up. Fred hadn't forgotten either. He took a wrinkled blank check out of his billfold, and wrote it out for a hundred dollars.

Dear Fred:

This is Joe and I have a unusual Request To make, I don't Like To Ask. I bought Some New Tools and IT Took ALL of my money, I am behind on my child Support Payments and without Notice They came To My house and Took me To Court and Then To Jail. what I need is a Personal Loan for $350.00 To get out of here. I'LL Put My Van or Tools up for Collerital If you consider This, ALL The People or friends are on a vacation or don't have any money. My Talents Shouldn't Be Locked up. ALL you can Say is yes or No. I don't want To spend 90 days in here or $350.00 To get out and work. I can Pay you back within 1 month, I've Learned a Lot here and been Reading Bible Related things. IT's given me a New Lite on Life If This is what it Took Thank you Sincerely,

Jail Address ⟶ Joe
701 Ball N.E.
I can get out any time when Grand Rapids, michigan
I pay it - Day or Night 49503

Letter from inmate

Pam Kleibusch

Fred has trusted so many people over the years. I recently stumbled across a note from 1982. He'd been visiting the Plainfield store, where a man approached him and asked if he could borrow twenty dollars for gas to get to Cadillac. Fred called me and asked me to write down the man's name and to jot a note, since he'd said he would repay the debt once he reached Cadillac.

Fred never got his money back. The man must have forgotten — or maybe he hasn't made it to Cadillac yet.

Jim Hilboldt

For fifteen years I served on the Meijer board of directors. Time and again I saw Fred make wise decisions. If there was an ethical issue in the gray area, he would quickly move out of the gray and into the clearly ethical. Whether it was an employee or corporate or public-sector issue, I could always trust and rely on his ethics and integrity.

A good example of how Fred liked to handle problems occurred in 1966. The original Thrifty Acres outlet on 28th Street and Kalamazoo Avenue was having growing pains, and needed to expand. But there was an issue with the parking lot: because of the topography, there were runoff problems during heavy rains. A neighbor had sued. Meijer's attorneys claimed the problem was "an act of God." A hearing had been set.

The neighbor was surprised when he entered the courtroom to see, instead of a battery of lawyers, just one man. Fred introduced himself and said, "I understand your problem. I think we can work this out." Several minutes of private discussion ended in a handshake. The case never came before a judge.

Chapter Thirteen

Creating a Culture

An institution is the lengthened shadow of one man.

— Ralph Waldo Emerson

Seventy percent of family-owned businesses never survive the second generation; the failure rate is 90 percent by the third generation. Meijer is one of the exceptions. There are three basic reasons for such a high attrition rate: plans for successors were never in place; the principles of the founder were never cemented in the heart of the company; most importantly, they didn't adapt to the changes in their business.

Hank, Fred, and Doug on ponies

Many of these changes, of course, involve technology; but they are mostly about fundamentals of business and human nature. When an organization feels too comfortable, and everything is nailed down, it is almost always a danger sign. What is usually missing is a relentless self-questioning. "How can we do better tomorrow than we did today?" is the question Fred has always asked.

Be Part of a Team

"Where there is harmony, there is strength. This applies to family, business and country." (Fred Meijer)

In 1987, when Fred and Earl decided to open the stores twenty-four hours a day, it never occurred to them to just issue a command. Instead, they set out to sell the idea to those people in store operations who would have to make it work.

Store directors, 1999

They had anticipated the initial reaction: "Are you crazy?" Didn't they realize that stores needed the nights to restock the shelves, mop the floors, and reset departments? Besides, security would be compromised, shoplifting would run rampant, and there would be a host of other logistical nightmares.

Pretty soon, however, the idea began to percolate. After all, there were customers who preferred to shop at night, many of whom worked second or third shifts. They agreed that they would wait until after the Christmas holiday, even though they would forfeit a lot of additional sales. Fred and Earl knew that it was important to give those who were responsible to make it work time to embrace this radical change from the way business had been done before.

In the end, everyone pulled together as part of a team. It was a perfect example of one of Fred's philosophies: "People are only loyal to things they help create or improve." There has always been a yearning in the human spirit to reach for new horizons. We can all recall those moments in life when we were part of a team effort that broke new ground, times when we felt enormously excited and invigorated. Early on, Fred had learned from his parents that the culture must be built around the customer; without them, there would be no employees or suppliers. The lesson of the three-legged milking stool is never far from his mind: he realizes that how the employees are treated is likely how they will treat the customers.

The 24-hour
supercenter

Don Koster

I started working for Meijer in 1947 at the age of fourteen in their second store located in my hometown of Cedar Springs, Michigan. Their third store in Ionia had just opened. A few years later I was transferred to the Division Avenue store in Grand Rapids, which was the furthest from my home. One day Fred came in and mentioned, "You sure have a long drive every day." The next week I was transferred to the Fuller Avenue store, which was much closer. Fred was always looking for ways to make things easier for us.

Phil Knoll

I started at the Holland store sorting bottles in the back room. This was in 1966, when almost all beverages were sold in glass bottles. I hadn't been there very long when one day a talkative man stopped and during our discussion told me he had a son who sorted bottles at the store on Michigan and Fuller in Grand Rapids. Years later, I found myself working in the advertising department with Hank Meijer, the other bottle-sorter Fred had been referring to that day.

Leonard Krampe

In 1950, the store manager at Cedar Springs left, and I was appointed to the position. I had been working at the Greenville store under two managers who really knew how to get things done. In Cedar Springs I observed that the bookkeeper was taking all day to balance the books, when in Greenville, at a much larger store, it had taken only two hours. I tried to talk to the bookkeeper about it, but she went home crying — and called Fred. The next day he came in and reassured me that she was indeed taking too long, but that I might want to consider whether I could run the store right now without her. He didn't tell me what to do, but he gave me something to think about. She stayed.

Jim Pranger

I had spent close to thirty years in retail management when I first arrived at Meijer. The first thing I noticed was that they were different from the other companies I had worked for. Everyone — from senior management to the hourly staff — welcomed me and went out of their way to help me get acclimated to the Meijer way of doing business.

There were new terms to learn at Meijer: "first assistant" meant "boss," "challenges" were formerly known to me as "problems," and of course, "Is there anything I can do to help you?" which I don't recall having heard in other companies where I worked. Moreover, people treated each other with dignity and respect, and the motivational language used to get the job done was always positive and non-threatening.

I soon realized that this positive spirit emanated from one man, who, through his example and directive, had set the hallmark of the Meijer business philosophy: Everyone should be treated with dignity and respect at all times.

Vendors receive the same level of respect. As a result, Meijer has enjoyed many advantages that most large public companies don't receive. The company can always be trusted to conduct business on a high ethical plane. Countless vendors with whom I have worked have commented on how Fred Meijer left a lasting impression on them. Many of these people have shared with me their fascination that the owner of a multibillion-dollar company can be genuinely interested in who they are, and thanks them regularly for helping Meijer achieve its business objectives.

Tim VanRavenswaay

All of our four kids worked at Meijer as soon as they were old enough to have a job. I wanted them to experience the Meijer culture before they left home for college and went on to their own careers.

Ben Negron

Prior to joining Meijer in 1984 as a produce trainee in the Ann Arbor store, I worked for a small chain of eight grocery stores. During the five years I worked there I saw the owner only twice and never had the opportunity to speak with him. In fact, word had it that he was not to be bothered.

You can imagine my surprise when, after working at Meijer for a few weeks, who should walk into the produce back room but Fred Meijer. He extended his hand and introduced himself, and for a moment I almost forgot my name. He asked me about my family and about myself and listened attentively as I told him about my parents, who were missionaries. That initial meeting made an impression on me. Here was a man with many stores and thousands of employees talking with me as if I was someone of great importance to him.

I've had the opportunity to visit with Fred ten other times since then (I've kept count), and he always asks me how my parents are doing. When I became a store manager, that first impression made me a better manager in terms of how I react to people no matter what their position.

Hire the Best

Meijer has management second to none, and they have management in depth. (*Supermarket Business,* May 1996)

In 1946, when Fred and Lena left on their honeymoon, their destination was Florida, with many stops along the way to check out grocery stores. In Cincinnati, Fred had made an appointment to see Bill Albers, the former president of Kroger, who was now running a successful chain of his own. Fred had a problem and he needed the retail sage's advice.

The meat departments in the three Meijer stores were losing money. In fact, the meat department had been a problem from the beginning. Hendrik and Fred did not know enough about meat to correct it, so they had made a lease arrangement with the butcher whereby he would own the department and pay 6 percent of sales to cover his overhead. That arrangement didn't prove satisfactory. When they had added the Cedar Springs store, they had gone back to trying to run the departments themselves, after they hired a different "meat man."

They paid this new employee a weekly salary plus bonus. However, with the third store opening in Ionia, things went from bad to worse.

Fred and Roland
Van Valkenburg
("Mr. Van")

Fred approached the butcher and told him that, since the meat departments were not profitable, they would need to reduce his pay by fifty dollars a week. Naturally, the butcher didn't think this was fair. He was now in charge of three meat departments, and doing more work than ever. He said that he needed to make $150.00 a week, or he would quit.

Fred and Hendrik talked it over. They both agreed that none of it sounded fair, yet they had nothing to lose. They might as well go broke in the meat department without him as with him; so they accepted his resignation. This was the dilemma Fred posed to Albers. His advice was that they needed a merchant, not just a butcher, to run the departments. It would have to be someone who could hire and fire people, who knew how to merchandise, and who could create ads.

Albers suggested that they not hire someone from a big chain like A&P, someone who was used to doing everything by the book and was not very creative. Fred was careful to take notes about everything Albers said. On returning to his office, he started asking around, and the name Roland Van Valkenburg kept coming up. "But he will never work for you," Fred was told. "He's used to running his own show, and has just sold his store and doesn't need the money." Fred and Hendrik sought out "Van," who told them just that. However, they were persistent, and the gruff older man eventually took a liking to the young upstart, Fred.

Okay, he said, he might be ready to go back into the business if the terms were right. Fred made the terms right in a hurry. The result was immediate improvement in the meat departments. Sales took off, overhead went down, sanitary conditions improved, and a sense of organization fell into place. Fred would reminisce later that that was the most profitable honeymoon he could have imagined. He realized that having the right people in the right jobs at the right time unquestionably made the difference between success and failure.

Harvey Lemmen

Fred has always looked within the company to promote people. He has always preferred to give existing Meijer employees the opportunity to grow. He believed that it was good for morale and that the best way to build a company is with people who you know share your philosophy. Fred also placed talent above education, and he didn't hesitate to promote someone into a new department if he thought that person could do the job. I was hired into the company as a bookkeeper in 1940, but I ended up working in store operations, warehousing, buying, and merchandising, even though I didn't have prior experience in those areas. Fred's philosophy gave many of us the confidence to give other people opportunities in new areas as well.

Harvey Lemmen

Fred nonchalantly stopped by one day and asked me if I would like to be chief executive officer of the company. I thanked him and then declined his offer. He thought for a minute, then asked me if I would like to be either vice or deputy chairman and chief operations officer. I preferred "deputy chairman" because I didn't like the word "vice." Just like that, I was the deputy chairman and chief operations officer, though I don't recall any fanfare or changes in my responsibilities at the time.

Earl Holton

Fred called me into his office one day. I remember having recently celebrated my twenty-sixth birthday. He asked me if I wanted Harvey

Lemmen's job. Harvey had recently been promoted, and I wasn't sure if I was ready to fill his shoes as operations manager.

I told Fred as much. He pondered my reaction for a moment before asking, "Then who do you suggest we promote to be your boss?" I quickly concluded that I was the man for the job. For a man who never went to college, Fred had a great handle on human psychology.

Mark Murray, *President of Meijer*

I'm often asked why I would give up the presidency at Grand Valley State University to accept the same position at Meijer. After all, academia and retailing aren't exactly sister vocations. The answer to the question goes back to my being an observer of the Meijer culture as a customer for several decades. Then, when I became president of Grand Valley, the evidence of Meijer generosity was everywhere, from the Meijer Broadcast Center to the Cook-DeVos Center for Health Sciences, which has a floor dedicated to Meijer.

Even though he had never attended college, Fred was active at

Mark Murray and store director Susan Merkle at the grand opening of the store in DeWitt, Michigan, 2007

Grand Valley events, and what was quickly obvious to me was his passion for learning. Soon we began exchanging books and comparing notes on books we had read. I was then asked to join Meijer's board of directors, where I got firsthand experience on the core values on which the company was built.

Even though my role as president of Grand Valley was deeply satisfying, and I thought long and hard about the transition, becoming president of Meijer, and becoming part of its culture, was an opportunity I couldn't pass up.

Fred's brilliance can be seen in the way he has selected, motivated, and mentored his management team. For more than thirty years under his leadership, there wasn't a single change in senior management except for retirements. The Meijer culture, which began with just the family members, now includes over 70,000 employees in five states, serving several million customers each week.

Delegate

"It's okay to delegate and it's okay not to delegate. It's pretending to delegate that's disastrous." (Fred Meijer)

Pam Kleibusch

When I started with Meijer, I didn't know a thing about the company or the Meijer family. Initially I thought, "This isn't my kind of work: it's just a job." I never thought I would be here this long, but when you work for great people who are always positive and who never criticize you, it becomes an easy decision to stay where you are.

Fred has never looked over my shoulder or micromanaged me. He's like that with everyone. Instead, he strives to hire the best person for the job, and then gives them the responsibility to carry out their duties.

Harvey Lemmen

In 1955 we opened our own warehouse to supply the seven Meijer stores that were operating at the time. We rented an old building on the northwest side of Grand Rapids, and soon everything was in chaos. After the warehouse manager quit out of frustration, Fred asked me if I would work in the warehouse and help to get things straightened out. I didn't know beans about running a warehouse, but I went there and started working.

After my first day at the warehouse, I suggested to Fred that we hire someone who knew what they were doing and could help us get straightened out. We hired a consulting company to which we'd been referred, and they had us back on track within a couple of weeks.

One night during this time, after everyone else had left for the day, I loaded a truck that had to go to a store in the morning (this was before we had hi-los). I didn't know anything about weight restrictions, so I just kept piling it in. Things were like that back then: we did whatever job needed to be done at the time, and we learned from our experiences.

Earl Holton

In 1955, I was asked to manage the newest Meijer store, which was Store #9 at the time (this was before Thrifty Acres). I was twenty-one, and very excited about the opportunity. In those days, each store had a small general merchandise department that was run autonomously by a director of home centers from the main office. This director had decided that store managers should not be given keys to the stock rooms.

The holiday season arrived, and one day a customer requested an electric fry pan that wasn't on the sales floor. I knew we had one in the stock room, so I used a screwdriver to take the hinges off the door, and made a sale that we needed badly at the time.

I informed my supervisor of my actions and waited for the other shoe to drop. Much to my delight, it never happened. Fred had learned of the incident, and instead of a reprimand, he made sure that all store managers were given their own keys to the stock rooms.

George Zain

In 1957, I was a salesman for the Armour Meat Company, and was given the Meijer account. At the time, they only had eight supermarkets. They are still my only account, 52 years and 190 supercenters later.

During those years, Fred always looked forward to attending the grand openings. On the two occasions he couldn't attend, he asked me to be his representative and pass out his trademark ice-cream cone cards.

Fred is a master at delegating and building self-esteem in others. It's an important attribute of his style of leadership, honed over many years. By empowering and showing confidence, he has proven that people will rise to the occasion in carrying out their responsibilities.

Communicate by Listening

"I believe I could run almost any company if I were wise enough to listen to the people in that company." (Fred Meijer)

Real communication happens when people feel safe. Fred's advice on more than one occasion has been: "Never punish learners if their motives are right." He believes that feedback is crucial to success, and that good communication means being approachable.

George Zain
and "Mr. Van"

Joe Stevens

Peter Drucker once said that great managers aren't those who speak well but those who know how to listen. Fred has the gift and patience of listening — not only to his managers, but to people from all levels of society.

Ray Leach

On Saturdays, Fred would spend time walking around the office where he would pop into someone's office and just start chatting. He would stop into my office, and his first question was always, "What's up?" Then he would ask about competition, people, where I thought we should build the next store, and so forth. His brain reminded me of a computer gathering information for future use.

Mike Holton

I was showing Anthony, a new Meijer team member, around the building. We went past Fred's office, and I introduced Anthony to Pam. Fred had a company V.P. inside, but Pam said I should take Anthony in anyway. I stuck my head in to say "Hi," and immediately Fred got up and came over to shake Anthony's hand. They were soon engaged in conversation. After a while, the other executive excused himself, even though I knew they were not done with their conference. Fred felt this new team member was more important than the immediate business at hand.

Mike Marcheski

I was managing a SuperValu store next to where a new Meijer store was opening. At that time, they were new to Chicago, and since they were going to be my main competition, I went to check them out at their grand opening. I was walking through the store when a man came up and asked how I liked it, and who I worked for. I told him I managed the store next door, having no idea he was Fred Meijer. He asked me if I knew Mike Wright, who was then president of SuperValu. He had met Mike on several occasions, and said he thought I worked for a good company. He asked questions about me and my family — not a word about business — and then gave me an ice-cream card, wishing me a good day.

Even though he knew I was his competitor, I felt like a guest. I left impressed not only with the store but with the man behind its name. I thought that if I ever decided to change employers, Meijer would be my first choice. I am now a Meijer store director.

Paul Boyer, *Former Meijer president*

I have witnessed Fred being asked his opinion on business decisions many times in my career. He is a master at answering such questions with questions of his own in order to simplify our challenges and help us to approach them from a different perspective. It's a technique I've seen him use many times.

Ken Brondyke

I remember many store manager meetings over the years when Fred would explain the condition of the company. He would share both the good and bad information. He would even get into personal issues, like the fact that Lena was all set financially in case something would happen to him or the company. There wasn't a question he was ever afraid to answer.

A few years ago a well-known doctor of psychology was conducting a seminar for retail business executives in Chicago. In attendance were several Meijer store managers, and the name Meijer came up. The professor, who had met Fred on several occasions, stopped and made a comment. He said that Fred Meijer had what he called a "pure ego": that is, Fred's personal satisfaction was derived from seeing the accomplishments of others and giving them credit.

Bill Whittaker

I remember Fred telling me one time, "When I visit your store I see it has my name on the front of the building. But when I leave, it's your store. That's the way the folks in Grand Haven think about it, and that's the way it should be."

One does not have to be around Fred very long to know how he feels about the subject. Speaking to a group of managers, he advised: "Be careful how you praise others. 'Thanks for everything' is meaningless. You must be specific. Also, saying that you're doing a good job to a poor performer is ridiculous, and it demotes the good performer who hears it." On another occasion he said, "It's surprising how much you can accomplish if you don't care who gets the credit."

Manage by Walking Around

> "We really have two jobs as management: to bring out the best in people in order to help them succeed, and to satisfy all our customers so they will want to come back and trade with us." (Fred Meijer)

In their best-selling book *A Passion for Excellence*, Tom Peters and Nancy Austin observe that the number-one managerial problem in America is quite simply that "managers are out of touch with what's happening on the front lines."

Fred is never comfortable viewing the company from the corporate office. He likes to mingle with the masses. It's an approach he has passed on to other top executives. The first thing he does when visiting a Meijer facility is to seek out the person in charge and say "hello." The manager is then free to go about his business or to walk through

Fred mingling

the store with him. He deplores the thought of sneaking around trying to find things wrong. Indeed, he especially enjoys catching people doing things right and recognizing them for it.

Terry Griffith

I was in my office one Saturday morning when Fred stopped by during one of his morning walks through the food areas. He's always made an effort to keep up with what's going on and to keep his finger on the pulse of the business.

I had just met with an employee who was upset about a certain issue, and I was wondering how I could deal with the situation in the best way possible. Fred asked me how things were going, and I explained my dilemma to him.

"When you're dealing with a person who has a problem, stay focused on the problem, and not on the individual," he advised. He told me of an experience he once had with an employee who had gotten in his face about a change in insurance coverage. Fred explained that he could easily have made the mistake of attacking this person by stating that, if certain employees were not abusing our insurance program, we could keep costs down and afford better coverage. He believed that approach would only have led to an argument from which no one would have benefited.

Fred instead explained to the person why the changes had to be made — that the benefit in question was not cost-effective in relation to the coverage. It was good advice that I never forgot.

Eva Bliss

My parents always taught me to address my elders as Mr. and Mrs. Since everyone at Meijer was on a first-name basis, it felt a little awkward until the first time I met Fred. I was sitting in my boss's office having a discussion, and there was a jar of nuts on the table.

Fred, walking past, spotted the nuts and asked if he could have some. He apologized for the interruption, introduced himself, and asked how things were going, while he enjoyed his snack. I was told this was a typical encounter — casual, warm, and friendly.

"I like to learn. I do not go to a store to pick up paper in the parking lot, but if I am in the parking lot, I pick up the paper. I do not come to shove the carts in, although if I come in, I bring in a couple of carts. I do not come in to supervise the store. If I happen to see something that I think should be done, I think it is my job to mention it, not to go back and end up with, 'Fred saw it. Why didn't he say something while he was here?' If I see something wrong in the store, it's my job to discuss it, but I am not looking for it. I am looking to learn. . . . It keeps me from being isolated in the proverbial ivory tower, so I can still understand what's going on." (*IHOW*, p. 166)

Pam Kleibusch

Fred has a fetish for following through on details. He always carries a notepad with him, full of things to do or to check on for someone. It is normal for him to call several times during his store visits to ask me to check on something, and when this happens, I often find that he has another person working on the same issue.

People always seem surprised when they get such a prompt reply to their questions.

Sara Hasbrouck

When I first went into management, Fred stopped by to congratulate me and to share some thoughts on being a manager. One thing he told me was that he felt he should never have to tell someone something twice.

Jim Stich

Soon after I began working for Meijer in 1994, at Store #60 in Columbus, we heard that Fred would be visiting the area. It was my day off, but I decided to be there in case he decided to stop by.

I met him at the doorway, and he seemed surprised to see me. "You're not supposed to be here on Thursday," he said. I explained that I'd heard he was going to be in town, and I wanted to be available to show him through the store. Fred smiled and agreed to walk the store with me, but first he offered to buy my lunch for coming in on my day off. On our way to the café, he invited several other team members to join us for lunch.

We spent the next couple of hours in the café, during which time he asked each of us about our families and our past employment histories before sharing a little bit about himself. When we finished eating, I expected him to ask me to walk the store with him, but instead he said he was leaving. He said, "Any director who comes in on his day off runs a good store."

Several years ago a major company was test-marketing a new line of dog food that they had hoped to introduce nationally. All the marketing bases had been covered for a successful launch. The packaging was attractive, advertising was eye-catching, the pricing was excellent — all of which was backed up by their retail sales force. At first the sales were better than expected; then they abruptly stopped. The company called in their market research people to find out what the problem was. When they finally talked to dog owners, they were told, "The dogs don't like it." Someone had forgotten to ask the dogs.

Show Integrity

"Live up to your promises. If you can't deliver, don't promise."
(Fred Meijer)

One day Fred was traveling back on the Meijer plane after visiting the stores in Indianapolis. There were always other Meijer personnel on board who were coming or going while doing business in various markets. On this occasion, one of the passengers was a new person working in the real estate department. During the conversation, Fred was explaining a real estate deal that he had committed to. The decision to purchase a certain parcel of land had initially looked promising, but circumstances had changed, and it wasn't such a good deal anymore. The new real estate man listened, then asked, "What's the problem? There's nothing in writing, is there?" Fred made it clear that something more than his signature on a contract had been given — his word.

Harvey Lemmen

When I first started with Meijer, one of my jobs was processing invoices in the office. Grand Rapids Wholesale was our main supplier, and one day one of the invoices was off by $10,000 — in our favor. I hadn't been there very long, but I knew that money was very tight and we weren't paying our bills on time. I asked Fred what we should do.

His reply was immediate: if we were charged $10,000 too much, we'd let them know in a hurry, so we should do the same in this situation. That may have been the first time Grand Rapids Wholesale had that happen to them, but it set the tone for me about what kind of company I was working for. I knew I was in the right place.

Pat Gavin

I was twenty-five years old when I was placed in charge of pharmacy operations for the company. We only had fourteen pharmacies in those days, but to me it seemed like a huge company. On my first day, Fred came to my office and just sat down to talk for a while. His intent was obviously to make me comfortable in my new position.

He also wanted to set a tone for my career. At that time, there was a lot of controversy circulating in the news about one of the largest drugstore chains in the country. Several of the executives had been convicted of improprieties involving billings to the federal government. One of their executives, who held a position similar to mine, was quoted as stating that he made the decision to do what he did based on pressure from his superiors to make the company profitable.

Fred said he wanted the company to be profitable, but he stressed that "profit is what you get for doing the right things." He insisted that if anyone ever put pressure on me to do something I thought was unethical, or worse yet, illegal, I should come to him immediately. Put ethics first, he said, and profits will follow.

Shortly after his visit, Harvey Lemmen dropped in to reinforce what

Fred had just said. A few hours later, Earl Holton just happened by and reiterated the same thing. Jack Koetje, my first assistant, later asked if I'd had any company that day. Of course, he knew that I had. I will never forget being visited by the three most powerful executives of the company on my first day on the job. Their message — to do the right thing — has proven helpful in dealing with many touchy situations since then.

In business, the blind desire to make money often compromises honesty and integrity. One has only to remember the headlines involving Enron, WorldCom, Tyco, Adelphia, K-Mart, and others. For Fred and the Meijer company, however, those core values have always been the cornerstone of the company's operating principles.

Chapter Fourteen

Leading by Example

Don't take people by what they say — watch what they do.
— Fred Meijer

F or many people, success is measured by winning: the first one to cross the finish line, survive the most games, make the most money, or collect the most trophies. But many of these winners, these would-be heroes, look better from a distance. Not so with Fred Meijer. The closer the scrutiny, the more his inner character is revealed. He lives a relatively simple life, consistently thinks of the needs of others, and doesn't put on airs. In other words, he teaches by example.

Pat Quinn
I had just been named president of Spartan Stores, and one of the things Fred had mentioned to me was the fact that he did not have reserved parking spaces at the Meijer offices. He said that those who got to work earliest should get the best parking spots.

At the Spartan offices, I found that there were thirty choice spots reserved for management. One of the first things I did was have all reserved parking signs taken down.

J. Hoppough Smith

It was a downpour, and I had just parked my car in the employee parking lot at the store. It was clear to me that I was going to be soaked before I got inside. Just then, a car pulled up with Fred behind the wheel and Lena in the passenger seat. "Can we give you a ride?" he asked. He and Lena were shuttling employees to the front door on that rainy day.

Phil Moore

We were at a Bill Knapp's restaurant with some friends one Friday night. The place was busy, and there was a twenty-minute wait for seating. We were eating when I saw Fred and Lena in the waiting area. I mentioned it to our friends. "That can't be Fred Meijer," my friend said. "If it were them, they wouldn't have to wait." When our waitress came by, I asked her. "Oh yes!" she said. "That's Fred and Lena. They come here on a regular basis, and they want to wait their turn just like everyone else."

Don Eberhard

The Meijer Fuller Street store was four miles from his home, but on Sundays, Fred would often ride his bike to the store to pick up a few things. One day, after he had done his shopping, he realized that he had left his wallet at home. Rather than tell the manager he would pay later, he rode his bike all the way home and back to pay for his groceries.

Buck Matthews

Early in my career in TV broadcasting, I often heard that Fred Meijer, despite his position and wealth, was a humble man. You know, the log-cabin stuff about growing up on a farm and delivering milk before school. It seemed like a good public-relations story.

What seemed less likely was that he and Lena lived in a modest house, drove used cars, and shopped for their own groceries. I learned the truth after I started hosting Meijer-sponsored "community parties." One time, when I was in the Alpine store, I felt a tug at my sleeve and there was Fred pushing a shopping cart.

Mike Lloyd, *Editor,* **Grand Rapids Press**

No matter how self-effacing and modest you may be, when your name is featured in huge letters on the front of multiple grocery stores, you are *not* just like every other company employee. But Fred taught me that there are small, very human ways for the man with his name on the door to connect to the people with whom he works.

In the early '80s, he gave me a tour of the new Meijer headquarters in Walker. Along the way he showed me his personal office, which was moderate in size and plainly furnished. He said the architect had originally included an executive washroom in his office. Fred said he flushed the bathroom idea. Being Dutch, he pointed out how expensive plumbing is to install and that his personal use of this facility wouldn't justify the cost.

"That's what I told the architect," he said. "The truth was, when I walk down the hall to use the same restroom as the people I work with, it's a clear message that I go to the bathroom the same as everyone else." He also said that those necessary trips got him out of his office and gave people a chance to talk with him. "Few things strip away the pomp and title of the corner office like a trip to the bathroom."

Fred's insight was a glimpse into his humanity and humility. His comments had a profound impression on me. When the executive offices at *The Press* were being redone, I was given the option of having a private bathroom, too. I turned it down. Fred was right.

Willet Smith

We have all had the experience of meeting people for the first time who were intimidating, and conversely, we have met those who made us feel comfortable. It is a unique persona that comes naturally to some people. Its outward signs are expressed in body language, facial expression, voice inflection, dress, mannerisms, and overall demeanor.

Such was the case the first time I met Fred. It was over fifty years ago. I was nineteen, fresh from the country, and had just been hired as a meat clerk in the office. My boss took me around the office to introduce me. Fred stopped what he was doing, looked me in the eye, and with a firm handshake welcomed me to the company. He concluded with, "Just call me Fred." It was a magical moment I will never forget.

Entry to the Frederik Meijer Gardens

At the Lena Meijer Children's Garden

Disk in the Form of a Desert Rose, by Arnaldo Pomodoro

Aria, by Alexander Liberman

Moving Rectangles, by George Rickey

Man-Woman, by Jonathan Borofsky

The Lena Meijer Conservatory in Autumn

Cactus at Christmas *(photo courtesy of Willem Mineur)*

Inside the Conservatory

"Butterflies are Blooming" exhibition in the Conservatory *(photo courtesy of Willem Mineur)*

Sunset over the Conservatory

Fred and Hendrik with a customer

Meeting Mr. [Hendrik] Meijer was a different matter. His white hair, meticulous dress, posture, and stature — with a gaze that seemed to take in everything — were intimidating. Nothing about him gave a clue that here was a man who had worked in the cotton mills in his native Holland ten hours a day for ten days just to earn a dollar. Pictures of him usually show him standing ramrod straight, with his arms folded across his chest, body language that communicates, "This is my space."

It wasn't long, however, before I learned he loved a good prank or practical joke. The contrast between the two men was remarkable. Here was a pair who were joined at the hip as they went about the business of the company, yet seemed so different.

Laurie Walton

I am claustrophobic, and had never flown on a small plane before, but I was asked to conduct some meetings in Columbus for our benefits department, and was scheduled to take the Meijer Flyer, a twelve-seater. I didn't know what to expect. When I got to the plane, my heart started to race and my stomach was churning. I swallowed, boarded the plane, and there was Fred. He asked if I wanted to face forward or backward. I wasn't sure what he meant, so I just took the first seat available, hoping I wouldn't get sick. He took the seat facing me, and, sensing my fear, talked to me all the way to Columbus.

Terry Griffith

I was to interview for a job in one of the Lansing stores, where I was to meet the district director in the cafeteria. I arrived early, ordered a cup of coffee, and was hoping that my nervousness didn't show. Meijer was a big company to me, even though there were only twenty-four stores at the time.

A middle-aged couple entered the cafeteria, ordered tea, and sat down at a table near me. "Are you waiting for someone?" the man asked. "You look a little nervous." I explained to him that I had an interview for a job, and that I was indeed nervous.

The man gave me a reassuring smile. "You should never be nervous about an interview," he told me. "Just do the best you can. Regardless of what happens, you will be all right in the end." This fatherly figure continued to talk with me for several minutes about interviewing and putting your best foot forward without worrying about the consequences. I felt more at ease as he wished me good luck and returned to his table.

Jack Koetje, the district manager, arrived soon thereafter. "Let me introduce you to somebody," he said, as he led me over to the table where the couple was seated. You can guess who it was.

I was shocked! I couldn't believe that Fred Meijer knew enough not to tell me who he was, and to offer helpful advice instead.

Ron Burnson

We were in the process of building the store in Highland, Indiana, in 1998, when Fred visited three weeks prior to our grand opening. He arrived, and the greeter — who didn't know who he was — inspected his briefcase as she was instructed to do in her training. Word spread like wildfire that he was in the store, and by the time I arrived at the front to meet him he had already started his tour. By this time, the greeter had heard that it was Fred Meijer's briefcase she had searched, and she was frantic. She was certain she would lose her job.

When I caught up with Fred, I explained to him how upset the greeter was over the incident. Without a word, he marched right back up front, shook her hand, and thanked her for doing her job.

Dave Poletti

I met Fred for the first time soon after I became director of supermarket operations following the death of Dick Stair. Dick was well-loved, with many years of experience, and I was the new kid on the block with some very large shoes to fill.

Fred walked in and introduced himself one afternoon as I was sitting in my office trying to figure out my new position. My heart dropped into my stomach, and butterflies the size of 747s began to swarm inside of me. However, it took only a minute for me to realize that this was a man of warmth and character. For ten minutes he shared stories about Dick Stair with me. I could have listened to him all afternoon.

Pat Gavin

Over the years, as vice president of pharmacy operations, I had the unfortunate opportunity to confront situations where health-care professionals were facilitating the improper use of narcotics and other controlled substances. A local physician, who at one time was a highly respected member of the medical community, decided to use his license to prescribe narcotics to anyone willing to pay his fee.

Our pharmacists quickly saw what was happening, refused to fill his prescriptions, and called me. It wasn't long before the doctor called, irate that we were infringing on his practice. He told me he was going to call Fred Meijer. I had been keeping senior executives informed of what was happening, so I went to Fred's office to let him know he could expect a call. I was in his office when the call came. He patiently listened to the doctor's tirade. When he was done, Fred said, "Did Pat and our pharmacists treat you with dignity and respect?"

"Hell no! They aren't filling my prescriptions. What are you going to do about it?"

"I'm not a pharmacist," Fred replied, "and I won't overrule them. In fact, I believe they made the right decision."

A few weeks later, a local TV station did an exposé under the title "Dr. Drugs." The doctor was eventually convicted, lost his license, and went to prison.

Helping Out

Last Friday, Mary Hammerstein of Lansing and her seven-year-old son emerged from the West Saginaw Highway Meijer store with two carts full of groceries. As Hammerstein herded the carts to her minivan and started loading up, an elderly man dressed in a suit and tie approached. He commented on the size of the order and offered to help her with the heavy lifting.

Hammerstein thanked the man, but said it wasn't necessary. The man said he knew it wasn't, but he wanted to help anyway. The man gently insisted. What could Hammerstein do but accept his gracious offer?

As he went to work, the man chit-chatted happily about groceries and minivans and this and that. He also gave Hammerstein's son a couple of coupons for free ice-cream cones. Then he offered to take care of the carts. Before he did so, he extended his hand and said, "By the way, I'm Fred Meijer." (John Schneider, "Helping Out," *Lansing State Journal,* June 14, 1994)

Ted Bedell

I received a frantic call from a clerk who was handling a customer complaint at the courtesy desk. I heard screaming and cursing in the background as I arrived at the courtesy desk, where two store detectives were also waiting. I took a deep breath and then asked the customer to calm down and to explain his problem.

Following a brief exchange of words and more threats and curses, I explained to the customer that if he didn't calm down I would have to ask him to leave. He informed me that he wasn't about to leave, and by now his arms were flailing and his face was red. The store detectives each took an arm and escorted the man kicking and screaming out the door. I was trying to regain my composure when I felt an arm on my shoulder. There was Fred, wearing a sympathetic grin.

"Isn't retailing fun?" he said as he gently pulled me off to one side. In his reassuring voice he asked if he could give a bit of advice. My mind was racing. I thought I was about to hit the door. After all, he had just seen one of his customers being dragged away.

"You know, Ted," he began, "I'm not here to judge your decisions — you guys run these stores and I try not to interfere. Under the circumstances, you probably did better than I would have. But here's a little advice I try to use in similar situations," he continued. "I've learned over the years that when someone is mad at me, I try to find some common ground where I can agree with them. In this case, let's say this guy tells you that Fred Meijer is stupid the way he runs his stores. I would look him in the eye and say, 'You're absolutely right. I'll call him for you tomorrow and tell him so.' You see, it's hard for someone to argue when you take all the wind out of their sails."

That was the best piece of advice I ever received about dealing with people. The best part was that he did it in such a way as to preserve my dignity and confidence.

Roger Horling

I started at Meijer on December 12, 1955, as the thirteenth employee in the warehouse. The company had just opened the tenth store and had moved its warehouse from the basement of the main store to an old foundry on the west side of Grand Rapids.

I remember the place as very dusty and cold. It was heated by a big gas furnace that didn't have a chimney, so the exhaust just blew into this big old building, but it was so drafty that it didn't make any difference.

Back then, businesses were required to take inventory for year-end tax purposes. Fred and Mr. Meijer came over that day to work with us. This was the first time I met Fred, and I thought it was strange that

The first Meijer warehouse

the owners of the company would be working alongside us in the warehouse.

At noon, Fred took us all out to lunch. Afterwards, someone noticed that his car had a flat tire. Not being able to find a jack, we all picked up one side of the car while he changed the tire.

Tim Zehr

One day a customer approached me and told me there was a gentleman in the parking lot picking up trash and gathering carts. The customer asked me if I knew who it was. I told her I didn't. Then she revealed her secret: "I know who it is — it's Fred Meijer!"

Sure enough, I got outside just as he was approaching the store with a couple of shopping carts and a handful of trash. I quickly reassured him that I would get someone right away to take care of these things, but he just smiled and said, "It's everyone's job to pick up trash and carts on their way into the store." The customer saw it, and I saw it: he was leading by example. To this day, I pick up trash or push a cart on my way into the store whether I'm at my own store or visiting another one.

Sandi Wagenknecht

Even though he'd had hip-replacement surgery the previous week, Fred came, along with Lena, to our grand opening at Store #168. After getting out of the car and into the wheelchair, he spotted some paper on the ground. So there he was, picking up litter from his wheelchair on the way in!

Jim Postma

It was a few weeks before Christmas, and the company was experiencing growing pains. We had opened new stores that year and the buyers ordered accordingly for the holiday season, which left the warehouse full from top to bottom. Merchandise was arriving faster than we could ship it out, and we had skids of product in the aisles, on the loading dock, and in truck wells.

Fred came to the warehouse and walked the aisles, speaking with the selectors and the hi-lo drivers. It was clear that he understood what we were going through and that he wanted to be accessible to us during a difficult time. It would have been easier for him to simply stay away until after the holidays when the problem was cleared up, but he was never one to run from or ignore a bad situation.

Joe McCormack

One morning we got to one of the Detroit stores about 10:00 a.m. It was a cold, wet, wintry day. Fred had always asked me to park farthest from the store so the customers would have the best parking spots. Walking toward the store, Fred and I came across a car full of high school kids who looked like they should be in class. They had gotten stuck by a drain hole covered with ice.

He threw me an elbow and said, "Let's give them a hand," so we pushed and got the car back on solid ground. They thanked us, piled in, and were ready to leave. As we walked away, Fred gave me several ice-cream cards and asked me to give them each one. They stopped as they saw me approaching. I handed them the cards, saying, "Mr. Meijer would like you to come back to the store and have an ice cream cone on him." Their jaws dropped to the floor. The driver said, "You mean that was Fred Meijer?" "Yup," I replied. "That was really cool!" he said. They parked the car and headed back into the store.

Dave Nesman

As a new Meijer employee, I had taken my day off to attend the grand opening of a new store. I had heard how big and exciting a new opening was, but I was not prepared for the reality. Arriving at the store, it took me fifteen minutes to find a parking space on the grass at the side of the road. Walking through the large parking lot, I saw a man directing traffic and helping customers find parking spaces. To my surprise, it was Fred Meijer. As I approached, I said, "Hi, Fred," and introduced myself as a new employee.

It surprised me when he asked if I would be willing to help him direct traffic. Later, he came over to me with someone to take my place. He handed me a Purple Cow ice-cream card and said we had done a good job and deserved a break. We had an ice-cream cone together, and then for the next hour I was his guest, walking the store, meeting customers, and being introduced to other team members and vendors.

Sid Allard

It was my second day on the job at Store #25, where I had been hired as a manager trainee. In the afternoon, an announcement over the P.A. system requested all managers to the service area. When I got there, I saw too many customers in line, and I was asked to start bagging. This was unusual for me, because at the company I had just come from managers didn't bag.

After I'd been working a few minutes, a man came up, took off his sport coat, and started working on the lane next to me. He was talking to customers and seemed to be enjoying himself. Once we got the lines down, he started to leave and I mentioned to him that he forgot his coat. He thanked me and asked what I did. I told him it was my second day, and I was still learning and a little nervous. He patted me on the back and said I was doing a good job. I later learned my bagging partner was Fred.

John Zimmerman

From time to time we would see letters to the editor regarding Meijer in the local paper. Some were good, and some were not so good. Whenever I saw a negative letter in the paper, I would do my best to beat Fred to that customer and try to win him or her back. Time and again, customers would hear me out and then tell me that they'd already heard from the company's top man.

Tim VanRavenswaay

I had moved to Kalamazoo to attend college. A retailing career was the farthest thing from my mind. I took a job as a night grocery stocker at a nearby Meijer store. I hadn't been there very long when, one morning, as I was hurrying to finish and get to my first class, a little lady came up to me and in a Dutch accent asked, "Young man, vhere can I find de baking powder?" Without looking up, I replied, "In aisle two," and I kept stocking shelves. A few minutes later a man came over and introduced himself as Fred Meijer. He said, "My mother still cannot find the baking powder. Would you please show her?" He went on to say, "It's always best if we take the customer to the item." He was gentle in giving me the first of many lessons that would serve me for the next thirty-seven years as a Meijer employee.

One day Fred stopped at a local car dealership on Michigan Street. It was 1957, and Meijer had just opened its fifth Grand Rapids supermarket. As he was looking around, the salesman tried to appeal to his ego: "A man of your stature should be driving our deluxe model over here," he said. It was the wrong approach. Fred didn't buy a car there.

Paul Boyer

For several years, company cars were furnished for senior management. A couple of rules were that the cars had to be American-made and that when they reached 60,000 miles, they were to be turned in — hopefully before any major repairs were necessary.

Whenever Fred was in the market for a new car, he would keep his eyes open for one of the company cars that was due to be turned in. On more than one occasion when mine was reaching its mileage limit, Fred would ask about the gas mileage, how comfortable it was, and any other attributes it may have had. He would then take it for a test drive. Thus my used car became Fred's new car.

He would promptly have the whitewall tires turned around. I think he felt whitewalls were a sign of affluence (which they were at one time). You could tell which car in the parking lot belonged to Fred — it would be the only one with blackwall tires.

Bob Summers

One day I received a call from the personal secretary of our banana supplier. This man owned several other companies, including an insurance company and a chain of retail stores. He had never met Fred and wanted to know if he, his son, and his executive V.P. could meet and have lunch with him.

I called Pam, Fred's secretary, and she handled all the details. I planned to meet our guests at the door and escort them to the dining area. They arrived in one of the biggest stretch limousines I have ever seen. I took them to the dining area, introduced them to Fred, and enjoyed lunch listening to these very successful businessmen.

Eventually, the subject got around to the new Frederik Meijer Gardens and Sculpture Park. Fred invited them to take a tour with him. They offered to drive and he agreed, but I knew he hadn't seen their mode of transportation. When we reached the lobby and saw the limo at the door, he called me aside and said to tell our guests that he had gone to get his car and they could follow or ride with him. They looked a bit puzzled, but agreed.

He pulled up and we all got in. Off we went to the gardens, five men in Fred's second-hand Buick, followed by this empty limo and the chauffeur, who must have been utterly mystified. I would have bet my paycheck Fred would never get into that vehicle, and I was right.

Great leaders in history have always led by example. This doesn't mean that everyone in the organization will follow the example. People are still free to make their own choices, regardless of what they observe or are taught. Nevertheless, consistent examples have a lasting effect.

Senator Feargal Quinn, *Owner of the Superquinn grocery chain in Ireland*
In 1987, my eldest son, Eamonn, and I visited Fred in Grand Rapids. The visit was an eye-opener for the two visitors from Ireland. Superquinn at the time employed about 3,000 people, and we were proud of that number, until I asked Fred how many worked at Meijer, and he said over 75,000.

On visiting one of his warehouses, I asked him what was the company policy concerning something technical and he said, "Feargal, with a company this size, I don't know all the details. Sometimes all I can do is set the tone."

I watched him for the rest of the day as we visited stores and shopping centers. Everywhere he went, he was "setting the tone." He never parked near the store, always at the back of the car park, rather than using a valuable customer space. He never walked to the store without a couple of empty shopping carts. He never passed a piece of paper on the ground without picking it up. He never passed an employee without a handshake and a word of thanks for their efforts. And he continued to give out "Purple Cow" ice-cream cards to customers as he thanked them for their loyalty.

I copied his Purple Cow token with a Superquinn "Doughnut" token for years. They were very well received and appreciated. However, when Fred took us to dinner in a restaurant in Grand Rapids, I thought I saw him give a tip of a Purple Cow to the waitress. I'm sure he was generous with a tip as well. I have been tempted to try the same with my "Doughnut" token in a Dublin restaurant, but have never plucked up the courage.

It was clear as we visited his stores and those of his competitors that we could see the difference. I believe it all came from his "setting the tone." Long may he continue to inspire.

Chapter Fifteen

Why Pay More?

I t was the fall canning season, and A&P was selling bulk vinegar for seventeen cents a gallon, far below the going price of twenty-five cents at other grocery stores in Greenville. Hendrik and Fred, determined not to be undersold, heard of a producer named Van Maldegan up near Grand Rapids who was too small to supply A&P, but had a surplus. They visited him at his warehouse on Fruit Ridge Avenue on the northwest outskirts of the city.

"I hear you've got a lot of vinegar," Hendrik said as they came in the office door.

"Yep."

So Hendrik asked, "Would you sell me some for nine cents a gallon?"

Van Maldegan, suddenly turning red, looked up at him. The wholesale price was a dime or more, and even A&P was getting seventeen cents a gallon retail.

Van Maldegan sneered. "You don't care whether we're losing money; you don't care about us at all. . . ."

On he went in his tirade against greedy merchants. Hendrik listened for a moment, then turned and walked out of the office, slamming the door behind him, and abandoning Fred to the irate vinegar man. Hendrik could not go far; Fred had the keys to the truck. A long moment later, he reappeared in the doorway. In a calm voice he said, "Mr. Van Maldegan, may I start over?" The vinegar man drew a deep breath and nodded.

"'I know the stores are getting twenty-five cents a gallon for vinegar, and A&P is now selling it for seventeen cents a gallon. What I'd like to know is if you would sell us a truckload of vinegar, ten fifty-gallon barrels, for nine cents a gallon, so that we can sell it for ten cents. That would really stir up the market, please the farmers, and bring in business. Will you help me?"

The vinegar man's expression softened. "You mean you'd be willing to haul it to Greenville, unload it yourself, and pump it — all for a five-dollar profit?" Hendrik nodded.

"Then I'd be glad to sell you my vinegar at nine cents a gallon." (*TY*, p. 164)

THURSDAY, AUGUST 25, 1938

We went to Grand Rapids and got a $479 grocery order and five more barrels of vinegar from Van's. We had a flat tire just out of Grand Rapids and had to call Eddie with Einer's truck to take off part of the load and help us change. We just got unloaded when it started to rain. [Fred's diary]

It was one of many early lessons he would learn from his father about buying by objective. The vinegar story was to become part of the Meijer lore passed on by Fred to many buyers and executives over the years.

"We were constantly overbuying," recalls Fred, "doing things like, 'Okay, if it's $2 a case for your normal list price, could you sell it to us for $1.90 if we bought ten cases?' If the vendor said, 'Yes, I'll give it to you for $1.90,' we'd say, 'Well, what if we bought 100, would you give it to us for $1.80?' If he said 'Yes,' we'd buy the 100 for $1.80."

As the lowest-priced stores in Greenville, the Thrift Market and the A&P vied for the business of farmers who bought groceries on their Saturday trips to town. As much as Hendrik tried, however, there were times when he failed to please some of those customers. In the late 1930s, both the Thrift Market and the A&P were licensed to sell oleomargarine, the cheap and still somewhat controversial alternative to creamery butter. Oleo appealed to the Thrift Market's welfare customers and others forced to stretch their dollars, but it was anathema to many farmers, some of whom had dairy herds themselves.

When a farmers' union decided to boycott stores that sold oleo, the Thrift Market became a target. A&P was too big to be intimidated by a local boycott, but an independent grocer was vulnerable. The president of the local union had a farm near Hendrik's, north of Greenville. Although he had been a steady Thrift Market customer, he refused to shop any longer at a store that exercised its license to sell oleo. Instead, he traded with a small grocer at a crossroads north of Greenville. The rural grocer did not dare to register with the state to sell oleo, even though some of his customers might prefer the cheaper spread. Rather than take out a license, he supplied oleo to those customers by buying it out of the dairy case at the Thrift Market, and signing his receipt as a wholesale purchase so he would not have to pay sales tax.

Soon more farmers began to trade with the oleo bootlegger. The farmers' union remained adamant, and so did Hendrik. Finally, however, after several weeks, they abandoned the boycott when it became apparent that they had failed to win the sympathy of other Greenville customers.

Whether the battle was fought over vinegar or butter or peaches, the outcome of the grocery store war, as Hendrik and Fred perceived it, turned primarily on the issue of low prices. They needed the lowest wholesale costs they could find. Hendrik argued with a Swedish immigrant supplier over the price of a load of oleo, and when they failed to reach agreement, he unloaded the product from his car and drove off in a huff to buy from another wholesaler.

TUESDAY, JANUARY 4, 1938

Dad and I went to Ionia and got flour today, and we went on to Grand Rapids (with trailer) and paid Grand Rapids Wholesale Grocery Co. $42 and got a $201 order. We saw Muller about the bread man (Jack), and we went to Swift & Co. Swift raised the oleo another half cent to eleven and a half cents, so we did not take their oleo, but got some from Good Luck Foods for ten and a half cents. [Fred's diary]

Salesmen often warned Hendrik that he was cutting his margins too thin. But he received their advice skeptically because he knew his prices irritated — even infuriated — his competitors, who frequently complained to salesmen as they made their rounds.

Maurie DeFouw, a salesman for Borden products, recalls: "Whatever A&P sold it for, that's what Meijer sold it for. It didn't make any difference what it cost them." Sometimes Hendrik was a bit reckless. Michigan's fair trade law required merchants to sell certain brand-name products at or above a minimum price. Among these was Miracle Whip salad dressing, which was many a grocer's staple. Its fair trade price was thirty-five cents, but competitors caught Meijer selling it for thirty-three cents.

"Meijer was the best customer I had," said DeFouw. "If we had a special promotion on a certain item coming up, I asked them how many they wanted. The biggest question always was, 'What's A&P going to sell it for?' A&P was the grocery business. Whatever A&P was doing, that's what Meijer would do. They couldn't have had a better pattern."

Along the way, Hendrik and Fred continued to learn things about buying. They did not hesitate to drive to Bay City for a deal on peanut butter, or to a little mill near Lansing for cheaper flour. As the price wars raged, the Thrift Market's customers came back. North Greenville residents were surprised when they found out that the new A&P could not improve on Thrift Market prices.

As the store grew, so did Meijer's campaign to match the prices of the ubiquitous A&P. Their advertising preached the low-price gospel: "The average family spends more dollars of their paycheck at a grocery store than at any other single store," one ad observed. "Three times a day most of us eat. That means three times a day you can either save or waste money. Did it ever occur to you what a saving like that means over the period of a year? Figure it out! Let's say you only save ten cents a meal, three times a day, 1,095 times a year. That saving alone would mean over $100 a year. If you think $100 or more extra each year might be useful, then the Thrift Market is your complete answer."

Harvey Lemmen

We had a relationship with a certain spice salesman who was a very nice guy and with whom we worked regularly. This man had developed a warm relationship with Hendrik, and they would often have coffee together. He had the exclusive spice business in our stores at that time, and we bought a lot from him. Eventually, another spice company made a great offer to us that our current supplier couldn't or wouldn't match. Therefore, we made a big change. This spice salesman was understandably upset. It was a tough decision, but both Fred and Hendrik always put the good of the customers and the company before business relationships.

"Why Pay More?" is more than just a slogan. It has been a way of life for the Meijer family from the beginning. Fred recalls: "I never bought a Coke for five cents in high school, because I didn't think I could afford it." However, his personal frugality stands in contrast to the money expended on his stores, which are bright and shiny, with immaculate parking lots and restrooms, and trucks that reflect the institution they represent.

Mike Lloyd

My wife and I were invited to a sneak preview prior to the grand opening of the Cascade Meijer store in 1984. The VIP guest list included community leaders, local politicians, building contractors, and many Meijer executives.

The night featured cake, punch, and speeches. Then every guest was encouraged to shop at the store. This was a "practice round" for the employees, tuning up for the expected customer surge at the official opening the next day. As "special guests," we were invited to take advantage of "grand opening" bargain prices. And nearly everyone pushed through the store behind shiny new shopping carts, loading up on the promised bargains.

My wife and I arrived at the checkout lane, coincidentally right behind Fred and Lena. I thought we had done the store proud, but Fred's cart was overflowing. I kidded him about buying so much. It was *his* store! His practical response: "With prices this low, we can't afford not to."

Guy Estep

My wife and I were shopping when I was approached by Fred, who was also shopping, and he asked if I could help him. Thinking that he wanted help with a heavy object, I followed him to the soap section, where he pulled out a ten-cent coupon for Dial soap. He wanted my help finding the soap.

Pam Kleibusch

Fred buys most of his clothes at the same place as his customers do — off the rack at a Meijer store. When he needs a type of sport coat that we don't sell, he frets about having to spend $75 on one out of a catalog. He just can't spend money on himself. He'd rather spend it on a statue for the Gardens. He's always maintained that clothes don't change the person. His friends, many of whom wear expensive suits, have ribbed him at times in the past, but he always says the same thing: "What I wear doesn't change who I am." It also gives him an opportunity to show off the Meijer clothing, of which he is very proud.

Bob Rasmussen

We were attending a business function at the community center in Greenville. I was sitting next to the mayor, who whispered to me, "I'm embarrassed! I've got the same suit on as Fred." The mayor had just bought his that day at Meijer, so I knew where Fred's suit came from.

Marv Grooters

Cordless phones were just becoming popular in the early 1990s, and Fred had decided to try one in his home. I went to his house, installed one, and he really liked it. He asked me how much it would cost to replace the other two phones in the house with cordless phones, and I told him about fifty bucks apiece.

He thought about it for a moment before deciding that phones with cords attached weren't so bad after all.

Doug Meijer

The summer before I started high school, we took a family business/pleasure trip to Europe. We were traveling through Belgium, and Dad started to look for a motel for the night. Hank, Mark, and I put our votes in for one with a pool. Dad is never one to pay extra for such luxuries, but he finally consented and found one with an outside pool.

We were excited and hastily changed into our swimsuits, only to find out that the pool was unheated and the water was chilly. To get our money's worth and not to disappoint Dad, we went in anyway.

Tim Nowak

For several years, I taught management training classes for entry-level managers. Next to our classroom was our Thrifty Outlet store that sold overstock office samples and one-of-a-kind items: it was sort of a big garage sale. It was not unusual for Fred and Lena to stop and check out the latest bargains; he would then usually come to our classroom.

I remember one time he stopped in to show the class an alarm clock he bought for $1.50. During these visits, he would ask what we were discussing, and next thing I knew, he'd be up front imparting wisdom and answering questions. Obviously, these new recruits were always excited at this unexpected opportunity to listen and talk to the man who owned the company they were now working for.

Tim Osbeck

I was promoted to travel manager at the time Meijer was expanding into Ohio and Indiana. Part of my job was to make hotel reservations for management and support staff. Fred stopped down to make it clear that he and Lena would be staying at the same hotels as everyone else, and that they were not to be given any preferential treatment. The hotels we used were not four- or five-star hotels. They were clean, affordable budget hotels.

Shortly after that conversation [with Fred], I got a call from a new vice president who informed me that he didn't stay in budget hotels. I told him that I couldn't overrule him, but wanted him to know that

Fred and Lena were staying at the budget hotel. All of a sudden, the vice president thought it might not be so bad after all.

Fred's thrift in his choice of cars is legendary. Once he found himself at a banquet sitting next to a lovely young woman who was wearing more jewelry than Lena owned. He was explaining how he liked to be frugal in his personal life, and he told her that he never bought a new car, but drove the company cars that executives turned in after they had put 60,000 miles on them. "As a matter of fact," he went on, "I'm really lucky, because Lena thinks the same way I do. I always tell her that I will buy her any car she wants, but she says she's perfectly content to drive used company cars."

"Wow!" said the young lady. "If I were married to you, I'd hate to tell you the kind of car I would pick."

"If I were married to you," Fred replied with a sly grin, "I wouldn't make that offer."

Bob Riley

In my sixth week on the job, I was commuting home to Chicago for the weekend, and I was driving a brand-new pool car from the company. In a freak occurrence, a semi coming from the other direction lost a huge tire, which hurtled across the median strip and hit my car like a bomb. I was lucky to be alive. The car was totaled. The only way to get back to Grand Rapids was to fly, so I found myself at O'Hare late that Sunday evening, waiting for the last flight, when who did I run into but Fred.

"What are you doing here?" I asked. He explained that he had been in Florida for a conference that had ended mid-morning, and that he could have gotten home earlier but had saved over $200 by taking the later flight. Then he asked, "What are you doing here?"

I was absolutely mortified! Here he had sacrificed half his day to save a few hundred dollars for the company, and I had to tell him that I had totaled a company car. As I sheepishly recounted my tale of woe, I was amazed at how he reacted. After making sure I was okay, he told me a story about how he was traveling with his family many years ago, and saw the same thing happen — only the tire rolled past their car without hitting it. In short, he couldn't have been more gracious, and he went of his way to put me at ease. Over the next seventeen years, I saw this on almost a daily basis. He was fierce as a lion when it came to the business, but gentle as a lamb when he was dealing with people at the company.

Betsy DeKorne

After our daughter Joan graduated from college, she moved to Washington, D.C., and a new job. One day, Pam called to say that Fred had to be in Washington the next day for a meeting, and asked if I'd like to ride along to visit Joan. We would be leaving on the company plane at 4:00 a.m. and coming back at 6:00 p.m.

I arranged with Joan to pick me up at the airport. She was driving a little yellow Volkswagen at the time. Upon arrival, it became apparent that Fred had no ride waiting, so I said, "You can ride into Washington with us, but it's just a little car." "That's no problem," he quickly responded. So with luggage and briefcase, we piled in and dropped him off at his destination — in between the limos and Cadillacs.

Mike Stewart

Fred was considering buying the Twin Fair chain in Ohio as part of his expansion, and was taking a personal tour of the stores. I was the Twin Fair manager in Marion.

Getting off the plane, Fred had looked up taxicabs in the phone book and found only one, Red Cab. He laughed as he told me that he had to hold his feet up in the air because part of the floorboard on the passenger side was missing, and snow and slush were splashing into the cab.

Throughout the decades of the 1950s, '60s, and '70s, Meijer employees enjoyed the highest wages and benefits in the grocery industry. It was an aspect of the business in which Fred took a personal interest. One member of the Meijer bargaining team in the 1960s remembers that Fred and Earl's objective prior to negotiations was: "We want to be sure our pay and benefits are as good as or better than our competition, because we have the best people."

Roger Horling

Early on, several of us drivers would help load and truck turkeys at Thanksgiving for Mr. Van, the meat director. He would always kid us and say, "I'm working with the highest-paid truck drivers in Grand Rapids." He was right. We were making five cents an hour more than the Teamsters.

Then a new breed of well-known, big-box, nonunion stores began infiltrating the markets Meijer was already competing in, and the wages they paid were far lower. It soon became apparent that Fred, much to his displeasure, would have to heed his own advice if he hoped to stay in business: "You must be in tune with the times to succeed."

Chapter Sixteen

Pennies and Inches

> For want of a nail the shoe was lost.
> For want of a shoe the horse was lost.
> For want of a horse the rider was lost.
> For want of a rider the battle was lost.
> For want of a battle the kingdom was lost.
> And all for the want of a horseshoe nail.

Shortly after Disneyland opened, Walt Disney was making an inspection of the park. He stopped to ride on the jungle cruise attraction, and he emerged furious. The ride was advertised as taking seven minutes, but he had timed it at only four and a half minutes. He ordered the ride lengthened immediately. In fact, no corner of the Disney organization escaped Walt Disney's obsession for meticulous attention to detail. He left a legacy so nurtured and ingrained in the organization that when it was discovered that a merry-go-round at Disney World was installed two inches off-center, Disney management insisted that it be corrected regardless of the cost. Attention to detail is one reason Disney World is truly a magical place for the 46 million guests who visit each year.

Donald Duck, Minnie Mouse, Pluto, and the other Disney characters are the enchantment of a Disney visit. Disney knows this and protects them fiercely. The most strictly enforced rule in the park is that no one outside the cast shall ever be permitted to see a character with his or her mask off. They are taught that never, under any circumstances, are they to break character. The illusion must be maintained.

Walt Disney knew that the total experience of colors, sights, sounds, and smell all had an impact on how the "guests" received the show. He knew that the tiniest of inconsistencies could undermine a host of favorable impressions, and he wasn't about to let that happen. That's why street cleaners at Disney World are given an extra three days of training at Disney University to ensure that they respond in a positive and helpful way to questions from departing guests.

John Barfield

One time a group of us went to the Dairy Queen for an ice-cream cone. I bet someone that if I dropped a penny on the ground, Fred would pick it up. I won the bet.

As this chapter title implies, the principle of attention to details is paramount in any truly successful retail business. Fred Meijer sums it up: "Retail is detail." And he communicates his beliefs day after day in both words and action. That's why he picks up trash and pushes an empty shopping cart into the store every time he visits. It is why the restrooms are clean and all the restroom doors push outward, so that no one has to grab a dirty door handle after washing up.

Pennies

In the grocery business, profit is measured by a fraction of a penny on every dollar taken in. There is a delicate balance between profit and loss. Any number of variables can easily tip the scales from black ink to red ink on the profit-and-loss statement.

Factors such as overexpansion, a new competitor, being out of the right items or overstocked on the wrong ones, lower sales than projected or higher expenses than planned, interest rates, the economy, the weather, and shoplifting — these are some of the details that determine the success of the business.

Don Nunn

When I started at Meijer, my first job was in the mailroom. One day I was asked to drive Fred to some out-of-town stores. Typically, he liked to drive himself, but when his mail and paperwork piled up, he would get someone to drive so he could work in the back seat.

Late that afternoon, he put his paperwork aside and climbed over the seat into the front. He started talking about the cost of doing business. He said: "You probably noticed that a lot of people in the stores carry a black marking pen in their vest pocket. Imagine if all of them working today, say 10,000, were to go home and empty the contents of their vests on the dresser, including these black markers, which cost maybe a dollar. Then the next morning, if they forgot to pick up the marker and got a new one at the store, it would cost the company $10,000. No one stole anything, and many would remember to bring it back another day, but at that moment the money is gone. The same with box cutters, pens, and all the other little items we use in our business."

Rick Zehr

One day, Fred and I were walking across the front of the store. He asked me, "Rick, what is the difference in cost between the paper bag and the plastic bag?" "I'm not sure," I said, "maybe a few pennies." He replied, "Maybe it would be a good thing to know so we can save on supply costs." Even though he knew the answer, he let me check it out for myself, and I always knew the cost of bags and other supplies after that.

Pennies were important for the Meijer family from the very beginning. In fact, it was a matter of a half-cent that caused them to lose their membership in the Red and White buying cooperative. They had lowered their price of milk to two quarts for fifteen cents; at the same time, the town's two other Red and White stores were selling milk for eight cents a quart. Those two stores complained to Lee & Cady, the organization's wholesale supplier, who sent a representative to give Hendrik an ultimatum: Raise your price or take down your Red and White sign.

Hendrik promptly got a ladder and hammer, went outside, took down the sign, and gave it to the astonished Red and White representative. It was not the first or last time that Meijer would be called on the carpet for being unfair competition, which caused Hendrik to muse: "No one considers the customer, but the customer has reason to consider Meijer."

The grocery business had always been characterized by a high rate of failure. A survey of the trade in Louisville, Kentucky, in 1925, showed that about 1,000 grocery stores in the city, including 800 independent operators, went out of business. During the next three years, at the height of prosperity in the 1920s, more than 1,000 grocery stores failed, a turnover rate of more than 100 percent. The vast majority of the victims were independents. Chains succeeded, not merely because they could command lower wholesale prices, but because they knew what they were doing in hiring, stocking, advertising, and a range of other retail skills. Among independent grocers, *Collier's* declared, there existed a "state of unbelievable chaos." A *Collier's* reporter summed up the ultimate truth of the marketplace: "A man has no God-given right to be in the grocery business." (*TY,* p. 132)

NOVEMBER 19, 1937

We are selling Swift canned milk sixty-four cents a case below cost.
We had to put on a limit of four cans per customer (five cents a can).
[Fred's diary]

"One time, Ellis Ranney came into the store and said, 'Why should I buy from you folks for cash when I can buy just as cheap from Svenson [a competitor] and get it delivered?' I said, 'Mr. Ranney, bring me some of your tapes.' He brought them in and threw them on the counter, and said he couldn't save much. So I figured them out — what we would have charged — and it was seventy-five cents less. He said, 'Well, there's only seventy-five cents difference.' I said, 'Gee, Mr. Ranney, it's fifteen percent cheaper. That's a lot of money.' That sold him. He was a banker." (*TY,* p. 132)

Harvey Lemmen

Before we opened our first Thrifty Acres store, we had only a grocery background and knew nothing about clothes or hardgoods. Therefore, we hired two executives from Arlan's, a successful discount chain at that time, to run that side of the business.

A large display of chocolate-covered cherries had been built for the grand opening, and Fred learned that a competitor had priced these candies one cent cheaper. He told this to the Arlan's man, who replied that the whole display couldn't be torn down for one cent. He soon found out that it could. It was just another lesson on the importance of not being undersold. Even though the two Arlan's executives were very intelligent and good at what they did, they didn't last long at Meijer because of our conflicting philosophies.

Abe Abraham

Fred was good about letting his managers run the stores, and very seldom interfered. He never pushed his people, but somehow he always knew what was going on. The one thing I remember is his being a stickler on his prices. His weekly ads proclaimed, "We will not be undersold," and he meant it.

Fred Meijer

My dad always wanted to know what type of merchandise we had for poor people. "What are we doing for the people who can't afford all that fancy food?" That's one thought that has always stuck in my mind.

Without a doubt the most unpleasant expense a business has to deal with is shoplifting, because it always involves a customer, an employee, or a vendor. It is estimated that shoplifting costs retailers eight billion dollars a year, and it is one reason that many companies fail. With profit margins being so slim, it is easy to see why. Hendrik had a discerning eye for shoplifters, and would often come up with a unique way of dealing with them. Once he noticed a regular customer who had some merchandise tucked in his jacket, and was in the checkout line. Squeezing past him, he patted the man's chest and said, "Say, John, you've put on some weight."

Al Waldorf

Fred and his dad suspected a prominent lady in town of shoplifting, and one day they caught her red-handed. Instead of making a scene and calling the police, they called her husband. I saw them all go into the office. No charges were filed and nothing was even mentioned. In a small town, this would have been devastating for the family, especially their kids at school. Even though Fred and his dad didn't like being stolen from, they felt that protecting the family's reputation took precedence.

Muriel Wise

One day I was working in the cash office in the front of the store, and Fred came over and pointed to a lady in the produce department. He said, "That woman has been pregnant for over a year!" Since this was out of character for Fred, I started to laugh, and his face turned red. He knew that the woman was shoplifting. She had a zipped pouch around her stomach under her coat, which made her look pregnant. I thought he was pretty observant to have noticed that.

Earl Holton

The warehouse manager called one day and told me that someone had stolen one of our semi-tractors. Of course, I immediately told Fred. "How did they do that?" he asked.

In those days, it was possible to find keys that would fit multiple ignitions. Apparently, someone had simply driven it away. We never did find the truck, but Fred didn't blame anyone. Instead, he chuckled at my discomfort at telling him about the loss and provided a typical down-to-earth reply: "I guess we'll just have to buy another one."

Jack McCarthy

While I was attending my first loss-prevention managers meeting, Fred came in. I'll never forget his message. He said, "It would be natural to become angry with a person who steals from us; however, most people who steal are not bad. They have only made a bad decision. We have all made bad decisions. We've done something we shouldn't have or said something we later regretted, and in some cases, people steal. It's wrong and they know better, but because most of them are good people, they deserve to be treated with respect."

He said that he realized some shoplifters are bad people, and we don't want them back, but most have only made a bad decision at that moment. If we embarrass them, they will shop somewhere else. So treat them well, be firm, let them know they did wrong, but also let them know they are welcome back. He went on to say, "You have a tough job, but a very important job in protecting the company."

Joe McCormack

One day I was sitting in Fred's office waiting to drive him some place. He was sorting his mail and shoved one letter over to me to read before he had even opened it. I recognized the name since it was from a former employee who was in a nursing home in Detroit. We had stopped there many times for Fred to visit when we were passing through. The man was on oxygen and was in pretty rough shape. What I didn't realize, as I read the letter, was that he had been fired for stealing from the company many years earlier. I always thought that was interesting that Fred would remain kind to someone he knew had stolen from him.

Inches

Fred Meijer

We built the first Thrifty Acres with five-inch concrete floors instead of the normal four-inch because we thought that if it failed we could sell the building to a car dealership. We built the next five stores the same way without thinking about it. Then we remembered why we did it in the first place, and we went back to four-inch floors. In the meantime, this one inch of extra concrete cost us thousands of dollars of unnecessary expense.

The grocery business has been categorized as a business of inches. Consider that twelve thousand new products are introduced into the marketplace each year, an average of a thousand per month; but the shelf space in the store remains the same. It is thus obvious that only a small percentage of these new items ever make it to the shelf in any given store. These precious few inches of shelf space are crucially important to the manufacturers in getting their products to the consumer.

Manufacturers with large advertising and promotional budgets and creative brand managers are very adept at finding ways to gain shelf space and increase their market share. An example is Tylenol, a highly respected brand for treating coughs, colds, and aches and pains. The occasional user may simply remember the days when a Tylenol tablet took care of everything, a one-size-fits-all remedy. Not so anymore. Now there are different Tylenol products for headaches, muscle aches, arthritis, allergy, coughs, colds and flu, and sleeplessness; they come in various sizes and can be taken in tablet, liquid, caplet, or gel form. There's a Tylenol that lasts eight hours, one that's rapid release, one for daytime, and one for nighttime. There's a Tylenol for men, women, children and infants — over sixty-five varieties, each with its unique packaging and UPC (universal packaging code) number.

Large manufacturers are able to create an instant demand for their new products by using heavy-saturation advertising and promotional campaigns. One need not watch television very long before this becomes evident; the same is true of the Sunday paper and the special inserts that drop out of it every week. All these new products must find a way to get on the shelf at the stores, thus presenting a challenge in shelf-space management.

Pennies and inches are the small but important details that Fred admonishes his team to constantly be on the lookout for. Where a penny has come to symbolize family shopping at reasonable prices,

Taking turns riding the ponies

the penny pony rides are now serving their third generation of little buckaroos.

You can ride in a racecar at another store for twenty-five cents, but that's equal to twenty-five pony rides at Meijer. This herd of ponies, which is constantly in motion and now numbers over 550, has been credited with enhancing many a parent's shopping experience with this promise: "If you're good you can ride the pony on our way out."

Fred Meijer realized this when he bought the first ponies many years ago, and even though a penny doesn't begin to cover the cost of the electricity and maintenance, he realizes it has been a worthwhile investment. It's often the last thing the child remembers on the way home. The only time he ever felt bad for having ponies in the store was in 1964, when the Greenville outlet burned down. He remembers kids crying because they thought the horses had burned up.

History is filled with examples of the importance of pennies and inches. During the California gold rush, two prospectors, Joshua Bauman and Dorval Fifield, staked their claim and started digging, hoping to strike it rich. They spent the next twenty years working the mine, earning a meager living, until Joshua finally died of exhaustion. Disillusioned, Dorval sold the mine to a neighboring prospector for a bucket of pennies. The new owner, on inspecting his new mine with a pickax, chipped away at the shale wall and quickly discovered, only two inches deep, a rich vein of gold. Two inches was the difference between a pail of pennies and millions of dollars.

Chapter Seventeen

A Fork in the Road

When you come to a fork in the road, take it.

— Yogi Berra

Alice was puzzled. As she searched for a way out of Wonderland, she came to a fork in the road. "Which road should I take?" she asked the Cheshire Cat.

"Where are you going?" the cat responded. Alice said she didn't know. The smiling cat gave her this reply, "If you don't know where you're going, any road will get you there."

— Lewis Carroll

With the explosion of the information age that began at the end of the twentieth century, Meijer faced a significant fork in the road. Deciding on what new technology options to embrace became critical, because it was expensive and the company couldn't afford the time wasted with bad decisions. Today, when you drive up to a McDonald's microphone and place your order, before you get to the window to pick up your food, your order has already gone to Colorado, been processed and sent back, all in a matter of seconds.

The bar code present on all packaging in stores today was unheard of in 1970. Early supermarket pioneers of technology saw that banks were clearing checks via a series of magnetic numbers and wondered why the same concept couldn't be used to scan grocery items at the checkout. A few visionaries were optimistic, but most were not — mainly due to the expense. It would cost $15,000 per checkout to install the necessary Point of Sale scanning equipment. The president of one company said that they would continue to use traditional cash registers, adding, "We can run our business out of cigar boxes just as easily and a lot cheaper."

Most manufacturers also balked. Now they would have to go through the expense of securing bar code numbers and re-labeling all their packaging. But it didn't take long for both sides to discover the benefits. Prior to bar codes and scanning, it took a product six to eight weeks to get from the manufacturer to the customer. That time would eventually be reduced to two days, resulting in huge savings in warehousing costs and improvements in efficiency.

Change, which means confronting new forks in the road, is never easy. Risk-taking is not instinctive, and old boomerangs are hard to throw away. Having grown up on a farm, Fred has often advised: "Don't be afraid of stepping in something soft. We used to follow the cows. When it was warm, it wasn't so bad. We need to see the future through a new set of eyes."

Fred and Earl Holton recognized the value of bar codes and scanning early on. But there was a problem. This new technology was a supermarket industry initiative designed for grocery products sold in traditional supermarkets. At that time, Meijer had the only stores in the country that also sold general merchandise, including clothing, toys, hardware, and tens of thousands of other nongrocery items through a central checkout. Fred, Earl, and a handful of other Meijer executives who recognized the value of scanning knew they had three choices: ignore the new technology, wait and see, or be the ones who would apply the technology to the general merchandise side of the business. They chose the third option.

Pat Gavin remembers being given the responsibility of overseeing the implementation of bar coding in the company. It was not an easy task convincing a group of already busy buyers that bar codes would ultimately make their jobs easier, but their support was necessary in order to help them convince their suppliers that they needed to bar-code their products. "I remember asking Earl to accompany me to one of the important meetings I was having with the buying staff," Pat says. "As a result, we were eventually able to achieve a 100-percent scanning rate on everything going through the checkouts." In 2009, America will celebrate its thirty-fifth anniversary "behind bars."

Another big fork in the road on the information highway was the use of credit cards. It all started in 1950: Diners Club introduced a single card in several cities that could be accepted by a variety of merchants as an alternative to cash. Twenty thousand people became cardholders that first year. The VISA card, issued by the Bank of America of California, followed four years later.

Credit cards were about to revolutionize the way Americans paid for their purchases. However, the use of credit cards for supermarket purchases did not come until later. In 1970, two supermarket chains, Ralph's in California and Jewel in Chicago, experimented with credit-card acceptance, then dropped it, deciding it wasn't worth the cost involved. This view did not change until 1991, when VISA announced a program offering the supermarket industry a reduced interchange fee for credit-card transactions.

Today, the average American has 6.6 plastic cards (credit and debit) and uses them for almost 60 percent of household purchases. In some ways, little has changed from the time the Meijer family opened its first store, when many of their customers' purchases were on credit, except that in those days, instead of scanning a plastic card, the grocer tallied the customer's bill on a credit sheet, or "due-bill."

Willet Smith

Meijer had just come out with its own credit card, and was promoting it to the public. The mechanics and transactions of co-branded credit cards are handled by an issuing bank, which, among other things, determines your line of credit.

My wife and I were shopping, and we decided to sign up for the card. There was a table and computer where someone would take your application and give you a temporary card. My wife was given a $1200 line of credit, but I only qualified for $600. That was a little embarrassing, so the next day I called the person in charge of the Meijer cards. "Michael," I said, "my wife got a $1200 line of credit, and I only got $600. How come?" He laughed and said, "What's the problem? Fred only got $300." He explained that if you don't use credit, the credit bureau doesn't have a history of how you pay. He was right. At least I qualified for twice as much credit as Fred.

Most of the arrays of choices we face every day are inconsequential; however, some of them have a monumental impact on our lives. In 1934, after applying to be a postman and still considering the prospect of being a full-time farmer, Hendrik Meijer was forced by circumstances into a decision that would lead his family down the path into the grocery business. After his high school graduation in 1937, Fred contemplated going to college with aspirations of becoming a history teacher. However, by then the spirit and excitement of the grocery business was so ingrained that he decided to stay with the family business. Hendrik cemented the deal by making him an equal partner. As the company grew, the choices of where to direct its expansion plans led to other crossroads: Should they concentrate on smaller towns or bigger cities? And in either case, which ones?

Nineteen sixty-nine will be remembered as a year of major historical events. Richard Nixon was sworn in as the thirty-seventh President and announced the first U.S. troop withdrawals from Vietnam, as hundreds of thousands of demonstrators marched in protest against the war. Sirhan Sirhan admitted in court that he had killed presidential candidate Robert F. Kennedy. Apollo 11, carrying Neil Armstrong, Buzz Aldrin, and Michael Collins, landed on the moon. The world watched in awe as Neil Armstrong took the first human steps on that previously lifeless orb.

In 1969, the Boeing 747 made its maiden flight. Dr. Denton Cooley implanted the first temporary artificial heart. It was the year of Woodstock, the first ATM, upsets in the Super Bowl by Broadway Joe Namath and the New York Jets, and in baseball's World Series by the "Miracle Mets." Golda Meir became the prime minister of Israel, and Yasser Arafat took the reins of the Palestine Liberation Organization. It was the year that the HIV-AIDS virus migrated to the United States via Haiti. And, after 147 years, the last issue of the *Saturday Evening Post* was published.

It was also an important year in the history of Meijer. On Wednesday, September 25, 1969, this full-page ad ran in the *Grand Rapids Press:*

We waited and watched, and then we decided. Beginning September 28, the Grand Rapids Thrifty Acres stores will be opened on Sunday. It was not a decision easily arrived at. We are aware of the strong moral convictions in this area against Sunday shopping. In fact, that conviction is shared by a large number of our own employees. But the facts are undeniable. Many people want the opportunity to shop on Sunday, and they express their desires in the strongest way possible, by shopping in great numbers at the many stores already open on Sunday. We cannot deny them that right. If we expect to stay in business, we must serve people when they want to be served. That's our job.

Of course, we will not force employees to work on Sunday if it violates their religious beliefs. Those who do work Sundays will receive two days' pay for their one day of work. If you do not agree with our decision, please remember that we must serve all the people of Western Michigan. We sincerely ask for your understanding in this matter.

Meijer, Inc.
Fred Meijer
Executive Vice President

Earl Holton

In retail, it is not enough to understand your business. You must also understand the communities that form your market. We weren't wrong to open on Sundays from a business perspective, but we had to approach the whole thing cautiously from a community perspective. People wrote letters to complain, and a few churches organized letter-writing campaigns or distributed preprinted cards to be sent to us. We made sure that personal letters got personal responses explaining our position, and preprinted cards got a form letter from Meijer.

We also did our best to accommodate team members whose religious convictions made it difficult for them to work on Sundays. It didn't take long to realize we couldn't always predict how team members would respond. I remember preparing to talk with one store manager who was quite religious. I approached the whole thing very cautiously because he was a kind soul and a true believer in his faith. His response taught me you should never anticipate another's behavior.

"If you decide to work," I said, "it would be this much overtime for you or whoever's in charge." To my surprise, he quickly agreed to work on Sundays, explaining that the additional income would permit his family to make a larger contribution to their church. (Earl Holton, *Learning to Lead*, p. 62)

Most people believed that this was the first time a Meijer store had ever opened on Sunday. Little did they realize that the seeds had been sown long before, in 1934, when that first store was open for business on Sunday.

Another decisive moment came in 1988, when the company decided to remain open twenty-four hours a day. There were also questions about how and where to expand the distribution system to supply a growing number of stores in new markets. As retailers have learned, supply-chain management is critical to a company's success. Having the products that customers want at the right place at the right time means the difference between success and failure.

Fred and the Meijer executives responsible for distribution recognized that three hundred miles was the maximum distance products could be trucked cost-effectively and in a timely manner. It was a lesson they learned by watching K-Mart's expansion in the 1970s. As the number of new K-Marts grew by the hundreds each year, each one further away from a distribution center, K-Mart started running into problems. An example was the new K-Mart in Little Rock, Arkansas, which was being served by warehouses in Fort Wayne and Detroit, over 700 miles away. This problem of distribution also affected the number-one supermarket chain in Michigan. Wrigley had an agreement with K-Mart to build a grocery store next to — and in many cases attached to — the K-Mart. But as expansion continued further west and south of Detroit, Wrigley was also caught in a logistical nightmare, which many observers believe proved to be its undoing.

In 1974 the sole Meijer grocery distribution center was moved from Grand Rapids to Lansing, a more central location, since more stores were being opened in the Detroit area. In 1993 the company built a 980,000-square-foot complex in Newport, Michigan, a small hamlet between Detroit and Toledo. The first Meijer distribution center outside of Michigan was built in 1994 in Tipp City, Ohio, just north of Dayton. By early 2008, four state-of-the-art distribution complexes, with a total of 6.5 million square feet, serviced the nearly two hundred Meijer stores in five states.

Jim Postma

Fred has always challenged us to continually look for better ways of doing things, and to keep our eyes open for changes in the industry. Once I told him about some innovations in warehousing that were being tested on the West Coast. He immediately encouraged me to book a plane ticket out west so that I could see these changes for myself. He told me that anytime I heard of something that could make us a more efficient, cost-effective operation, I should go check it out.

Forks in the road included decisions on diversification. In 1973, unable to convince Levi Strauss to allow the sale of the popular Levi's brand of jeans in Thrifty Acres stores, Meijer built free-standing outlets called Copper Rivet. This worked all right for a while, but finally Levi's executives balked, saying that they wanted an exclusive store

"My first store was successful right off the bat. Made me want to open more. So I did."

that would sell only the Levi's brand. The brand was at the height of its popularity at the time, and so Sagebrush stores were born.

Sagebrush ads featured a prospector called Sagebrush Zeb, who touted the merits of Sagebrush for a decade before this successful venture, now amounting to forty stores, was sold in 1988. At about the same time, Meijer purchased Jean House, a chain of women's specialty clothing shops located in malls. These shops continued to be developed under the names Casual Court and Tansey.

These were busy times for the company, with seemingly endless opportunities offered by many diverging roads. Beginning in 1991, two other retail formats arose. Two former Meijer supermarkets that were being closed, along with two additional store leases, were converted into a drug discount chain called Spaar (from the Dutch verb *sparen*, meaning "to save"). Though the stores showed respectable sales, the company knew that they would need dozens of them to succeed. Meanwhile, corporate energies concentrated on the new Thrifty Acres format; thus, two years after its inception, Spaar quietly disappeared.

In 1981, responding to K-Mart's national success, Meijer decided to test the waters by opening several conventional discount stores under the name Meijer Square. The response was encouraging. These smaller stores, without perishable food departments, did not have the heavy start-up costs that the big Thrifty Acres format demanded. They looked so encouraging that when a floundering discounter based in Buffalo, New York, called and offered to sell its two Twin Fair divisions, one in Ohio and one in New York State, Meijer agreed to buy the fourteen Ohio stores, which were located mostly in strip malls in the Cincinnati area. However, the decision to buy them was not unanimous with the Meijer management. Fred Kistler, the former vice president of finance, remembers sitting with fourteen other executives in a conference room for three hours discussing the pros and cons of the proposed purchase.

Finally, everyone was asked to submit a written vote. When the votes were tallied, there were twelve against and three in favor. Fred announced that the results were that they would do the buyout. The reason he didn't buy both divisions of Twin Fair was because he'd always told Harvey and Earl that if either of them disagreed with him, he would not overrule their decision. Although they didn't like either division, they decided to use their veto power sparingly, and keep the damage to a minimum.

The Twin Fair acquisition took the company south of the Michigan border for the first time. Meijer, accustomed to occupying a unique niche with the Thrifty Acres stores, soon found it was forced to run stores in a new market where shoppers were having a hard time pronouncing the name. The Meijer managers wanted to run the newest and best stores in the country, but it wasn't working out. As the leases began to expire, they sold, closed, or replaced the Twin Fair stores

A Twin Fair store

with full-line Meijer stores. The experiment provided an initial foot-hold in the Ohio market, and today Meijer operates forty supercenters in that state.

Amid all this feverish activity, Meijer was testing other kinds of businesses: a free-standing fast-food restaurant dubbed Thrifty Kitchen; auto centers that carried tires, batteries, and automotive accessories alongside the rapidly expanding number of gas stations. Meijer tried an outlet store called Source Club, but it was unable to compete with Sam's Club. Meijer dabbled in the financial business, opening a dozen Michigan savings and loans. Then there were men's suit departments, floor coverings, appliances, lumber, Chinese restaurants, video arcades, drive-up pharmacies, and mail-order prescriptions.

Despite the frequent failures of these ventures, the company has succeeded because Fred has heeded his own advice about being a risk-taker.

Tim Lesneski

In the late '90s, drive-through pharmacies were a new concept being tried in several parts of the country. Since our pharmacies at the time were not located on an outside wall where the pharmacist could see and talk to the customer, we recommended using pneumatic tubes like you see at drive-through banks. After a few months, I was asked to give a report to management, and the report wasn't very good. In fact, the concept wasn't working. One of the members expressed his dissatisfaction about the failure, and I thought, This is just the beginning of what's about to come. About then, Fred joined the conversation. In his calming way, he thanked us for not being afraid to try something new. He closed the meeting saying something I will never forget. He said, "We should be trying and failing at new things all the time. This is how we learn, and this is how we invest in our people as they learn along the way. We shouldn't be afraid to be risk-takers."

Yesterday, Americans filled their prescriptions at a local drugstore; today, 75 percent are being filled somewhere else.

Fred's advice parallels that of a number of great achievers who came to similar crossroads in life. In 1914, when Thomas Edison was sixty-seven years old, his laboratory was destroyed by fire, demolishing much of his life's work. His son, Charles, found his father calmly watching the scene. The next morning, Edison looked at the ruins and exclaimed, "There is great value in disaster. All my mistakes are burned. Now I can start anew." Three weeks later, Edison managed to deliver the first phonograph.

Of the Fortune 500 companies, only ten are privately held. The biggest reason for a private company to go public is to raise capital. In December 1980, for example, Apple Computer's initial public offering valued the company at $101 million; ten years later, it was capitalized at $15 billion. Fred and the Meijer family have resisted the temptation to become a public company; instead, they have chosen to reinvest the profits in the company rather than paying dividends and answering to stockholders. Many have suggested that Meijer could have been a national company by selling stock, as Sam Walton chose to do. That is probably true. However, Hendrik and Fred never set out to be the biggest. They just wanted to make a living at something they enjoyed. Did going public ever cross Fred's mind? Sure it did. In 1978, during the Carter years, he seriously considered the idea — then emphatically dismissed it.

Any successful enterprise has its suitors, and Meijer has had its share of would-be buyers. Fred remembers that one of the first of those was an A&P representative. When he asked what it would take to buy the business, Fred threw out what he thought was an exorbitant figure. "Okay," said the caller. Taken aback, Fred added, "And I would need to run the company." Again, an affirmative reply. By now Fred knew this was serious, so he politely dismissed the caller. Then there was the overture from Joe Antonini, the CEO of K-Mart, and three calls from Sam Walton, which Fred did finally return in order to decline to meet with him. There have been offers from overseas conglomerates and several national chains. The answer, however, has always been the same: it's a path the family has chosen not to take.

Great leaders are decisive and creative; they know how to negotiate unexpected realities. As a young man, Abraham Lincoln commanded a small squadron of the Illinois militia. Never having been a leader before, he hadn't learned the commands for close-order drill. One day, as he was marching his troops across a field, he noticed that they were rapidly approaching a fence row with only a small opening. They were marching six abreast, and he was trying to recall the command that would get his troops through the opening in proper military fashion. Unable to think of it, he called a halt and said, "Fall out, take a ten-minute break, and then fall in on the other side of this fence."

Chapter Eighteen

Dodging 500-Pound Gorillas

First Retailer: Is it true the alligators won't get you if you're
   carrying a torch?
Second Retailer: That depends on how fast you carry the
   torch.

D odging 500-pound competitors started the day the Meijer
family opened its first store in 1934. Their gorilla of that decade was the great Atlantic and Pacific Tea Company. A&P's
roots went back to pre–Civil War days, when two unlikely partners,
George F. Gilman, a prosperous entrepreneur, and George H. Hartford, a twenty-six-year-old from Augusta, Maine, shook hands on the
docks of New York City to seal their new business venture. Hartford
had presented this idea to Gilman: buy tea direct from Chinese plan-
tations, which would cut out all the middlemen and drastically undercut the market. Tea was selling for $1.50 a pound, a staggeringly high
price at the time. Hartman's plan would allow them to sell quality tea
for less than $1, and, with enough volume, still show a healthy profit.
And so, with Gilman being the financier and Hartford running the
business, A&P was born.

   By 1865, the Civil War had ended, and A&P had five successful tea
shops in New York City. During the next ten years the company added
more stores, a mail-order business, and home-delivery wagons, which
delivered not only tea and coffee but other household items. By 1879,

the company had more than a hundred retail stores, and their product lines had expanded to include sugar, milk, butter, flour, baking powders, and other sundries. The company created its own brand, Eight O'clock Coffee, which reigned as the number-one brand of coffee in America for the next seventy years.

In 1901, George Gilman died unexpectedly, and George Hartford became sole owner of the company, along with his two sons, John and George, Jr. By 1907, A&P's annual sales were eight million dollars, and growing rapidly; by 1912, the Hartfords owned over 400 retail stores and offered extensive product lines to their customers. The company next started its own canning factories and manufacturing plants, and it introduced many products under the A&P brand.

During the next two decades, the company exploded into a retail giant that ran more than 16,000 stores. At least one A&P stood on every main street of every small town east of the Mississippi. So great was its power over suppliers that Congress passed several antipredatory laws specifically aimed at the practices of A&P. In the meantime, thou-

A mid-1930s A&P store
(Photo courtesy of the Shelby Needham Collection, Marion, OH)

sands of small stores were forced out of business by the company's superior buying power. Because it could give customers lower prices, they kept coming.

In 1934, Greenville had two A&P outlets a few blocks down the street from the newly opened North Side Grocery. In the spring of 1937, A&P announced plans for another twenty stores, enlarged and improved, in and around Grand Rapids. Their competitors could not afford to match A&P's prices because their wholesale costs were usually more than what A&P was selling the items for.

> Hendrik and Fred would often drive to A&P in Grand Rapids to pick up items to sell at the North Side Grocery, all the while hoping they wouldn't be recognized. Once they needed wallpaper cleaner, and A&P's price was lower than their wholesale cost. They bought a dozen cans in Grand Rapids to take back to Greenville and sell themselves. The A&P cashier was surprised to see someone buying so odd an item in quantity. The white-haired customer, rather fastidiously dressed in a dark suit, had a hint of ministerial bearing about him, so the cashier ventured to inquire, "What are you going to do with all this, clean a church?" With a sly smile, Hendrik replied, "In my father's house are many mansions."

After saturating the larger cities with new supermarkets, A&P fixed its gaze on small-town expansion, including Greenville, and store owners trembled. Some closed their doors, knowing they couldn't compete. Not Hendrik and Fred, who drove to Grand Rapids, Big Rapids, Muskegon, and Charlotte to see what A&P was doing. Fred had never been inside an A&P store before his father went into the grocery business. Now father and son both became students of the huge chain's success. Everywhere they went, they carried a tape measure. In Grand Rapids they studied the aisles at the A&P on Grandville Avenue and measured the shelves in the store on Stocking Street.

Sometimes they conducted their research clandestinely. On other occasions they had the blessing of the A&P manager, who amused himself by divulging his chain's techniques to a small-town merchant with a heavy Dutch accent. Either way, Hendrik saw exactly how he might set up a supermarket, where the meat and produce went, what aisle was best for bread or cereal, where the cookie counter belonged, and so forth.

"The new A&P stores went first class. The new store planned for Lafayette Street in Greenville (the town's smaller, older A&Ps would be closed) would be located in a new building. And the chain's acquisition of new equipment meant bargains for buyers of the old. Hendrik bought five used A&P meat cases. They were not as shiny and modern as the newer models, but they cost only twenty-five dollars each, and they enabled Hendrik to boast that the expanded Thrift Market had the biggest meat department in Montcalm County." (*TY*, p. 156)

In a bold move, they decided to confront A&P head-on, doubling the size of their store. Their business grew, and by the time the dust settled, Greenville had five fewer grocery stores, and Meijer had the highest volume in Montcalm County.

In 1949, when Meijer began to build stores in Grand Rapids, A&P was still by far the biggest competitor. In addition, the market was dominated by a local grocery chain called Eberhard's. L. V. Eberhard, the owner (always known by his initials), was an austere and astute businessman who was bent on securing the best locations. His stores would usually open with whatever was the latest trend around the country. For example, he introduced Grand Rapids' first air-curtain door at his Wealthy Street store. The Eberhard stores were also enthusiastic purveyors of S&H green stamps, a powerful motivator for housewives in those days, because they could be redeemed for premiums — without the need to spend any additional cash.

In fact, a conversation with L. V. was a major reason Meijer had decided on Grand Rapids for expansion. A few years earlier, Fred had happened to be seated on a plane with L. V. as they traveled to a grocers' meeting in Chicago. As the plane took off from the south side of Grand Rapids, L. V. called Fred's attention to "all those new houses." The message was clear: new houses translated into customers. Grand Rapids was enjoying the prosperity of the postwar boom.

Meijer decided to enter the fray in the big city of Grand Rapids even though they would be facing A&P, Kroger, and Eberhard's as solid competitors. The family opened eight supermarkets in Grand Rapids during the decade of the 1950s, with their three "county" stores being the only initial source of cash flow. The company was only marginally profitable during that period.

Entering the decade of the 1960s, the next real test came when Meijer opened its first Thrifty Acres store. That move greatly expanded the sphere of competition, which now was made up of all general-merchandise competitors, including the largest retailers in America, Sears and K-Mart. Now Fred and Hendrik found themselves sandwiched between the upscale Sears Department Store, the anchor of a large mall just down the street, and the new discount K-Marts that were springing up all around them with a middle-range assortment of general-merchandise products and prices.

Sears, a company begun really by accident in 1886, had become an American institution by that time. When most general stores received their goods by train, Richard Sears was a railroad station agent in Redwood, Minnesota, and he received a shipment of watches from a Chicago jeweler that the intended customer didn't want. Sears purchased the watches and sold them himself. That worked so well that he ordered more and subsequently quit his railroad job. He moved to Chicago, where he met Alvah C. Roebuck, and the two formed a partnership in a catalog business, which they named Sears, Roebuck & Company.

The company was an instant success. By 1894 the Sears catalog offered 332 pages of products available through the mails. It soon developed a reputation for quality products and customer satisfaction, while it took advantage of increasingly reliable mail delivery. The following year the catalog grew to 532 pages. This laid the groundwork for customers being able to buy nearly everything for the home from a catalog. Soon the company was offering entire house kits: they were called Sears Modern Homes, and they were shipped on railroad cars. By 1940, one hundred thousand had been sold.

The first Sears retail store opened in 1925 in Chicago. After World War II, the company built department stores in suburban shopping malls and quickly became the largest retailer in the United States. Americans would soon be acquainted with the Sears brands: Kenmore appliances, Craftsman tools, Die Hard batteries, and Allstate insurance, which Sears began in 1931. A national advertising campaign featured the slogan, "There's more for your life . . . at Sears."

During the decades of the 1970s and '80s, the company that became Meijer's fiercest competitor was K-Mart, originator of the "blue light special." But the history of K-Mart was different from that of either A&P or Sears. It was the offspring of an already successful five-and-dime chain. Sebastian Kresge had opened his first dime store in Detroit the year before the turn of the twentieth century. Known as S. S. Kresge, the company quickly expanded across the Midwest and became a publicly traded company on the New York Stock Exchange in 1918. (Wal-Mart did not become a public company until 1972.) Recognizing the culture shift that was taking place in the late 1950s, the company introduced its K-Mart discount stores in 1962. These new stores quickly outpaced the Kresge dime stores in sales. Fueled by the established parent company with both capital and seasoned general-merchandise management, K-Mart was in a prime position for expansion. By 1975, it was the biggest discounter in America, eventually boasting more than 2,000 stores. In Michigan it was Meijer's biggest competitor.

A few years earlier, Meijer had started to build stores in the suburbs of Detroit, K-Mart's backyard. K-Mart executives took note of the insolent little upstart from the other side of the state. In fact, they let it be known that wherever Meijer built a store, they would build one across the street, and they did a pretty good job of keeping their promise.

It was July 1987. The rush and excitement of the Fourth of July had just passed. Shortly after lunch on Friday, the telephone rang on

Fred's line on the fourth floor of the Meijer office. Pam Kleibusch, his administrative assistant, took the call and gave the usual greeting. A man on the other end introduced himself as Joe Antonini, whom Pam immediately recognized as the chairman, president, and CEO of K-Mart.

"What can I do for you, Mr. Antonini?" she asked.

"Is Fred available? I'd like to speak with him." His intention was to set up a meeting, and he offered to come to Grand Rapids.

Realizing that if the president of K-Mart showed up in a Meijer corporate office lobby that was usually full of buyers and sales representatives, it would fuel a rumor that would vibrate throughout the U.S. business community, Fred offered instead to drive to the K-Mart headquarters in Detroit. They arranged a meeting for the following week. Before arriving, Fred stopped at the Meijer store on Coolidge Avenue to walk through as he usually did, visiting with customers and team members. Then he got back in his car and proceeded a few blocks up the road for his meeting, having already surmised what Antonini had in mind.

The impressive multistory world headquarters of K-Mart took up several blocks. As Fred pulled into the parking lot, he noted the energetic activity associated with a very successful company. Parking in one of the parking spaces farthest from the entrance, as was his custom, he noted the reserved parking spots for K-Mart executives near the entrance. The lobby was busy with sales reps waiting for their appointments with their buyers, but hardly anyone paid any attention to someone they assumed to be one of them. However, two Proctor and Gamble reps gave him a second look. He overheard one say to the other, "No, it can't be," and they went back to their discussion about their newest product.

He announced himself to the busy receptionist, who gave him a second look when he said that he had an appointment with Mr. Antonini. A secretary promptly appeared and escorted him to the elevators that would take them to the tower where the top echelon resided. There he was cordially greeted with a big smile on the face of the most powerful man in the retail business, Joe Antonini himself. Other executives and secretaries working in nearby offices, trying not to be conspicuous, got a glimpse of their boss's guest and could only imagine who he might be.

After the usual exchange of pleasantries, and Fred's polite refusal of a proffered cup of coffee, the subject turned to John Glenn's recent orbit of the earth. Both men were careful not to get into any discussion that could be construed as collusion. They seemed comfortable with each other as their chat continued.

Sensing that the time was right, Joe got down to his reason for the meeting. Being careful in choosing his words so as not to offend, he posed a hypothetical question: If — just if — Fred ever considered selling his company, K-Mart would like the first right of refusal. A dollar offer was never put on the table, nor any proposal about whether Meijer would be run as a separate company, nor the nature of Fred's involvement in the resulting entity.

Fred didn't even try to suppress the smile that crossed his face. He had figured on something like this. But he thought that the way the offer was made was an interesting approach.

"Mr. Antonini," he said, "I thank you and am flattered by your hypothetical question, but we're not interested in selling to anyone. Even if we did, who knows, you may not be here to finalize your offer." It was over that quickly. The whole discussion took thirteen minutes: the overture had been made and politely rebuffed. They shook hands. It was the last time the two would see each other. And Fred's comment proved to be prophetic: Joe Antonini was dismissed by the K-Mart board a few years later.

Ray Leach

In 1967, Fred and I attended a produce seminar in Phoenix, Arizona. One of the other attendees was the owner of Farmer Jack, the biggest chain of grocery stores in Detroit. We were not in the Detroit market at the time, and he didn't know who we were. He was bragging about making plans to build stores in Grand Rapids the following year. I remember Fred whispering to me that he should spend more time listening and less time talking.

Farmer Jack did build three stores in Grand Rapids shortly after that, but they closed less than two years later.

With Lake Michigan separating them from Wisconsin to the west and the Upper Peninsula and Canada to the north, Meijer felt it had to expand to the east, which would mean the Detroit market. The competition there proved to be fearsome. K-Mart saturated the area with blue lights. The city had large malls strategically located, with a Sears anchoring each one. Then there were the national grocery chains, including Kroger and A&P, along with hometown favorites such as Wrigley, Chatham, Great Scott, and Farmer Jack, all of them firmly entrenched.

A Detroit analysis

Some retailers will probably say Fred Meijer is crazy. After all, Detroit is notoriously over-stored already, with six cutthroat grocery chains. And why should Meijer succeed as a mass merchandiser in K-Mart's backyard — where Arlan's, Miracle Mart, Yankee, and others have failed? The answer is a riddle: by being both smaller and bigger than the competition. (*Detroit Free Press,* May 31, 1974)

Detroit became a national hotbed for price wars that would eventually result in the closing of Chatham, Wrigley, and Great Scott. Though it was battered like everyone else, Meijer survived, and Detroit played a key role in the company's subsequent growth.

As if competing with the biggest and best retailers in the world weren't difficult enough, the decades of the 1980s and '90s would spawn a whole new kind of competitor, known in the industry as a "category killer." Whereas the big department stores and mass merchants might designate 10,000 square feet of retail space for toys, Toys R Us would build a 40,000-square-foot store for just toys, adding variety and selection to this single category. Also adopting this model were Staples for office supplies, Best Buy for electronics, PetSmart for pets, Lowe's, Home Depot, and Menards for home improvement, Auto Zone for automobile parts, Gander Mountain for sporting goods, Blockbuster for videos, and many others.

K-Mart saw the trend emerging and attempted to be everything to everybody, mostly by acquiring struggling companies. By the mid

1990s, K-Mart operated eight "category-killer" divisions, including Office Max, Sports Authority, Borders Books, Builder's Square, Pace Warehouse clubs, and Payless drugstores. In less than ten years they would close or divest themselves of all of those companies, losing perhaps a billion dollars in the process.

Loren Fairbotham

In 1988, Cub Foods, a Minneapolis-based food chain of large, high-volume supermarkets, entered Kalamazoo, opening a big new store near the one I was managing, with intentions of adding more. I was given carte blanche to make sure they didn't take our business. Every morning I would check their prices to be sure ours were as good as or better than theirs. One day, as was often the case, Fred was in the Cub store and noticed that their bananas were cheaper. He asked me about this. I explained that since their produce wasn't moving, they had a lot of overripe bananas to get rid of. Their customers were not going to be happy with spoiled bananas. Since our bananas were clearly superior, I hadn't reduced the price.

He listened, and then explained his philosophy about meeting prices on our items regardless of the quality being sold by the competitor. After a few months, Cub closed its new store and didn't build any more in Michigan.

The chairman of SuperValu, parent company of Cub Foods, later told Fred that Meijer was the toughest competitor they had ever encountered.

The ultimate gorilla in every retailer's mind today, and for good reason, is headquartered in Bentonville, Arkansas. At the turn of the twentieth century, the relatively small country of England could boast that the sun never set on its empire. A hundred years later, Wal-Mart can make that same claim: as of 2008, Wal-Mart operates more than 7,000 stores in fourteen countries, including China, with its 1.2 billion potential customers.

In 2001, Wal-Mart became the largest company of any kind anywhere in the world. Its two million employees represent the largest private-sector work force in the world; its technology and computers control more data than anyone outside the U.S. government; and only a handful of world governments, military included, have bigger payrolls. If Wal-Mart's sales, $400 billion, were measured as gross national product, it would be the world's twenty-first largest country, right behind Switzerland. It currently sells over 50 percent of all mass merchandise and is the number-one grocer in the United States. It is expected to reach one trillion dollars in sales by 2018.

Wal-Mart went flying past K-Mart in 1990. That was also the year that Wal-Mart built its first store in Michigan, in what would become the beginning of close-encounter competition that would spread to all five states in which Meijer has stores. First it was the traditional Wal-Mart, selling general merchandise and a limited line of groceries; but by the early 2000s, this rapid growth included supercenters as well. In the United States, with few exceptions, there are no Wal-Mart stores more than sixty miles apart. In 2001, Wal-Mart accelerated plans for scores of new supercenters near current and future Meijer store locations.

Toughest Food Fight in Modern Supermarket History

The above title refers to the upcoming clash of supercenters in Michigan that will pit incumbent Meijer against insurgent Wal-Mart stores. Meijer, based in Grand Rapids, Michigan, has several interesting dynamics, among them is that it's 70 years old. It now operates more than 150 stores, it is privately held, and it is the originator of the supercenter concept. It is impossible to walk into a Meijer without realizing immediately that Meijer supercenters are the model upon which Wal-Mart based its supercenters. Now those two companies are about to clash as Wal-Mart pours supercenters into Michigan. Meijer is getting ready. It has already instituted a couple of rounds of job cuts so it looks like there will be quite a battle ahead. (*Supermarket News,* November 22, 2004)

Since 1980, there have been over 150,000 retail bankruptcies. In order to remain a healthy and growing company, Meijer has continually had to adjust to the competitive environment around it. Many companies have gone out of business because of their inability or unwillingness to make tough decisions that are painful in the short term. People who invent and perfect concepts such as Fred and Hendrik did with one-stop shopping do not generally enjoy their advantage for long, because when good ideas work, others will copy the concept.

Paul Boyer

When Wal-Mart announced that it would expand aggressively into the Midwest, thereby competing head to head with us, we knew a transformation was necessary. We also understood that such change would involve many tough and unpopular decisions that we wouldn't have considered in the past.

Many of these decisions have been especially hard on Fred, and often he has been tempted to override others and say no. But he has always understood that the future success of the company would be at stake if he did so. Fred has shown time and again that being a real leader means keeping pace with the times even when it hurts.

Jim Postma

Everyone was concerned when Wal-Mart first began putting up supercenters near our Meijer locations. It felt like David and Goliath to have to face the largest retailer in the world. After all, they had a reputation of cutting costs on everything they did, including wages and benefits, and that meant Meijer would have to go through a major transformation that would be gut-wrenching and emotional, since we would be forced to reduce costs to compete with them. That required laying off hundreds of good people.

I remember Fred saying that this challenge was a matter of life and death for Meijer. He asked us to transform Meijer, not because anyone wanted to, but because it was necessary in order for us to survive as a company. He reminded us that in any facet of life or business, it's not how you start that counts, but how you finish.

Chapter Nineteen

Ain't Retailing Fun!

Choose a job you love and you will never have to work a day in your life.

— Confucius

There's nothing like being part of a winning team that's having fun.

— Fred Meijer

Have fun! Leadership isn't always serious.

— Fred Meijer

Mary Radigan

When Fred Meijer tells his managers to have fun, he means it. He took the stage at the Welsh Auditorium during the company's Outlook convention to stress the importance of reaching for success, while at the same time having fun. "Take your work seriously, but don't take yourself too seriously, and it will bring out the best in everybody. Leadership doesn't have to be serious to be effective." To prove it, he teamed up with Alberto Hidalgo, a store greeter in Goshen, Indiana. Hidalgo, an entertainer all his life, plays the keyboard and sings to Meijer shoppers as they enter the store. The audience cheered the Hidalgo/Meijer duet as

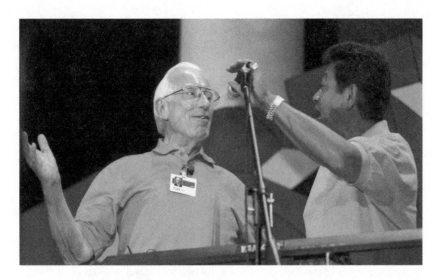

Fred and Alberto (*Photo courtesy of the* Grand Rapids Press)

they sang "People Who Need People," despite the rookie singer's trouble hitting the right notes. They brought down the packed house consisting of 3,000 Meijer employees and 1,100 vendors, with their finale of "Happy Trails to You." (*Grand Rapids Press*, July 31, 1997)

Fred Meijer is always looking for opportunities to have fun. Rick Wenzel remembers celebrating the fifth anniversary of the Owosso-Corunna store he was managing at the time. Fred and Lena came to join in the festivities. "The next thing I knew, Fred was dancing in the center aisle with Ruth Kroske, a greeter and one of the original team members. Everyone was clapping and having a good time. A newspaper photographer was there, and their picture was on the front page of the local paper the next day." On another occasion, Fred was caught skipping rope down the center aisle of the Bay City store.

Mike Frattini

We were about to open our new store in Lancaster, Ohio, and as always, we held meetings for all the store employees to acclimate them to the Meijer culture and share other information necessary to running the store. We usually invite a couple of speakers from the Grand Rapids office, so I called Hank Meijer and asked him to come. The theme for that particular meeting was the "Fabulous Fifties." Two of the more daring team members in charge got me an Elvis costume to wear, complete with wig and glasses. For the two speakers, they had the wildest sport coats emulating Lenny and Squiggy from the *Laverne and Shirley* sitcom that was popular at that time.

Lancaster, Ohio, is a very conservative community, so many of the new team members didn't know what to expect. After all, they were being paid to learn about running the store. When Hank arrived, much to our surprise, Fred was with him. There I stood in my Elvis outfit, and you could have heard a pin drop. Fred and Hank immediately put on the Lenny and Squiggy outfits, and the place erupted with laughter. The ice was broken. They got their message across proving you can have fun and still do your job.

While Fred was not a natural prankster growing up, his dad, on the other hand, was always ready on a whim to spring a practical joke on

Hank, Mike Frattini, and Fred reliving the 1950s

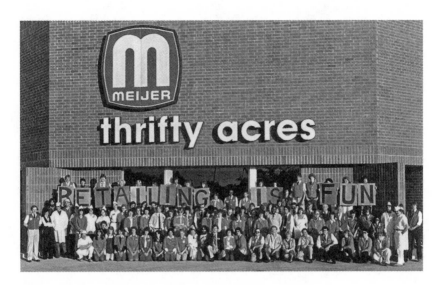

Saginaw team members with "Retailing is Fun" sign, 1982

an unsuspecting friend, and Fred was always a willing spectator. One time, in the barbershop, a customer offered to pick up the tab if Hendrik would cut off all the hair of a friend he knew was coming. The man came in and settled in the chair. "Your hair is getting awfully thin," Hendrik informed the man. "If I put on some Vaseline and massage it and cut it back a little, it will grow in stronger." The man grunted his approval. Hendrik tipped the chair back, turned it away from the mirror, and proceeded to shave the man bald. When everyone in the shop saw what had happened, they doubled up with laughter, including the instigator, who had tears streaming down his face, while the hapless victim howled with rage. Another time, Hendrik took a friend's bike and put it in front of a second-hand store with a "For Sale" sign on it. But the jokes worked both ways. One day, Hendrik went home for lunch, and when he came back, he saw all his equipment and furniture on the curb with a sign saying, "Barber wanted."

> "My dad and I had more fun than two people are entitled to have." (Fred Meijer)

Fred was walking through the grocery-buying department one day, and the buyer showed him new dog candies in a glass dish: they were called Lolli Treats, were colorful and about the size of lifesavers, and they looked like candy except they were for dogs. About that time, Hendrik walked by with two unfamiliar gentlemen. Fred took the dish and asked his dad if he wanted to try these. Hendrik replied, "No thanks, but maybe our new sales tax inspectors would like some." As the men reached to help themselves, Fred had to quickly fess up to his joke.

On more than one occasion, Fred has said that he feels sorry for those who cannot have fun in their work, whatever it might be. Unless there is absolutely no other choice, he'd advise them to seek out a job that gives them some enjoyment and satisfaction.

Dani Goen

At a Marketing Department luncheon in 1994, my future husband, Glen, was to be the host, and we were scheduled to be married that weekend. Glen had invited two guests from the Grand Rapids Symphony to be our speakers. Fred heard about the luncheon and asked if he could attend.

Unbeknownst to us, some of our fellow marketers were plotting a mock wedding. You can imagine our embarrassment when Glen's boss, Rob, announced our wedding ceremony. Steve Van Wagoner hopped up front to play the part of the preacher, while two other marketers started playing the wedding march on kazoos. All I could think was, "Oh no! Not in front of Fred." Fred didn't miss a beat. He stood up and said, "Well, somebody needs to give the bride away. That's my job." He walked me down in front of the preacher.

Steve asked if anyone had any reason why we should not be married. My friend, Patti, was eight months pregnant at the time. She stood up crying and said, "I do, and you can see why." By now everyone was hysterical, including our guests from the Symphony.

It was a day I won't soon forget. Every time I would see Fred after that, he would call me his adopted daughter.

(The story doesn't end there. Patti, my pregnant friend, picks it up.)

Patti Saganski

A year later, my husband and I were at O'Hare airport in Chicago. We were in the waiting area ready to board our flight back to Grand Rapids. In walked Fred and Lena, who were taking the same flight. As soon as he saw me, Fred said to Lena rather loudly, "Look, that's the woman who doesn't have a father for her baby." Lena immediately tried to shush him. My husband had a shocked look on his face and said, "Who is that man, and what is he talking about?"

On the way home, Fred started telling the story to everyone on the plane, and they were having a good time joshing with him, including the stewardess. As people left the plane, Fred stood with the pilots and gave everyone a Purple Cow ice-cream card. I'm sure glad my husband had a chance to hear the rest of the story. Fred, by the way, gave him two ice-cream cards.

Pat Gavin

Fred always loved to tell jokes and try to trick people in good fun. People didn't always know when to take him seriously and when not to.

I was invited to a store directors' meeting shortly after I was hired into my office position. I was introduced to the group as the new person that was responsible for the pharmacies. I was only twenty-five years old at the time, and there were some friendly comments about my being so young. Fred heard this and said, "Pat is my other son. We thought the pharmacy job would be a good one for him." He was then interrupted by something else and never had the chance to say that he was joking.

The rumor spread like wildfire through the company. I didn't want to embarrass Fred or Lena, so I told him about it. He laughed and never took back his story. I'm sure Hank, Doug, and Mark were surprised when they heard they had another brother.

Brian Breslin

One day Fred stopped by my office. Somehow the subject got around to the Panama Canal. He said, "I'll bet you a dollar that the Atlantic mouth of the canal is further west than the Pacific mouth." I quickly took the bet, knowing that the Atlantic is on the eastern seaboard and the Pacific is on the west coast. He smiled, and we both went to look for a map. Sure enough, he was right! Folding the map, he said, "I'll give you a chance to get your dollar back. I'll bet you that Reno, Nevada, is further west than Los Angeles." By now, thinking he might be using reverse psychology, I took the bet, only to find I had lost again. So I gave him two dollars.

The next day, he brought me a glass frame with my two dollars inside and the inscription, "To Brian Breslin, in memory of the Panama Canal and Reno, Nevada." He chuckled as he gave me this advice: "Never bet unless you know the answer."

Harold Hans

Several of us were flying on the company plane — Fred, Dick Stair, Bill Smith, and I. Bill was wearing a new hologram watch that, when tilted just right, displayed a strange-looking eye on its face. This was at a time when Proctor and Gamble's logo was being criticized as a satanic symbol by some religious groups. Fred, sitting across from Bill, said, "Haven't you heard, Bill? Your watch has the evil eye." Surprised, Bill asked him what he meant. "Well," Fred went on, "it's been in the news that the eye on your watch is a satanic symbol. Haven't you read about that?" Dick and I didn't miss a beat. We both confirmed it. "It's been all over the news. Where have you been?" Bill quickly took off his watch, and we never saw it again.

Howard Dean, *President, Dean Foods*

I was visiting the Meijer office with our local manager, walking down the hall, when Fred approached. I happened to be wearing a new tie that my wife had just given me for my birthday. It was one that had cows in the pattern. Fred stopped to talk and was admiring my tie. He told me he used to have to milk and take care of the family's cows when he was growing up.

"You wouldn't want to trade ties, would you?" he asked. Now, as any good businessman knows, it's pretty hard to tell one of your biggest customers that you would rather not, so I said, "Sure." So here we are, standing in the hall, trading ties as we're talking and people are watching. That was more than twenty years ago. I'm sure my wife paid at least thirty dollars for my tie. I'm also sure his tie came out of a Meijer store for around three dollars. Every time he saw me after that he would remark on how well Lena liked his new tie.

Thomas Haggai, *Chairman and CEO, IGA Inc.*

Being a Meijer competitor, I had become good friends with Fred over the years. We were both attending a food convention in California before the beginning of warehouse membership clubs. Sol Price, an acquaintance of mine, had just opened one of the first Price Clubs. He was making headlines, and of course everyone at the convention wanted to see the store.

Sol was not about to let his competitors get inside to snap pictures, ask questions, and take his ideas back to their companies. I told Fred and a mutual friend from Australia, John David, to be ready to get picked up at 8:00 the next morning, and I would see that they got into the store.

I didn't dare call Sol because he had already turned down hundreds of requests. I rented the biggest limousine in the city, and gave the chauffeur instructions to pick up Fred and John, drive to the store, and park at the front door and just wait, which he did. A crowd soon gathered. Sol and his managers came out, saw the excitement, and assumed he had two very famous people — foreign ambassadors maybe, movie stars, politicians perhaps, he wasn't sure what. He welcomed them into the store, thanking them for coming, but was too embarrassed to ask who they were.

Loren Fairbotham

Fred asked me and several others to join him for lunch in the cafeteria during his visit to our store. Several of us ordered chili, and Fred ordered coleslaw as well. After we were seated, Fred started putting coleslaw in his chili. I must have had a strange look on my face, because the next thing I knew, I had coleslaw in my chili. Everyone at the table quickly put their hands over their food knowing they could be next, while laughing their heads off. I must confess, it tasted pretty good.

Gary Knight

It was a busy Friday night, and I was running the cash register in the party store at Store #24 in Lansing. This was back when most Meijer stores had separate party stores located on the main store concourse.

The line at the checkout kept getting longer, and about that time Fred came in. I knew who he was, but he had never met me. Never one to be intimidated, I said, "If you're going to just stand there, you might as well help." His face lit up with a big grin as he took off his coat and started bagging. He stayed until we finally got caught up.

I figure that was the most expensive bagger I ever had helping me, but he did okay.

Roger Horling

Whenever one of us truck drivers saw an approaching car flash its headlights and someone waving, we knew it was probably Fred. One day, I was training a new driver when this happened. He asked, "Who in the world is that crazy guy?" "That's the man who owns this truck," I answered.

Two of the people who know Fred best are Joe McCormack and Carol Alexander, longtime employees who started at entry-level jobs but got drafted from time to time to drive Fred to the stores.

Joe McCormack

I had just graduated from high school and applied at the Meijer office for my first job. They had an opening in the mailroom, and I was told to report to work the following Monday morning.

The first thing my supervisor told me was that I was going to drive Fred Meijer to Detroit. I wasn't sure I had heard right. I was eighteen years old, didn't own a car, and had never been to Detroit. If you have never had a panic attack, let me assure you, this will do it! I met him at his office, introduced myself, and addressed him as Mr. Meijer. He let me know that calling him Fred was fine. I told him of my concerns, but he assured me that everything would be okay.

I was so white-knuckled that by the end of the day my hands hurt. We visited a number of Meijer stores and got home at 9:30 p.m. When we pulled into the office parking lot, I asked him if I could get into the office to use the phone. He said sure, but asked why. I think he knew the answer. I told him I had to call my mother to come and pick me up. He said that wouldn't be necessary, and handed me the keys to his car. When I got home, my mother was waiting for me, concerned that I hadn't called. I hadn't told her where I was going — probably a good thing. She looked out at the driveway and asked where I got the car. I told her. She had a panic attack, and took the keys for safekeeping until I could get the car back the next morning.

On another occasion, I was driving Fred home from one of those long days visiting stores. It was about 10:00 p.m., and we were on 28th Street waiting for the light to change. I was busy checking my watch and thought I saw the light change. I hit the gas and rammed the car in front of us. Their trunk popped open, and their antenna bounced off our hood. Fortunately, no one was hurt.

The police came, and the other couple and I sat in the back of the police car while they filled out the report. The policeman asked where they were coming from, and they said they were just shopping at K-Mart and going home. I answered that I was just driving Fred Meijer home. Everyone looked at me. When I told him, still sitting in the backseat reading the paper as if nothing had happened, he said, "You didn't have to hit them just because they were shopping at K-Mart." He sent the couple a fruit basket and insisted on paying for my ticket.

Carol Alexander

One day I received a call from Fred, who asked if I could come to the Meijer Gardens as soon as possible. Not knowing what to expect, I arrived to see police cars parked everywhere. There was Fred with President Jimmy Carter, and he wanted to introduce me to the President. During the introduction, all I can remember saying was, "You have all

JIMMY CARTER

September 24, 2002

To Carol Alexander

It was a pleasure to meet you during my visit to the Meijer Gardens and Sculpture Park. I am glad that I was able to learn about them directly from Fred. He and Lena are amazing people. Please continue to look after them.

With thanks and warm best wishes,

Sincerely,

Jimmy Carter

this security and all Fred has is me." He laughed, and the next day I received a note from President Carter thanking me for taking such good care of Fred and Lena.

Bob Strodtbeck

We were in the middle of the Meijer yearly Outlook show at the downtown convention center. I was working security, and walking in the back parking lot, when I saw one of my colleagues looking around. I asked him what he was looking for. "A tall blonde," he said rather sheepishly. It seems that Fred had driven in that morning and handed his keys to the first person he saw, whom he described as a tall blonde. It turned out that the tall blonde worked at a nearby restaurant and had nothing to do with the convention center. She did, however, wonder why a stranger had given her the keys to his car while she was on a smoke break.

Fred meets his double at a Meijer Outlook show: same clothes, glasses, watch — right down to the name badge.

Don Clark

It was Saturday, and a friend and I had just finished doing some body work on my car. I was working for Meijer in the real estate department at the time. I had just started to spray paint the car when my daughter came out of the house to tell me that I had a phone call. Well, one thing you never want to do is stop in the middle of a spray paint job, so I said, "Tell whoever it is that I'm too busy to talk right now."

I proceeded to spray, and she came out a few minutes later, got on her bike and started to ride off. I stopped and asked her who had called, and she nonchalantly replied that it was Fred Meijer. I ripped off my paint goggles, ran into the house, and dialed the number. It rang once before a voice said with a chuckle, "Hi, Don." This was before caller ID.

Jim Pranger

Fred used to be asked to be a celebrity walker in numerous charity walks. Prior to such occasions, he would often visit my office with a grocery bag filled with shoes from home. He would take each pair of shoes from the bag and ask me which ones would be best for him to wear in the upcoming walk. He bought only Meijer's private-label shoes, and since our walking shoes were made for us in a Rockport factory, I could confidently attest to the fact that all Meijer label shoes were warranted for longer than the 5K walk on which he was about to embark.

Jim Walsh

Fred knew we had a couple of horses, and he loved to ask me questions about them, and tell stories about growing up with horses. He told me of how as a youngster he had delivered milk in a wagon pulled by horses, and how, on one occasion, the team got spooked and ran off, tipping over the wagon and spilling all the milk in the process.

One day, he mentioned that he was going on vacation with his family to a ranch out west. He asked me if he could test ride one of our horses before he left, and I scheduled a time with him, but not without some reserve. After all, he was seventy-seven at the time and had recently undergone hip surgery.

To make me even more nervous, he mentioned that Lena probably didn't know what he was up to. As he rode away on the horse, all I could think of was, "This is going to be a long afternoon."

Rob Ver Heulen

A few years ago we were in Colorado for a sculpture show. We had spent the entire day outside in 100-degree heat, and I couldn't wait to get back to the air-conditioned hotel room for a cool, quiet evening. Fifteen minutes later, the phone rang. It was Fred. He suggested I meet him in the lobby with a notepad so we could visit stores. He was eighty-five at the time.

I never saw a purple cow. I never hope to see one;
But I can tell you, anyhow, I'd rather see than be one.
— Gelett Burgess

Gelett Burgess may never have seen a purple cow, but he never shopped at Meijer either. In addition to the penny pony rides, the other Meijer icon that is synonymous with having fun is the Purple Cow ice-cream card. Fred and Lena have passed these out generously to kids of all ages. Lena personally signs each one she gives out. Fred estimates that they have distributed over 500,000 in the past four decades. Former Michigan Governor James Blanchard once yelled across a banquet room his request for a card. Jay Van Andel and Rich De Vos have lined up for their freebies. Summoned to the White House, Fred presented ice-cream cards to Jimmy and Rosalynn Carter. Even presidential brother Billy Carter got one. Generals Colin Powell and Norman Schwartzkopf have ice-cream cards, and, on the international scene, so does Queen Beatrix of the Netherlands.

Fred uses the cards as icebreakers. "You can always tell when Fred is in the store because the Purple Cow suddenly gets busy," commented one store director. The cards have no expiration date, and he once told a customer in Indianapolis, "You have fifty years to redeem that." The man replied, "Fifty years? I'll be with the Lord by then." Fred handed him another card, "Well, in that case, here's one for the Lord, too."

In 2004, a couple of longtime friends and Meijer customers, Glen Smith and Jessica Pilat, decided to visit the 163 Meijer stores that were part of the chain at that time. They planned their trips to the five states in between full-time jobs. Incredibly, they covered those miles in day trips, spending only one night on the road. In that stretch, they visited twenty-two Meijer stores in forty-two hours, obtaining a cash receipt at every store. When asked why, they said it was simple: "Meijer is our happy place. When we walk into a Meijer store it feels like home."

Fred's Purple Cow
ice-cream card

The Meijer company heard about their venture and surprised them with gifts and gas money. But their biggest thrill was having dinner with Fred. "We're not used to people, let alone a corporation, rolling out the red carpet," Glen said. "We were overwhelmed. It's the reason we consider ourselves Meijer's biggest cheerleaders."

Chapter Twenty

From the Mailroom to the Oval Office

I n the course of an active and successful career, Fred has had occasion to meet with many of the world's leaders. However, though he is utterly respectful of their position, he does not rearrange his personality to fit the social class of those he meets. Whether it's a president, a secretary of state, a queen, a prime minister, or a general, he comports himself in much the same way he would with a new employee or a stranger on an airplane. There's an immediate friendliness, a respect for the dignity of the person he's speaking to, and an uncomplicated directness in the way he behaves. People who don't know Fred sometimes find it surprising.

Pam Kleibusch

Fred and Lena have met with many world leaders and famous people over the years, but they've always kept things in perspective. I have taken calls from presidents, governors, foreign heads of state, movie stars, sports celebrities, and business tycoons. I have confirmed meetings at the White House and Buckingham Palace. Through it all, they have remained two of the most down-to-earth, unpretentious people you could hope to know.

Fred and Lena with Lady Bird Johnson

Joe McCormack

I was driving Fred to the airport one day when he mentioned that he was going to a meeting with some other business and civic leaders to talk with former President Gerald Ford regarding a new museum being built in his honor. I asked Fred how he would address him — Mr. President, Mr. Ford, or Jerry. Fred said that was a good question. It was the end of the discussion, and I forgot all about it.

A week later, I was sorting mail in the mailroom, and in comes Fred, like he does every day, to get his mail. He hands me a napkin. Written on it was "To Joe: Best Wishes, Jerry Ford."

That was my answer. What an impression that made on me! Here I was working in the mailroom at Meijer, knowing I was a topic of conversation between Fred and the former President of the United States. I still have the napkin.

Pat Quinn

At a business conference, I was to be picked up at the airport by the hotel van. When I got in, there was Fred. Two of the other passengers were Charles Schulz, creator of "Peanuts," and Joe Garagiola of baseball fame.

I remember Garagiola saying that he had had the "Breakfast of Champions" that morning — two aspirins and orange juice. Fred, of course, was right at home with these celebrities. It's one of his gifts.

Henry Witte, *Honorary Consul of the Netherlands for West Michigan*

Grand Valley State University had invited Ruud Lubbers, the prime minister of the Netherlands, to come to GVSU in connection with the dedication of a Dutch Carillon at Allendale. The thinking was that the president of Grand Valley, Arend Lubbers, shared a last name with the prime minister. They thought it would be kind of interesting to have

Fred likes to look you in the eye.

Ruud Lubbers dedicate the carillon. There was a luncheon at Kent Country Club with the ambassador and his wife, the prime minister and his wife, and a group of supporters.

I introduced Fred and Lena to the prime minister, and they started chatting. Fred still speaks a few words of Dutch, which he was trying out on the prime minister. It was not necessarily the Dutch I would speak in a formal situation, but they were having a good time with it. Then Fred said, "Mr. Lubbers, I don't know how long you're going to stay in Grand Rapids, but if you can, you should stop in one of our stores." Then he reached into his pocket, pulled out a Purple Cow card, and offered it to Lubbers. "And if you go there," he said, "this will let you get a free ice-cream cone."

I don't know how often he did that with world leaders, but I think it was a fairly regular occurrence.

Rick Zeeff

In the spring of 1994, I had the pleasure of opening the first Meijer store in Indiana — in Mishawaka. Fred and Lena would visit often to see how things were going. On one such occasion we were walking through the store when Fred was paged for a phone call. He grabbed a phone in the seafood area while I waited for him nearby. A few minutes passed, and then he handed me the phone. "Someone wants to speak with you," he said. I greeted the person on the other end of the line, and then I heard the distinctive voice of President Gerald Ford saying, "Hi, Rick. You have quite a boss there!" After a moment of stunned silence, I was able to talk again. President Ford explained that Fred wanted him to speak with me because I probably didn't have many opportunities to chat with a former president.

It's not only with famous and ordinary adults that Fred works his charm. He frequently engages the very young in conversation as well, singling out children for special attention.

Fred and John Taylor

Dave Plasman

At my thirtieth anniversary party, which was held in the office, I was talking to Fred when my four-year-old granddaughter, Haley, came in to be among all the "big people" there. Fred immediately focused on her. He got down on his knees so he could look her in the eye, and they carried on a conversation. She and I will never forget the royal treatment she got that day.

George Zain

After our son Tom returned from a college exchange program in Russia, Fred called and asked if he could visit with Tom to learn more about the country. He was planning to take a trip there, and wanted to learn as much as he could. Later, when a group of Russian students were our guests during a stop on their tour of the U.S., he learned of their visit and asked Tom if they would like to be his guests for a day for a tour of the Meijer stores. He and Lena then in- vited them to their home, where they had a lengthy discussion

Fred and Lena sitting in President Ford's chair at the dedication of the Ford Library in Ann Arbor, Michigan, April 27, 1981

about their respective countries. Before they left, Fred gave each of them one of his trademark Purple Cow ice-cream cards, some of which are probably still floating around Russia, waiting for the first Meijer store to open there.

A food systems student at Michigan State University had a very positive reaction to Fred's presentation in his classroom.

Mike Keller

I just wish everyone who is down on the establishment, and thinks businessmen are just out for the almighty dollar, could have talked to this man. He really restored my confidence in the basic humanity of a businessman. His opinions on many issues were valuable: pledging to hire the hard-core unemployed; treating each employee as an individual and recognizing his or her personal worth; promoting the best people for the job, regardless of race or sex; taking a stand on issues he believed in, whether widely accepted or not; finding problems in the company even before consumers complain; recognizing that people are everything — the backbone of the company; not publicizing all the charitable works performed just to build up a good name. He really is the kind of person I'd like to know better.

Of course, Fred is not always that successful with students.

Nov 27, 1990

Dear Mr. Meijer,
Thank you for taking the time to visit Sibley School. I learned nothing. But it was good speach.
Sincerely
Amanda

Letter from Amanda Kishman

Chapter Twenty-one

Human Rights

Learn to enjoy and respect each other's differences.

— Fred Meijer

As a young man traveling the country a century ago, Hendrik Meijer swung a sledgehammer in the state of Washington, breaking up pig iron at a foundry in 115-degree heat. Men of seven different nationalities worked alongside him. They washed in the same bucket and ate the same food together. "We all got along fine," he would recall years later.

Even when he was growing up in a row house in his hometown of Hengelo in the Netherlands, prejudice was never an issue. A Jewish family lived next door, and every Saturday morning the father would rap on the wall to signal to Hendrik that it was time for him to light their fires, because it was against their religion to work on the Sabbath. He also worked for a spinner who was Catholic and said that he had "never known a finer man."

Whenever he heard someone condemn a whole race of people, it always upset him. "There is good and bad in all races," he would say. He tried to imagine how black people must feel, knowing that if he had been born black, he would not be allowed to wash in the same bucket or eat at the same table as whites. Hendrik had a great love for America — with all its opportunities and diversities. He traveled the country, never working at a job for more than six months, until he found what he was looking for in West Michigan. "You don't have to travel the world looking for peace of mind," he said. "You can find that place in yourself if how you live your life squares with your conscience." When he died in 1964, he left behind a legacy that he had nurtured and passed on to his son: "Respect and dignity for all."

Fred grew up listening to his parents as they discussed racial prejudice, but mostly he observed the interaction between his family and the few black families who lived in town. This was only seventy years after the civil war — one lifetime — and America was still highly segregated, almost completely in the South, but also in the North. In Greenville, the few black children were allowed to attend the public schools, but their fathers were relegated to jobs as common laborers. Hendrik was the only barber in town who would cut their hair. On one occasion, Fred was the only white man in town asked to be a pall-bearer at a black funeral.

Max Guernsey

One day, I was riding with Fred, his father, and some insurance company people from out of town. We had made an inspection at the Ionia store, and had stopped at a restaurant for lunch. During the meal, Fred saw a black couple who were Meijer customers, and he went over to speak to them. The people from the insurance company were shocked, and I remember one of them asking Fred, "You associate with those people?"

Another time, I had just built a large display of kidney beans. The brand name was Old Mammy, and featured a picture of a portly black woman on the label. I had all the labels facing outward as usual, when Fred walked by. He stopped, turned a can around, and said, "We're selling kidney beans, not Old Mammy." I rebuilt the display with all the labels facing inward.

"Remember how you *don't* like to be treated." (Fred Meijer)

In 1952, two years before the Supreme Court declared segregation unconstitutional, and five years before federal troops had to be called in to integrate the public schools in Little Rock, Arkansas, a situation came up that would officially break the color barrier at Meijer. There was an opening at the office for a receptionist. Harvey Lemmen, who would later become the company president, came to Fred and said that he had three good candidates for the job, but there was one he would like to hire.

"So what's the problem?" asked Fred.

"She's black," Harvey replied. He went on to say that some of the office staff had seen him interviewing her and were already talking about separate toilets. Fred told Harvey he would handle it, and he began talking to the other employees — about thirty in all — one at a time.

"I told them," Fred said later, "that a black lady had applied for the receptionist job, and she was qualified. 'What do you think?' Some said, 'I don't care, but others might not like it.' I said, 'I'll put you down as *you don't care.* I'll be asking the others, so you don't have to speak for them. No one was willing to admit they didn't want to work with a black person. I told Harvey to go ahead and hire her, and she did a great job." Later, the office manager and the personnel director were black men.

The first black manager working in the stores was Russ Johnson. Fred wanted some of the store managers to attend a seminar being put on by the Super Market Institute, which was held in the fancy Edgewater Beach Hotel in Chicago. Thinking Russ might be the only black man in attendance, Fred called the hotel and was told that it wouldn't be a problem. To be on the safe side, he assigned one of the older, more seasoned store managers to be in charge, with instructions that if Russ got insulted or didn't receive the same service as the others, they were all to pack up and come home.

Fred's commitment to breaking the color barrier encountered everything from bewilderment to admiration to open hostility. However, another thing that his father had taught him was to confront problems head-on. He is fond of telling the story of when Hendrik worked a brief stint in a Chicago foundry. Being surrounded by big, burly foundry workers wasn't conducive to the free flow of opinions. But Hendrik wasn't one to hide what he was thinking, and one day his assessment of a local political situation earned the wrath of a particular workyard bully. The man declared his intention to beat Hendrik to a pulp if he dared to show up in the parking lot after work. Hendrik did show up, much to the admiration of his fellow workers, and proved to everyone not only that the bully was mostly bluff and bluster, but also that Hendrik had the courage of his convictions.

"My lesson from that story," says Fred, "was that if you have a problem, just look it in the eye and confront it. Don't look away and pretend it isn't there or hope it'll go away. An honorable leader has to be driven, always, by conviction."

As a result of these convictions, the company at one time spent $200,000 to settle a lawsuit brought by a white employee who was fired for making disparaging remarks and refusing to work with a black manager. It cost a lot of money, but there was no way Fred wanted someone with that attitude working in his store.

At about that time, there was an incident in Kansas that would change the face of America. Oliver Brown was a welder for the Santa Fe Railroad, as well as an assistant pastor of his church. He had a daughter in elementary school named Linda. Every day Linda would walk six blocks to catch a bus for a one-mile ride to her school, Monroe Elementary. One day, Oliver Brown decided to enroll Linda in Sumner Elementary, a school that was only seven blocks away. Linda recalls sitting outside the principal's office while her dad was talking to the school administrators, and hearing raised voices. After a time, her dad reappeared and Linda learned that she had been denied admittance. Not because of anything she had done, but simply because she was black. Oliver Brown, with the help of the NAACP, filed suit against the board of education of Topeka, Kansas. The case was heard before the U.S. District Court in 1951. The court listened to the case, but citing a previous Supreme Court ruling, *Plessy v. Ferguson,* it ruled against Oliver Brown and for the board of education of Topeka, Kansas: Linda would not be allowed to attend Sumner Elementary, an all-white school, but had to continue to attend Monroe Elementary, an all-black school.

Oliver Brown was convinced that a travesty of justice had taken place. He appealed to the U.S. Supreme Court. In 1954, the court heard the case of *Brown v. Board of Education, Topeka, Kansas.* Chief Justice Earl Warren, in reading the unanimous decision of the court, said: "We then come to the question presented, does segregation of children in public schools, solely on the basis of race, even though the physical facilities and other tangible factors may be equal, deprive the children of minority groups an equal educational opportunity? We believe that it does. We conclude that in the field of public education, the doctrine of 'separate but equal' has no place. Separate educational facilities are inherently unequal. We hold that the action brought by the plaintiff has been deprived of the legal protection of the laws guaranteed by the fourteenth amendment of the constitution of the United States." With that decision, the laws of segregation in public schools had changed forever, not just for Linda Brown, but for all black children and for minorities everywhere.

Abraham Lincoln, *Republican State Convention,*
Springfield, Illinois (June 16, 1858)

"A house divided against itself cannot stand." I believe this government cannot endure permanently half slave and half free. I do not expect the Union to be dissolved — I do not expect the house to fall — but I do expect it will cease to be divided. It will become all one thing, or all the other. Either the opponents of slavery will arrest the further spread of it, and place it where the public mind shall rest in the belief that it is in the course of ultimate extinction; or its advocates will push it forward, till it shall become alike lawful in all the States, old as well as new, North as well as South.

Fred recalls going into a discount store in Florida. He was looking for the bathroom and came to the one marked "Ladies." Assuming the one next to it was for men, he was surprised when that one was also for ladies. Going back to check the names on the doors, he found there were two marked ladies and two marked men, all having a little blank spot in front of the name. He realized then that someone had covered up the words "White" and "Colored."

Friday, December 7, 1967

Dear Mr. Meijer:

As the President of the local chapter of the NAACP, I am writing in behalf of the members of this chapter, to let you know how much we appreciate the help that you are giving to the Negroes in Grand Rapids.

I was attending a meeting of the Negro Leadership Conference, and one of your employees told us about the meeting that you had with him and some other Negro employees who work for your company.

We, the members of the NAACP, are more than willing to work with you and other officials of your company to help improve and change the attitude of the white race towards the black race.

As members of the NAACP, we try to encourage more Negroes to do their shopping where they can observe a large number of their race working for a company that cares.

We would like to invite you to join the NAACP. As you know, this is an integrated organization, but we have very few white members in our local chapter. We would consider it an honor to have you as one of our members.

Yours respectfully,
(signed)
Jerome Sorrells,
President, Grand Rapids NAACP

In Grand Rapids, Fred's anti-establishment, feather-ruffling heritage surfaced quite often. He was an active member of the NAACP and the Grand Rapids Urban League, where he served as one of only two white members on the board. His strong convictions didn't stop with minorities; he also backed equal treatment for women. His sister, Johanna, had been the first store manager at the Cedar Springs store; his mother and his wife had helped run the business. When Hendrik died in 1964, Fred insisted that his mother become chairman of the company. Because of his activism in the Urban League, he spearheaded the integration of the Grand Rapids Rotary Club, nominating its first black member; and he nominated one of the first two female Rotarians. There was opposition, to be sure, but it was all familiar territory to someone who had worked to allow women in the Rotary back in Cedar Springs in the 1940s. Fred had joined that civic club in 1942 as one of its twenty-two charter members. When he proposed the idea of female membership, there was strong opposition, and it would be years before opinions would change. He remembers hearing one club member saying, "I don't care what Fred Meijer thinks, there ain't gonna be no blankety-blank females in this club while I'm here."

That eventually changed, and three years after women were admitted, there was a woman president at each of the clubs to which Fred belonged: Cedar Springs, Ionia, and Grand Rapids. "They breathed new life into the clubs," he recalls, "and many things were accomplished that might never have happened otherwise."

Paul Boyer

We had recently installed a new conveyer pricing system in the warehouse, and the manager was giving Fred a tour. This manager was justifiably proud at how well the new system was working, and he credited his staff — made up mostly of women at the time — by saying that "the girls are really doing a great job."

Fred smiled and asked the manager why he referred to them as girls. Puzzled, the manager replied, "Because they like to be called girls." "That's probably true," Fred said. "But just in case a few of them don't like it, I'll bet none of them would mind being called ladies." He said it in a way that preserved the manager's dignity, but taught a valuable lesson.

Someone once observed that Fred really enjoys standing up for the underdog, and that is a reputation he is proud of.

Molly Jordon

My late husband and I were attending an Urban League dinner. We got there early and seated ourselves. Pretty soon three people approached and asked if they could join us. It was Fred, Lena, and Fred's mother. We started talking, and I referred to them as Mr. and Mrs.

Meijer. Fred said, "You call me Fred and I'll call you Collie and Molly." With both of us being black and raised in the deep South, we were taken aback.

Fred asked Collie what kind of work he did. Collie told him we had a shoe repair business on Baxter Street. Right away, Fred asked if we would open a shoe repair shop inside the Plainfield Avenue Thrifty Acres store, then under construction. Collie looked at me, and we readily accepted.

This all took place fifteen minutes after meeting Fred and Lena. There were no applications, no inspections, no reference and background checks, just a handshake. We opened a shop in the store, where we had a successful business for the next eighteen years before we retired. Fred and Lena stopped by often, and we became very good friends. On our last day, they gave us a retirement party in the conference room of the store.

If there is one word that exemplifies Fred's feelings for all people, it's "dignity": dignity for all human beings, plus the respect they are entitled to by virtue of their humanity.

Collie and
Molly Jordan

Ernie Escareno

A number of us were in the break room of the store when Fred came in and joined us. One of the employees started talking about certain nationalities (I'm Hispanic, Fred is Dutch). I tried to kick the person under the table to get him to stop. With each comment, Fred would defend the ethnic group being mentioned, and would look at me for approval.

Two days later, a company memo came from the office saying that ethnic slurs and jokes were not allowed in the workplace. I was really impressed with how quickly Fred moved on something he thought was inappropriate and unhealthy for the company.

In Goshen, Indiana, there is a large population of Amish, many of whom are Meijer customers. In the parking lot, among the car parking spaces, Meijer has built hitching posts and a horse shed. Whenever Fred would visit the store, it was there that he would go to engage in conversation, swapping stories of how he and his father traded, raised, and worked with horses on the family farm when he was a youngster.

He has often mused that if white people were a little darker and black people a little lighter, we wouldn't know the difference. The point is made by a good friend of his, Joe Stevens, who is Jewish. During World War II, Joe was able to pass himself off as Polish under the noses of the Gestapo, who didn't know the difference because his skin was the same as theirs. He tells his story in his book *Good Morning,* which Fred and Hank helped to publish in 2002.

"We used to call Indians 'savages,'" Fred says, "and then we took their land and homes. Our treatment of the Chinese in this country wasn't much better. We brought them here to build our railroads, and when that was done and we didn't need them anymore, we called them 'yellow dogs.'"

Fred and Lena's compassion for others extends beyond race and color. Visitors to the Frederik Meijer Gardens and Sculpture Park, when entering the children's section, are greeted with Kirk Newman's *Children of the World,* a project Fred and Lena commissioned and supervised. These eleven children, standing and playing together, repre-

Kirk Newman's *Children of the World* (Photo courtesy of Bob Strodtbeck)

sent various races and disabilities, including a child who wears leg braces and one with Down Syndrome. "It is our hope," says Fred, "that when future generations visit this display, the tour guides will explain the importance of getting to know and appreciate people who may be different from them."

November 19, 1992

Dear Fred,

On Sunday, November 15, one of your greeters caught my eye. He was a young man, in his twenties, seemingly proud of his red vest and strapped into a wheelchair. He also was to stamp door receipts for packages brought into the store. Afflicted with what seemed to me to be Cerebral Palsy, he had a difficult time manipulating the stamp and his speech was slow and labored yet precise and well-composed. Working without assistance, he performed well by any measure.

Of many things that can be said, I feel the contribution Meijer is making to this person's self-esteem is of primary importance. Further, it tells me something about the management of your company. Oh sure, the cleanliness of your stores and the competence of your staff speaks volumes, but that's the usual stuff. The prominent placement of this person reflects a concern, sensitivity and commitment that goes beyond revenues per square foot and such mundane tasks of daily operations.

(signed)
Thomas Wheeler
Rochester, MI

In 1963, Fred was appointed to Michigan Governor Romney's committee for the handicapped. He was President Johnson's appointee for people with disabilities.

The education Fred received from his parents regarding respect for everyone regardless of their race, creed, gender, or other difference placed a responsibility on him that he readily accepted early in life. Many times it has meant going against the status quo. Someone once mentioned to him that his convictions took a lot of courage. Going with the flow, as a businessman, would have been a lot easier and less costly. "We tend to make courage too dramatic," he says. "Courage is just trying to do the right thing in every situation. If we do, we'll sleep better at night."

Chapter Twenty-two

Things I Might Have Done Differently

> To make no mistakes is not in the power of man; but from
> their errors and mistakes the wise and good learn wisdom
> for the future.
>
> — Plutarch (AD 46–120)

In a career that spans eighty years (he began peddling milk when he was eight), it is astonishing that so many of Fred's actions and decisions turned out so well. It would be even more astonishing if he hadn't frequently had second thoughts, wondering whether he did the right thing, whether things might have turned out better if he'd gone in a different direction. When he mentions regret, it's usually that he wishes results had been better, not that he's sorry for what he has done. And of course he has a clear sense that when you make choices in life, you have ruled out some possibilities while others become inevitable. One man can't live two lives, except in his imagination.

A Post Office Pension

He remembers his dad writing to Johanna while she was still in college, telling her that he had applied for a job with the U.S. Postal Service. At that point Hendrik was still cutting hair while trying to run his new grocery store on the side. "He wanted security with a pension," says Fred. "He had failed in two types of farming, and he had failed in some other things. He was making four dollars a week in the barbershop. If he could just get twenty dollars a week as a postal carrier, with a pension to follow, it would be utopia.

"And if he had gotten that job in the postal department with a pension on the end, he would have chucked the whole grocery business a year or two after we started it. But he failed to get the postal job, and as you can see, things turned out all right."

College

Fred often says that he would probably have been a history teacher if he had not gone into the grocery business. When he graduated from high school, his sister Johanna was still studying at the University of Michigan, and he might have considered going there, too. But the year was 1937, the Great Depression had not lifted, and he was needed in the family business. So he didn't go to college. Always inquisitive, with a nearly flawless memory and a tireless determination to learn with or without a classroom, he educated himself in the ways of business and the world at the same time. The years he spent building the business with his father provided invaluable lessons for him.

"I'm sorry I didn't go to the university or college," he says, "because I have a feeling that I would love to interact with the good minds that are in a university. But I also understand that those people are few and far between. You have to put up with a lot of mediocre and pedestrian people along the way that are no more deep thinkers than the folks we deal with every day. I am probably fantasizing, thinking what I would like to have gotten out of a university rather than being realistic. That

Pondering

is one thing about regret. What would I have to trade [a university education] for? Would I trade it for five years of working with my father? No way! So really I don't regret it. I guess I just wish I had what I had, plus more. Life can't deliver you ten days in a week."

Vietnam

The Vietnam War was long and divisive. During its ten-year duration, many Americans died for their country, and many other Americans expressed their strong opposition to the continued conflict. Fred was among the latter: he believed that America had lost its way in the jungles of Southeast Asia. In fact, he remembers clearly the day of the antiwar protest called the March on Washington. It was October 15, 1969, and an estimated two million people had gathered in the nation's capital to commemorate the deaths of American soldiers and to protest the continuance of the war. On that day, Fred found himself going to the White House, where prominent retailers were holding a meeting with President Nixon. He was intensely aware of the march, partly because his oldest son, Hank, was among the protesters. He remembers thinking, as he rode from the airport to the White House, "I really should be across town with Hank." Not wanting to be a crusader, however, he participated in the meeting with President Nixon instead, a decision he doesn't really regret. Still, he thought, Hank was right to protest.

WOTV

In a lengthy television interview done near the end of 1984, Fred was asked whether, looking back over the years, he would have done anything differently.

"Yeah," he replied without a moment's hesitation, "I would have bought WOTV. I could have bought it a while back for somewhere from six to eleven million dollars. They would have financed it, and I could have sold it later for sixty million. What a deal! I didn't have nerve enough to tackle it. All I had to do was take on the equivalent of mortgaging two stores in those days, the debt of two stores. But. . . ." (Interview with WOTV, Grand Rapids' NBC affiliate)

Twin Fair Stores

In the early 1980s, Fred became interested in buying the Twin Fair chain of grocery stores in Ohio. The two top executives in the Meijer company, Harvey Lemmen and Earl Holton, didn't think it was a very good deal, and they tried to talk him out of it. They discussed the situation for quite a while, going back and forth, and at one point Fred told the two of them that he would give them veto power over whatever decision he made, if they felt strongly about it. He was reprimanded for that by Art Snell, who was the company's chief legal counsel. Snell thought that an executive should make the final decisions. "But I did make the final decision," replied Fred. "I told them they had veto power."

As it turned out, the veto power only went so far. Lemmen and Holton agreed, more or less, that they could afford to buy one-half of the Ohio chain, fearing Fred would buy the whole thing otherwise. They ended up buying only half, and it was still a bad deal. "Later on," says Fred, "I twitted them for letting me do it. They were right, and I was wrong."

Wal-Mart

"If we had sold out to Wal-Mart back when they were trying to buy us," Fred says, "we could probably have done very well financially. That's certainly what happened with Drayton McLane. We might have had more money than we have now. But I wouldn't have been happy with it, and I don't think our family or our associates would be either. Even though Wal-Mart is a tough competitor for us, I'm ecstatic with the way it has turned out."

The Embarrassment of Riches

"For years," says Fred, "I think we spent too much putting up our buildings, we had too much overhead, too many expenses of every kind, including labor. Now I don't blame the unions for that — they were just looking out for their workers, as they should. They were taking advantage of our many good years of business. We suffered from an embarrassment of riches." This phrase is the title of a book by the historian Simon Schama that he has read and loaned to many friends. The book discusses life in the Netherlands during the Dutch Golden Age. One of its contentions is that Dutch society, while achieving great wealth, also felt somewhat uncomfortable with its attainment.

For many years, people at Meijer had not felt much pressure from the big national competitors, especially in Michigan. They were flying below the radar, and that meant making money more easily than they would have if, for example, Wal-Mart had moved into Michigan in a big way. Wal-Mart was holding back on its development in the state partly because it had hoped to buy the Meijer chain, and it did not want to waste money putting in stores that would become redundant. Once it became clear, by the mid-1990s, that Meijer would not be selling to them, Wal-Mart began competing in earnest, as did Target; both companies used the supercenter concept they had taken from Meijer.

Now, suddenly, the sizable overhead costs, which had been manageable in the previous business environment, were no longer sustainable. It became necessary to cut back significantly. In the first years of the twenty-first century, Meijer found ways to reduce the cost of its buildings by about one-third, but it wasn't enough. The company also had to lay off more than two thousand members of its management team, a trauma that deeply affected the company and everyone associated with it.

"It was like cutting off a limb to save the patient," says Fred. On the day when most of the layoffs were announced and offices were being cleared out, though he was no longer involved in day-to-day activities and had not made this decision himself, Fred still felt personally involved. He came down to the corporate offices to speak with some of the people whose jobs were being terminated, and he remembers it as one of the most difficult days ever in the life of the company. A reporter for the *Grand Rapids Press* saw him in the parking lot that day.

Mary Radigan

Meijer, like many other local companies, was going through a painful period of downsizing. This was a tough time, I knew, especially for

Fred, as the company had experienced six decades of growth where layoffs were rare.

I was assigned to write the story for the paper, and decided to go to the Meijer corporate office the day most of the layoffs were to take place. As it happened, Fred was in the parking lot talking to the employees as they were leaving. I pulled up beside him and asked if I could talk to him. Thinking I was one of the employees, and not recognizing me at first as a reporter, he got in the car. I started asking questions and taking notes, and then he realized I was from the *Grand Rapids Press* and writing a story. He remained very gracious and continued to answer my questions, explaining that sometimes the future of a company necessitates unwanted and unpopular decisions. After the interview, he continued talking to the employees even though, I knew, it was painful for him to do so.

Speaking to a group of employees in 2006, Fred thought back on the results of the layoffs.

"All you folks here for the awards banquet know a lot of what we did. Some of your friends got caught up in it. Some of your good friends were terminated or reassigned, and it's always a painful thing. But we had to do it. We had to cut the overhead from 22.5 percent to 18.5 percent, and we're almost there. I am very bullish about the future.

"Of course, when you're my age of eighty-six, you live in the past a lot. But you also have to live today, and you also have to live for the future. I didn't work in this business that long to see it go down the drain. And so, with the new competition, we always have to find ways to meet it. That's what we're doing, and that's what makes our company healthy. I'm proud of everybody, that we did such a fantastic job. If you didn't . . . if we didn't do these things, then we'd go the way of other companies, and go out of business.

"So I think we've got a bright future. I wish I was forty years old again, or fifty, rather than eighty-six. But I'm not. I can't live it over. So my hope is that we can keep up the good pace and do what we have to do to build a good future for you and for us and for the company."

Chapter Twenty-three

The Quiet Samaritan

F red has often been honored publicly for his charitable activities, and has long been a willing donor to a multitude of civic causes. In 1982, he was honored by Grand Valley State University with a doctorate in Humane Letters. He has received other honorary degrees, and in fact has been offered more of them than he has been able to accept. He has served governors and presidents on advisory commissions. His and Lena's names grace many prominent buildings throughout West Michigan. While he freely admits to feeling a certain pride at receiving these public expressions of respect and appreciation, he recognizes that there's another kind of kindness — privately expressed and often not known by the general public. This kind of charity brings no public praise, does not advertise itself from the rooftops of the city, and offers no gratification to the ego. And yet it is in some ways a more important expression of altruism.

By their nature, the acts of a quiet Samaritan usually go unrecorded. Many of them — donations to help children with special needs and the institutions that nurture them, scholarships for promising students, seed money for clinics, enrichment programs for inner-city children, support for historical or scholarly pursuits, a smoothing of the road for servicemen, much-needed assistance given to refugees from foreign wars or civil unrest — are silently treasured by the recipients. It may be that many others have long been forgotten. In either case, the purity of motive grants an unsullied dignity to these selfless acts. The following are a few examples of Fred's kindness that were written down.

Curt Buchholz

My wife's grandfather, Leo Swartz, was a friend of the Meijer family during the Depression. In fact, Hendrik Meijer sold Leo his barbershop in 1934 so he could start the Thrift Market, the first of the Meijer stores.

Right up until his death at age 99, Leo would get a phone call from Fred every week. One afternoon around the Fourth of July, I got a call from Fred. He had just spoken to Leo, who talked about how hot it was in the house. Fred wanted to know if I would go to the local furniture store, buy an air conditioner, and have them install it and send Fred the bill.

Larry Gratz

Shortly after I had been promoted to manage the Greenville store, Fred stopped by and said he would like me to meet Mr. Sims, who I found out was one of Meijer's first and most loyal customers. Mr. Sims was 90 years old, and lived alone. Fred would always visit him whenever he came to town.

After introductions, we spent the next hour just talking. On the way back, Fred asked if I would check on Mr. Sims from time to time. This request turned into a wonderful experience for the whole family.

Fred and Mr. Sims

Our sons, young at the time, learned the satisfaction of assisting older people as they raked leaves and shoveled sidewalks, while my wife and I would do light housework and repairs. Then we would hear stories from Mr. Sims about the "good old days" over a cup of hot chocolate.

Olga Van Cleef

In 1958 my husband and I and our two boys, ages two and three, emigrated from the Netherlands to Grand Rapids to seek a better life, and to try to forget our experiences of World War II. We had both lost our families in concentration camps, and we ourselves had survived different concentration camps. To immigrate at that time, one needed a sponsor, and because my husband was in the military police after the war, the police chief of Grand Rapids, Dewey Beaver, agreed to sponsor us. We arrived in Grand Rapids, where he had rented a house for us, but we had little money and no jobs. One of the first places he took us was to the Meijer store on Michigan and Fuller, which was also the main office at that time. The chief introduced us to the Meijer family, and he must have told them about our situation. The next day I answered a knock on the door, and there were three Meijer grocery boys with bags and boxes of groceries. I distinctly remember that some of the staple items like flour and sugar lasted us more than sixteen months.

Not long afterward, our car broke down at the same time that we had some other unexpected expenses. My husband, John, went to the Meijer Credit Union located in the Meijer office to try to get a $1,000 loan, a sizable sum at the time. Fred walked by, saw him sitting there, and said, "John, you don't look so well today. What's the problem?" After he told him, Fred escorted John to see the Credit Union manager, and asked him to loan John the money. Fred suggested that he could pay it back at his convenience, which we did within a year. These are just two of the many kindnesses shown to us by the Meijer family over the years.

In 1962 I got a job at the first Meijer Thrifty Acres store on 28th and Kalamazoo, where I worked for the next twenty-five years before retiring. During those years Fred and Lena would look me up whenever they were in the store.

When John passed away, Fred and Lena attended the funeral.

Harv Koetje

My family watched as fire destroyed our home during one of the worst snowstorms of 1979. The next morning, I called my boss and told him I wouldn't be in that day. Two hours later, he showed up with the personnel director. Fred Meijer had heard about the fire and pulled them out of meetings to see what he could do to help.

At the time, we had four children — including a special needs son — who were attending three different schools, and our insurance company wanted to put us up in the next town. Of course, this would be a logistics nightmare.

Meanwhile, Fred called around searching for a mobile home to put on the site temporarily, which everyone said couldn't happen in the middle of January in Michigan. Two days pass and I'm back in the office when my wife calls to tell me that there were trucks, workmen, heavy equipment and a brand new 70-foot-long, three-bedroom mobile home out in the street. Within the week we were all together living on our back lot while our home was being rebuilt.

Fred stopped by several times during construction to make sure we had everything we needed. When our new home was finished four months later, the mobile home was gone as quietly as it appeared. We never saw a bill, and very few people ever knew.

Gabe Ensenat

In 1996 I joined Meijer from a public company that was not "people-focused." My first encounter with Fred and Lena came at a retirement dinner for Henry Nyeholt. My first reaction was, Wow, the owners of the company at a retirement for the V.P. of softlines. I was walking in with my wife, and we came in the same time that Fred and Lena did. I introduced myself and referred to him as Mr. Meijer. Remember, I came from an environment (K-Mart) where we referred to everyone as Mr. or Mrs. He said, "Call me Fred," and introduced his wife as Lena. He then asked me where I came from and welcomed me to the company.

Martin Shelly

As a lines manager at the Ann Arbor store, I was occasionally in charge during my boss's time off. One day while I was in charge, Fred and Lena visited the store, and they invited me to sit down for a break. I prepared myself to answer questions about the business — sales figures, profit numbers, and such. Instead, Fred asked me about my family and my life. I mentioned my hope to transfer to one of the soon-to-be-built Indianapolis stores so that my young daughter, Bethany, who has been deaf from birth, could attend the best school for the deaf in the nation. "I think we can make that happen," he said. A few months later, I put in for a transfer, and it was immediately accepted.

Mike Stewart

In 1984, I was selected to open Store #51 in Findlay, Ohio. Fred told me that there were several people living in Findlay with whom he and Lena had ties. One of these was Karen Dubois, who was from Amble, Michigan, and had once been Lena's babysitter. Karen was 90 years old, and had moved to Findlay to live with her grandson. She lived to be 105, and every time Fred came to town, he would make a point of visiting her.

The first time he took me to meet Karen, he found out she had never been in an airplane. Even though she was wearing her bathrobe and slippers, we took her out to the Meijer plane and flew around the

Karen Dubois and Lena, 1990

town, giving her a bird's eye view of her house and the store. She had a blast!

Karen was not able to do much at her age, but what she did enjoy was knitting afghans. Fred made arrangements for me to have thirty-five skeins of yarn delivered to her about every other month. Karen would use these to make afghans, which I would pick up, paying her forty dollars apiece. Fred would send me the money. He once told me he and Lena had a closet full of afghans, but as long as she enjoyed knitting he would give the yarn to her and keep buying.

Judy Dense

In the spring of 1986 my husband, Jim, was diagnosed with a liver condition that would require a liver transplant, and so he was put on a waiting list for a new liver. Our biggest challenge would be getting to the hospital in Pittsburgh in the short amount of time required for such a procedure — if and when a liver became available.

We prayed about our dilemma, and then one day Fred visited Jim's office and graciously offered the use of the corporate plane. Thanks to this generous gift, Jim had a chance to see our sons grow up, and he worked for Meijer for another fifteen years as well. Our prayers of blessing for Fred, Lena, and their family continue.

Tim VanRavenswaay

I had been asked to manage a new Detroit-area store that was having problems. After discussing it with my wife, who was expecting, I decided to take the job. A few months later our daughter was born with spinal meningitis, and because of this we felt we needed to move back closer to our doctor and our family until things became more stabilized. I discussed it with my district manager, who was not a happy camper. "We just paid you big bucks to move here," he said, "and I'm not going to give you a transfer." The next day Fred happened to call to ask about our daughter's condition and if there was anything he could do. I told him about our wanting to move back. This was a week before Christmas, and two weeks later I was given a transfer.

John VanKuiken

It was 1989, and my wife and I were on vacation and traveling through Georgia when I had a severe heart attack. I was rushed to the hospital in Atlanta, where I remained in intensive care for several days. I longed for home and to be near my own doctors, but I knew I couldn't ride all that way in a car.

Before I had too much time to fret, and to my complete surprise, the Meijer plane arrived to pick me up. To this day, I wonder how Fred even knew about my problem. He never took any credit for this generous act. He did send flowers, and he called and wanted to know if there was anything else the Meijer family could do. You can imagine how loyal I felt working for such a person.

Gabe Ensenat

I was relatively new to the company, having just come from K-Mart, when our son became seriously ill with a heart problem. He was in intensive care, and the prognosis was bleak. Fred somehow heard about the situation and came by to say he wanted to help.

He had us flown to the Cleveland Clinic on the Meijer plane, and made arrangements with the specialists to operate on our son. I'm convinced that his action saved our son's life.

I've always believed that God puts people in our lives just when we need help. My family will be forever grateful that there are the Freds of this world, who put people before business.

Chapter Twenty-four

Giving Back

Money is, in essence, only a technique for the extension of love in space and time.

— W. H. Auden

I would rather have it said "He lived usefully" than "He died rich."

— Benjamin Franklin

F red Meijer does not really think of his charitable giving as un-usual generosity, which is how the world might well see it. He thinks of it as trying to create a complete life for himself, his family, and his community. "If we enjoy the past, then we ought to contribute to the future," he says. "It's as simple as that. I don't call that being generous."

However, he does recognize that there's something different in his perspective. He recalls an occasion when a prominent businessman told him, "If you worked for me, even if you were my son, I'd fire you. You're too darn idealistic." He came by that idealism honestly — by watching his parents.

As an early example of the family's involvement with community projects, Hendrik Meijer worked hard on the board of the Greenville Hospital to build a new structure that would replace what he saw as a

Fred with fellow members of the Improvement Club, 2008.
Back row, l.-r.: Peter Cook, Ralph Hauenstein, Dick Young, Earl Holton,
Chuck Royce. Front row: George Cope, Bill Martindill, Fred, Arend Lubbers,
Bill Schroeder. Missing: Dr. William Sprague, Jim Carpenter.
(Photo courtesy of Bob Strodtbeck)

potential firetrap. It wasn't just the nightmare he'd once had about losing Fred in a hospital fire; it was concern for the whole community. Hendrik raised $9,000 in 1941 for a thirty-bed addition to the original house. A few years later, he and his family spearheaded another fund drive. Lena and Fred's sister, Johanna, went out in those early days, along with other members of the family, eventually helping to collect $365,000 for a modern structure. "I'm sure the Gibsons and the Ranneys gave a lot more money than we did," says Fred, "but we did our best, and my dad saw it through on the board."

However, by the time the new building went up, in 1952, the family and the company had moved to Grand Rapids. "We never had a chance to use that hospital," says Fred. "But that doesn't mean my dad wasted his time. When we got to Grand Rapids, we enjoyed the fruits of somebody else's earlier work, when our children were born at Butterworth. So I don't really think of it as generosity; I think it's just a way of looking at life. Each generation builds for the next one."

The once-new Greenville hospital of 1952, however, was not really adequate to the requirements of the twenty-first century. So it became necessary to put up a new addition. A fund-raising drive begun in 2004 was to add a three-story wing, about 48,000 square feet, to the existing hospital, which had by then been acquired by Spectrum Hospitals of Grand Rapids. The new wing was to cost $17 million, a goal reached by February of 2005, in part because Fred and Lena made a significant financial gift.

Because of their generosity, they were asked about the naming of the new wing. "I put my mother and dad's name on it," says Fred, "because it was really his dream." The Hendrik and Gezina Meijer Surgery and Patient Care Center opened on May 24, 2006. The gleaming new facility was an important part of Hendrik Meijer's dream — in more than one sense of the word.

In other words, the generosity of the Meijer family is not new. It goes back to the earliest generation in America. When the Meijer Corporation was honored by the state of Michigan in 2004 for its Community Rewards program, the state listed not only the millions of dollars given to more than 4,800 local schools, churches, and community organizations; it also mentioned the National Kidney Foundation, the American Red Cross, various children's hospitals, and other organizations that had benefited from the company's contributions and volunteer efforts.

Michigan also recognized that these efforts are part of a seventy-year history of charitable giving and school partnerships. "It's quite an honor to be named for community involvement," said John Zimmerman, a former company spokesman, "and it boils down to the philosophy that Fred and his father always had. They felt it important that a community should be better off because they have a Meijer store in the neighborhood."

A list of some of the bequests Fred and Lena have given to communities in the region and the country indicates the broad sweep of their charitable interests, from medicine to education to the environment and the arts.

Among the projects that have particularly engaged their interests are the Fred and Lena Meijer Heart Center in Grand Rapids, the Hendrik and Gezina Meijer Wing of Spectrum United Memorial Hospital in Greenville, the Lena Rader Meijer Emergency Department of Kelsey Hospital in Lakeview, the Meijer Majestic Theater (home of the Grand Rapids Civic Theater), the Meijer Public Broadcast Center and Frederik Meijer Honors College of Grand Valley State University, the

Lena Rader Meijer Emergency Department
May 2008

Lena Rader Meijer Emergency Department, Kelsey Hospital, Lakeview
(Photo courtesy of Spectrum Hospital)

Fred Meijer Chair in Dutch Language and Culture at Calvin College, and the Lemmen-Holton Cancer Pavilion in Grand Rapids.

A passion for interaction with the natural world led Fred to become an advocate for the rails-to-trails movement. Among his projects are several significant trails in central and western Michigan, including the Hart and Flat River Trails and the Fred Meijer White Pine Trail State Park. He was also instrumental in creating the Fred Meijer Nature Preserve at Pickerel Lake.

Such lists from a long life could encompass many more schools, universities, organizations, and institutions, but among so many, some, such as the Gerald R. Ford Presidential Museum, Goodwill Industries, and the Urban League, particularly benefitted from Fred's energies as well as his philanthropy.

A summary of bequests to a host of organizations and causes over the years, no matter how lengthy or impressive, does little to show the level of involvement Fred has had with many of these activities. In the years before he began to withdraw from the day-to-day management of the increasingly immense business he had begun with his father, he began to allot a great deal of his time to charitable activities. However, even after his "retirement" at the age of seventy-five, he never quit going in to his office at corporate headquarters.

Fred has served as a trustee or on the board of directors of a host of local, state, and national organizations, always bringing his unique perspective to their causes. It should be no surprise that he spent time serving professional organizations such as the Food Marketing Institute, the National Association of Food Chains, the Grand Rapids Chamber of Commerce, and the Economic Alliance for Michigan. He was asked to sit on the boards of several banking institutions, including Michigan National Bank and the Federal Reserve Bank of Chicago, which he balanced nicely with a term as Vice President of his local PTA. He has served on the boards of Mary Free Bed and Spectrum Hospitals, the Emergency Medical Services Advisory Committee, and Michigan's Comprehensive Health Planning Unit.

These activities were seldom a simple matter of writing a check to a worthy cause. More often, he also dedicated his time, energy, and imagination. He has helped with fundraising for institutions by asking his large network of friends and associates to join in the project, so that the money he gave was multiplied by the generosity of others in the community. He has come up with ideas to expand or enhance the reach of the project. He has helped clarify questions people might raise about goals and methods. He has helped cut through red tape in ways that only a man of his stature, experience, and wide circle of friends could do. Although the amount of time he has given was limited by his other obligations, his energy and imagination have been virtually boundless, and the nonfinancial gifts he gave were of the utmost importance to many of his benefactions. In other words, Fred was not a drive-by donor.

A few brief stories serve as examples of the myriad ways in which he helped change the face of his community and the nation.

Gerald R. Ford Museum

Well before Grand Rapids' Presidential Museum opened in 1981, Fred was one of the community leaders intimately involved in helping to create what would eventually be a significant national institution. He was a member of the Gerald R. Ford Liaison Committee, was the vice-chair of the Museum Development Committee, and chair of the Site Selection Committee.

Mary Ann Keeler

Fred and I served together on the Site Selection Committee for the Gerald R. Ford Presidential Museum. I was passionate about a downtown presidential museum, and he, after three or four sites had been rejected because they were too small, too expensive, or too complicated to obtain, turned his thoughts to some land on the East Beltline that he owned. I felt that would never do. "It must be downtown," I said, and I found another site on the west riverbank. We were both determined to support our favorite sites. Fred thought there might be canals underneath my chosen site. I didn't think so, and my husband, Mike, paid for borings to be done to prove there weren't. All the members of the committee saw the problems with the river site — eminent domain, getting the city fathers to okay it, and so forth. But that didn't deter me one bit.

I went out to Fred's office on Walker and said to him, in pretty forceful terms, that it couldn't be on the East Beltline, it had to be downtown. I was very upset. In a quiet tone of voice, Fred said, "You know, if any of my employees talked to me as you just have, I would fire them." At that moment I was awfully glad I didn't work for him, but he preserved his dignity and mine by being the perfect gentleman he always is. I can't remember what I said, nor what he said next, but we have been great friends ever since. Mike and I have enjoyed wonderful times with Lena and Fred. He also gave me full credit for finding the site, and was very generous about it.

The East Beltline site later became the Frederik Meijer Gardens and Sculpture Park, which I cheered from the beginning. It was a perfect match: on the East Beltline in all its glory, a joy for all ages, a place for meditation, for respite, for learning, and for happiness.

On one occasion, when former President Ford was in attendance at a meeting, several local members whispered among themselves that they wondered whether Ford was planning to be buried at the museum. Since the former President was still a youthful sexagenarian, they were afraid it might be indelicate to ask him about it directly. When Fred heard the questions, he took direct action. Why would anyone be embarrassed to ask such an honest, universal question of a man known for his straight talk? Without hesitation, Fred walked

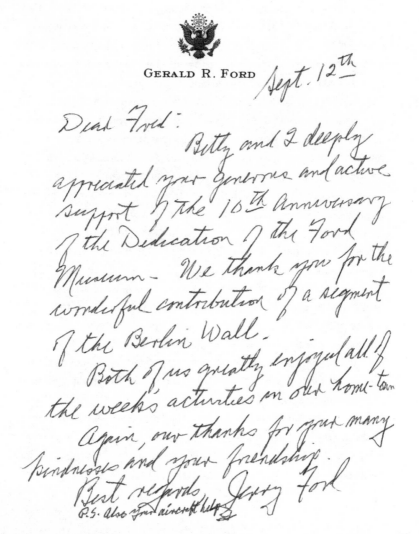

GERALD R. FORD   Sept. 12th

Dear Fred:

Betty and I deeply appreciated your generous and active support of the 10th Anniversary of the Dedication of the Ford Museum — We thank you for the wonderful contribution of a segment of the Berlin Wall.

Both of us greatly enjoyed all of the week's activities in our home-town

Again, our thanks for your many kindnesses and your friendship.

Best regards, Jerry Ford

P.S. Also for aircraft help

A note from Jerry Ford

across the room and asked the former President, "Have you decided where you'd like to be buried?"

"Here in Grand Rapids, of course," was Ford's immediate, smiling answer. Issue resolved. Plans for the Ford Museum from that point on included an area set aside for the eventual interment of Gerald R. Ford. It was to be visited by many of the world's leaders along with thousands of local mourners when, in January 2007, the nation's Thirty-eighth President was laid to rest along the peaceful banks of the Grand River.

Berlin Wall

When Fred was born in 1919, the Soviet Union was just organizing itself in a flurry of battles, coups and countercoups, and a widespread bloodbath in the aftermath of World War I. In the years after World War II, the opposition between the communist way of life and that being pursued in the West grew increasingly tense. In a memorable speech on October 15, 1946, Winston Churchill told the world:

"From Stettin in the Baltic to Trieste in the Adriatic an iron curtain has descended across the Continent. Behind that line lie all the capitals of the ancient states of Central and Eastern Europe: Warsaw, Berlin, Prague, Vienna, Budapest, Belgrade, Bucharest and Sofia; all these famous cities and the populations around them lie in what I must call the Soviet sphere, and all are subject, in one form or another, not only to Soviet influence but to a very high and in some cases increasing measure of control from Moscow."

For most of Fred's life, that "Soviet sphere" was a basic fact of history, a hostile force poised just over the horizon, with its nuclear missiles aimed in our direction, as ours were aimed at them. It often seemed unchangeable, as if it were woven into the fabric of existence. But the once-impregnable empire began to unravel in the late 1980s, and by the end of the decade, under Mikhail Gorbachev's leadership and with strong encouragement from many Western powers — Europe, the United States, the Vatican, and strong dissident elements in Poland and elsewhere, strengthened by the Helsinki Accords that President Ford had negotiated in 1975 — what Ronald Reagan had called the "Evil Empire" finally came to a stumbling conclusion.

One of the most potent symbols of the Iron Curtain had long been the Berlin Wall, its infamous guard towers with guns and dogs and bristling razor wire separating East from West in Germany's most important city. When the wall came down in 1990, it served to underscore the biggest governmental and ideological collapse of the twentieth century. Fred wanted to bring a symbol of that change to Grand Rapids.

"With the exception of the CIA," he says, "I'm probably the biggest buyer of the Berlin Wall in the United States." First, he paid $20,000 for a three-ton, eleven-foot-high segment of the wall. It was placed in front of the Ford Museum, and it was dedicated on September 6, 1991, the tenth anniversary of the museum's founding. Former British Prime Minister James Callaghan was there, along with former West German Chancellor Helmut Schmidt, Gerald Ford, and Fred Meijer. "We feared," said Callaghan in his dedicatory speech, "that those in East Berlin would be forever and always shut off. We should have had more faith."

Schmidt called the wall "a ridiculous piece of concrete," and praised Ford for his role in the Helsinki Accords, which he said encouraged early reformers within the Soviet bloc, setting the stage for what followed.

As the Berlin Wall came under siege, the cover of *Time* magazine had shown a portion of the wall with the name "Meijer" spray-painted prominently across it. The Grand Rapids Meijers and the company had no connection with the graffiti artist, apparently a Dutch visitor who shared their common surname. But once Fred saw it, he wanted that segment of the wall as well. The New Jersey businessmen who were then selling souvenir chunks of the wall knew they had a captive customer when Fred contacted them. Their price for this segment of the wall was a firm $50,000, which he finally paid. That piece of Cold War history now stands in the Van Andel Public Museum in Grand Rapids.

Vietnam War

Gerald Ford was President at the time the Vietnam War ended, in the summer of 1975. It was a moment of sadness and defeat. One particular televised news drama etched itself into the minds of Americans: the image showed the last American helicopter taking off from the

Left to right: Former British Prime Minister Lord James Callaghan, President Gerald R. Ford, Fred, and former German Chancellor Helmut Schmidt, 1991, posing in front of the eleven-foot, 6,000-pound piece of the Berlin Wall that Fred purchased and donated to the Grand Rapids Public Museum. (*Photo courtesy of the* Grand Rapids Press)

roof of the embassy while a crush of people clambered onto a steel staircase, trying vainly and desperately to get away from the deadly scene playing itself out on the streets of Saigon below them.

In October 1994, on a commercial visit to Vietnam, Hank and Mark Meijer found themselves in Saigon, now called Ho Chi Minh City, and as they were being shown the sights, Hank asked their driver to stop at the former embassy. Walking amid the messy ruins, he spotted that infamous steel staircase, rusting and unused on the roof of the building. Upon returning home, he suggested to Fred that the staircase might be an acquisition for the Ford Museum. Fred brought it up at the next meeting of the museum board. Henry Kissinger, who also serves on that board, argued strenuously against getting the stairway.

"Why would you want to remind visitors," he asked, "about this horrible chapter in American history?"

Kissinger's argument and Fred's response turned up in the pages of *Time:*

Somewhat startled, Meijer held his ground. "Henry, if we don't acquire the ladder, it will end up in the bowels of the Smithsonian." To which an annoyed Kissinger shot back, "That's a good place for it."

Then the ex-president spoke up for his old friend Meijer, likening the "freedom ladder" to the concrete slab from the Berlin Wall that adorns the museum's entrance. "No one knows more than I how humiliating it was," Ford reminded his Secretary of State. "As you recall, I had to sit in the Oval Office and watch our troops get kicked out of Vietnam. But it's part of our history, and we can't forget it." The decision was made to get the ladder. "To some, this staircase will always be seen as an emblem of military defeat," Ford notes. "For me, however, it symbolizes man's undying desire to be free." (*Time,* April 24, 2000, p. 40)

Thereafter, the stairway, roped off, has stood in a hall of the Ford Museum, its eighteen metal steps leading upward and ending in a blank wall.

Preserving Our History

Gordon Olson

In 1987, I was appointed city historian by the Grand Rapids Historical Commission. In that capacity, I was to "collect and preserve the city's history," as well as raise some of the funds needed to do the work.

Shortly after taking the job, I was confronted with a major challenge when a local photo studio announced it was closing after sixty years. It had an inventory of one million historical negatives; a priceless trove of the city's history was in jeopardy. I had two weeks to raise the $10,000 needed to purchase the collection, and I immediately began approaching potential donors.

I did not know Fred, but had been told that he generously supported community projects. I made an appointment, and Fred quickly put me at ease. He listened to our "pitch" and said that preserving our history was important, and he would be happy to help. Fred's quick affirmative response encouraged us to speak to others, and we were able to raise the funds in time.

Hardly a day goes by that someone doesn't use that collection, which has provided images for historical books and documentaries, and the story does not stop there. Fred said something else that day. "When you have other projects, come back to me. I'll help if I can."

I have taken advantage of that offer for other projects. His support has helped produce a video of Grand Rapids' African-American trailblazers, created a fund to gather and transcribe oral history, and a book and video about Vietnamese refugees who came to Grand Rapids after the fall of Saigon, to name a few. The history of Grand Rapids will be preserved for future generations, thanks in part to Fred.

Grand Valley State University

Arend Lubbers

I remember walking into Fred's office many years ago, meeting him for the first time. I had made this appointment to ask for a donation to the college. First we talked politics, then economics, religion, and art. Thirty minutes into the meeting I had to remind myself that this was a busy man, and I was there to ask for money.

Finally the conversation turned to my job, and that gave me the opportunity to pop the question. Back then, parting with money was more difficult for Fred than it is today. At the time Meijer was still struggling with their new one-stop concept that we all know today. I think he gave me $5,000. He thought that was a sizable gift. I did too, and I was happy.

That was the beginning of a generous relationship between Fred and Grand Valley over the years; and to think that it came from a man who never attended college.

Arend Lubbers

One day in 1971 I received a call from the chairman of the committee to establish public broadcasting in Michigan. He wanted to know if Grand Valley would like to have the license for public television in

West Michigan. He went on to say that ours was the largest geographic area in the state without public television.

We at the university recognized that this was a once-in-a-lifetime opportunity, but with our expansion plans at that time, we had no idea where we could come up with the necessary funding. A decision had to be made quickly. Funding was found from the federal government (through the help of Jerry Ford), the state legislature, and West Michigan donors, including Fred Meijer. Later, when the broadcasting facility was moved from Allegan to downtown Grand Rapids, Fred gave the lead gift. In recognition of his many contributions, the new broadcast center was named for him.

The *Grand Rapids Press* reported the event: "On May 25, 1998, thousands of children were in attendance to help celebrate the opening of the Meijer Public Broadcasting Center located on the downtown campus of Grand Valley State University. President Arend Lubbers recognized Fred Meijer for the gift that gave public broadcasting a new name in West Michigan."

Arend Lubbers

In 1996 our expansion plans for the university included finding a suitable campus site in Holland, Michigan, twenty-five miles away from our home campus. While not sure of where we would find the land or the necessary money, we started looking anyway.

I was checking out a location adjacent to a Meijer store and learned the property belonged to Meijer. While I was standing there contemplating my next move, a Meijer truck drove by. Painted on its side in bold letters were the words "Why Pay More?" That was all the inspiration I needed. I took the epiphany back to the university board for consideration. And after a few lively conversations, the land was donated to the university. On August 26, 1997, we dedicated the new Meijer campus in Holland, where we gave special thanks to Mr. Meijer and the Meijer Company for the contribution of land that helped make the new campus possible.

Hurricane Katrina

When Hurricane Katrina struck New Orleans with deadly force on the morning of August 29, 2005, the Meijer Company immediately took steps to help. There were significant cash donations, given by the company and by customers who donated through the Meijer website. But the most immediate step was when the Meijer Company dispatched trucks loaded with food and water, which arrived at relief centers in the South before government aid had been mobilized.

Fred and Lena Meijer Heart Center

When Spectrum Hospital decided, in 2003, to add a state-of-the-art heart center to its operations in downtown Grand Rapids, it began a fund-raising campaign for a hundred million dollars. It must have seemed only natural to ask Fred to be a part of that project. He had for years shown his interest in the quality of health care, and had served on Spectrum's board for many years. He was also the beneficiary of heart-bypass surgery, which returned him to health after an earlier bout of cardiac difficulty. The amount of the Meijer bequest was not published, but it included funds to be used for a nearby cancer center as well. The cancer center has since been named for Harvey Lemmen and Earl Holton, two past presidents of Meijer who were Fred's friends and partners through more than five decades of work.

But the naming of the heart center for Fred and Lena was not originally in Fred's plan. He had hoped to name it for Desiderius Erasmus (1466-1536), the Dutch humanist philosopher and theologian. Erasmus, with his extensive writing and learning, was one of the most important voices in bringing the fruits of the Italian Renaissance to the northern part of Europe. The fact that he had a humble birth — he is thought to have been the illegitimate child of a poor Dutch couple — did not deter him from developing his considerable talents, and he was for years one of the most illustrious scholars of the European continent, fiercely critical of the church that had once ordained him as a priest and determined to see the fruits of learning applied in every walk of life. During his lifetime, and partly because of his influence,

The Fred and Lena Meijer Heart Center
(Photo courtesy of Spectrum Hospital)

the Netherlands began to go beyond its old ways, and to enter what would one day be called the Dutch Golden Age. It was a time of unparalleled accomplishment for this small country in northern Europe.

Best known are the Dutch achievements in the arts, with leading figures such as Rembrandt and Vermeer. But there were also revolutions in economic development, as the Vereenigde Oostindische Compagnie (Dutch East India Company), the world's first large joint-stock corporation, took charge of bringing goods from all over the world to the doorstep of Europe. Then there was world exploration, including a thriving settlement on the island of Manhattan (then called New Amsterdam). In science, Antoni Van Leeuwenhoek's development of the microscope followed close on the heels of work by the lens-grinding philosopher Baruch Spinoza. The scholar Timothy Brook calls this era of Dutch history "the dawn of the global world." It was a new world that Erasmus, with his multitude of interests and his wide renown, had helped bring into existence. To commemorate Erasmus's shining intellect, as well as his Dutch background, Fred had hoped to honor both Grand Rapids and the memory of the great scholar he had long admired by helping to give the city an Erasmus Heart Center.

It was not to be. Almost everyone else involved in the project — friends, family, and Spectrum board members — thought the name was too strange, too far from everyday knowledge and experience. They wanted the familiar and well-loved names of Fred and Lena to be engraved on the front of the new building. So that is what won out in the end. Fred gave up his crusade for the Dutch philosopher, with a few regrets, and continued to support the vision and purpose that were revitalizing yet another area of downtown Grand Rapids.

Civil Rights

Having been imbued since childhood with the sense that all people must be treated with dignity, regardless of their circumstances, Fred has been a longtime member of the Grand Rapids Urban League. The Meijer Company has for years promoted the hiring and advancement of blacks and Hispanics within the corporation, and Fred has worked on many of the same issues throughout the community. "Meijer was doing a fantastic job of hiring black people before it was fashionable," says Paul Collins, a Grand Rapids artist, "so when he talks about dignity, he means it."

One simple way Fred emphasizes his point is to tell the story of a time years ago when Lena saw a woman slap her child for stuttering. He compares that reaction to an employer denying a job on the basis of sex, race, or physical disability. "When we don't give people a chance, it's a slap in the face," he says. "Everyone wants dignity. There is little dignity in being at the bottom of the income and social ladder. We can make a difference, if we all give it our attention. I can't do it alone. You can't do it alone. We can do it together." This is a commitment he has lived out in many ways. "I've never tried to be a crusader," he says. "I have strong beliefs, but I don't generally try to push them on others."

On a shelf in Fred and Lena's home stands a collection of small figures in bronze. One that is especially meaningful to him is an American Indian figure, the great nineteenth-century leader Nishnabe Gemau. For years, says Fred in explaining the statuette, we have used Indian names for our cities and streets, our subdivisions and developments. We have appropriated their land and made it our own. And yet Grand Rapids had no memorial to specifically honor their culture.

He wanted to help change that sad reality. In addition to donating the money necessary to have a statue made, he spent a good deal of time meeting with representatives of the Chippewa, Potawatomi, and Ottawa tribes, learning about their history and trying to make sure the statue he was commissioning would be an accurate reflection of the era when Great Lakes Indians had this land to themselves. He learned about leggings, headdress, ceremonial activities, and a host of other things about the culture — all in the interest of preserving this part of our history. In September 1992, a life-sized statue of Nishnabe Gemau was dedicated in Grand Rapids' downtown Centennial Park.

The Heartland Trail

Fred has always thought that people in the city are in need of green space where they can stretch their limbs and their minds in ways not easily found in cities. "Ninety-five percent of folks live in the city," he says, "and never get to experience the rural areas surrounding them." He goes a little farther when he refers to keeping one's "mental stability" by spending time outside of the noise, congestion, and great human drama of the city. By getting out of the city, even for a short time, by riding a bicycle or taking a walk, a person can help to maintain his or her own sanity.

That's why, in 1994, Fred made a landmark donation of $265,000 to help purchase an abandoned rail line in Greenville, Michigan. This would become the Fred Meijer Heartland Trail, stretching from Greenville to Alma, a walking and biking path of more than forty-one miles. The many trails established through his generosity help preserve a sense of bucolic tranquility that is often missing in lives saturated with the constant din of the city. One of them, the Fred Meijer White Pine Trail, is scheduled to run from Grand Rapids to Cadillac: on completion, it will be the longest state park in Michigan. For a while, because of his extensive activities, especially in reclaiming unused railroad right-of-ways, Fred was called the "Johnny Appleseed of trails."

The Zoo

Not all of Fred's pet projects work out the way he would like. Philanthropy on the scale that he practices it must involve the people of the region, and if they don't agree, it is simply necessary to muster the grace to go along with community sentiment. In the summer of 2004, Fred offered Grand Rapids Township a 165-acre golf course that he had purchased on east Leonard Street, together with $25 million in cash, to build a wildlife park. The goal was to replace the aging zoo at John Ball Park with a state-of-the-art facility that would treat animals well and would provide enrichment and education for the public. He brought in national experts, such as the well-known primatologist Jane Goodall, to help develop a plan for the careful treatment of animals that would be housed there.

"I'm not sure I'm entirely in favor of zoos," Fred said at the time, "especially when they are so often sad, inadequate places for animals to live. But if we're going to learn about these animals, and learn to treat them better in the wild, a really good zoo is probably the best place to start." His gift of the land and money would have gone a long way toward creating such a place, but there was a condition attached to his offer: the community would have to make a commitment as well, to support the idea with its tax dollars by passing a millage increase to ensure that a high-quality zoo could continue to operate in the future.

The land on which the golf course was situated, not far from the Frederik Meijer Gardens and Sculpture Park, had belonged to Fred for some years by that time. He had initially purchased it because the owners were planning to use it for housing, and Fred thought it might make sense to save it for potential future civic purposes. The idea of a wildlife park was not in his thinking at that time. "So I let three years go by because I had no idea what to do with it. Then all at once the discussion comes up about the zoo, so I thought maybe that would be a good thing."

Fred did not peddle his idea as a high-pressure salesman might. In discussing the impending township millage vote, he said: "People should vote their conscience, and they shouldn't do anything that hurts their family, or their future. And if their family and their future don't include a wildlife park, I think we all should respect that. All I want to do is offer the community something, and have the community take what they want. If anybody thinks it's not an asset, or there are other priorities, they should vote the other way." (*Grand Rapids Press*, August 1, 2004)

The millage vote failed to pass, and the wildlife park did not happen. It was a disappointment to Fred, but it did nothing to diminish his commitment to improving the community. He simply moved on to the next venture. "The world goes on as if nothing happened at all," he says, in an approximate quote from his favorite poet, Carl Sandburg.

United Way

Pat Quinn

In 1987, Fred was the chair and I was the vice-chair for that year's United Way drive. To kick off the campaign, it was suggested that we appear on TV for the news media, each wearing a jacket with our respective Meijer and Spartan logos, the jackets our truck drivers wore.

On the morning of our appearance, I remember driving up in my company car, a Cadillac, while he drove up in a nondescript Chevy, obviously a company pool car with a number stuck in the rear window.

They arranged to have Fred and me with our backs to the camera, washing the windows of a school bus. On cue, with the announcer talking, we were to turn around to reveal our identities. This got a lot of laughs over the next few days, and that year we set a record for the campaign.

Celebration on the Grand

Mike Lloyd

Each fall, tens of thousands throng to downtown Grand Rapids for "Celebration on the Grand" weekend. It's a major community event, sustained by corporate financial donations, support and staffing from the city, and hundreds of man hours from area organizations, clubs, businesses, and volunteers.

"Celebration on the Grand" was originally planned as a one-time event tied to three "openings": the dedication of the Gerald R. Ford Museum, the move of the Grand Rapids Art Museum into new quarters (the former Federal Courthouse), and the sparkling overhaul of the dowdy Pantlind Hotel into the Amway Grand Plaza.

The stars aligned perfectly for such a celebration, with dignitaries from around the world attending that special week in 1981. That glamorous first year gave momentum to continuing the event a second year. The focal point then was inaugurating the second Amway hotel tower.

After that, interest among community leaders waned. Fred had already agreed to be chair of Celebration when the leadership committee voted to cancel the event. My boss, *Press* Publisher Werner Veit, was on the committee and informed me of the vote. I felt the committee of CEOs made a decision at an executive level that forgot about the grass-roots support the event had at the "worker-bee" level. Werner encouraged me to talk to Fred, who had been a major contributor and supporter — in addition to being the chair of a cancelled event.

Fred's response: "We have every reason to be proud of Grand Rapids. It's a special place. Many people at Meijer are proud to live and work in Grand Rapids." He had no problem stepping aside. "Others can — and should — carry the program forward," he said. "The thing about oligarchs," he said, "is that sometimes the old garchs need to get out of the way and let the young garchs take over."

His enthusiastic willingness to hand over the reins to a new generation is a major reason so many people continue to enjoy Celebration on the Grand all these years later.

Theater

Built in 1903, the Grand Rapids Civic Theater played a crucial part for more than a century in showcasing the downtown cultural experience in Grand Rapids. But by the early twenty-first century it was showing its age. Its structure was no longer safe in many respects, and it was a persistent challenge for the theater's volunteers and professionals to present the kind of technologically sophisticated shows that were necessary for its survival. Consequently, Grand Action, a private development group, undertook a $10 million renovation. The hope was that a gleaming new facility for the theater and its educational activities could also spark a kind of renaissance in that area of North Division Avenue, which had not enjoyed quite the cachet of so many other areas of downtown Grand Rapids.

Among the things that concerned Fred about the building was the condition of the balcony. When they began carefully examining the upper level, structural engineers found significant defects in its holding capacity. Furthermore, it was difficult to get to, especially for people who might have difficulty handling the stairs. There were a couple of cost overruns because of the renovation of the balcony's support structure and the new elevator shaft, but Fred cheerfully covered those costs. "I think we've made the balcony very user-friendly and much safer," he said. "When you get older, you realize people have certain limitations."

Meijer Majestic Theatre, home of the Grand Rapids Civic Theatre

"All in all, I feel good about it," he added. "We've always enjoyed Civic Theatre productions. They needed a fine showplace." (*Grand Rapids Press,* Sept. 17, 2006)

Fred and Lena, who contributed more than half of the cost of the Civic Theatre's renovation, were the guests of honor in the fall of 2006 when the updated facility, now named the Meijer Majestic Theatre, was unveiled. Hollywood and Broadway composer Marvin Hamlisch headlined the show.

Opera

Mike Lloyd

Opera Grand Rapids had taken a flying leap of faith by scheduling a Wagner opera, *The Flying Dutchman.* Wagner's works are big-time opera but not big-time box office. The company hoped to boost ticket sales by bringing in internationally famous soprano Martina Arroyo as the show's headliner. She was signed to a hefty contract before the question came up of how to pay for her performance — and maybe the company.

Knowing Fred's background as a member of the Schubert Club, his love of opera, and the fact that he is a Dutchman, I asked if Meijer would underwrite Ms. Arroyo's performance. Without hesitation, Fred said yes. Then he asked if it was possible that, during her visit in Grand Rapids, he could have his picture taken with her. He'd bring the camera, he said.

I set up a lunch for Fred and Lena and a few other supporters of the opera in a private room at the Peninsular Club. In the dramatic fashion of a true diva, Miss Arroyo made a grand entrance. Her voice was as sonorous when she talked at lunch as when she was singing on stage, and Martina enthralled everyone, first with opera stories and then telling Fred about her first visit to a Meijer store. She loved it.

But the crescendo came when she looked across the table at Fred and asked if *he* could do her a favor. Would he agree to have *his* picture taken with her? No egos — just shared happiness. Each thought the other was the star.

Legacy

When asked what he would like people to think of him after he is gone, Fred sometimes tells the following story:

"Winston Churchill is buried in his hometown. Near his grave is a little tombstone that says, 'Here lies Mary Smith. She did her best.' She did her best. Did Winston Churchill always do his best? And if they both did their best, given their human failings, isn't Mary Smith just as important a human being in the scope of history as Winston Churchill?

"What I would want people to say about me is, 'He did his best as he saw it.' And hopefully the world was a little better."

Chapter Twenty-five

Frederik Meijer Gardens and Sculpture Park

A thing of beauty is a joy for ever:
Its loveliness increases; it will never
Pass into nothingness; but still will keep
A bower quiet for us, and a sleep
Full of sweet dreams, and health, and quiet breathing.

— John Keats

A t the age of seventy-five, when most people have begun slowing down and simplifying their lives, Fred began the largest philanthropic project of his life, the Frederik Meijer Gardens and Sculpture Park. As he withdrew from the daily operations of the business that he had shepherded for so many years, he consciously began to cast about for activities that would engage his talents and energies.

Charles Royce, *Friend*
In 1990 we accompanied Fred and Lena on a historic Mediterranean cruise. We saw Mount Vesuvius, Pompeii, Mount Etna, Alexandria, Jerusalem, Rhodes, the Acropolis, Ephesus, and Crete. But the high point of the trip was our visit to the Babai Gardens in Haifa, Israel. Fred had always been fascinated by sculpture, and had collected a number of pieces by Marshall Fredericks. I will always believe that seeing the

Aerial view of the Meijer Gardens during the groundbreaking ceremony, 1994
(Photo courtesy of Bob Strodtbeck)

Babai Gardens may have been the catalyst Fred needed to help create the marvelous attraction now named for him.

The Meijer Company initially acquired the property on which the Gardens now stand for the purpose of building a new Meijer store. The store was to occupy some fifty acres of land on the East Beltline, a busy thoroughfare not far from where I-196 and I-96 flow together. Just five minutes from downtown Grand Rapids, it was a perfect retail location. Behind the proposed supercenter's acreage lay a back section of the property, seventy acres of low wooded hills, a small stream, two fields that had once been farmed, and a huge wetlands area. This back property was not suitable for retail uses, but the company had purchased it along with the front parcel.

A group of local residents expressed vociferous opposition to the new store location, so the Grand Rapids Township authorities were moving very slowly in the zoning approval process. However, Fred still believed that the company would get the necessary permissions. He went so far as to put in an access road for the property (since the voluminous store traffic could not flow directly onto the East Beltline), together with water and sewer mains large enough to serve the needs of a 200,000-square-foot emporium.

While the Meijer Corporation was struggling with its plans to use the property, the West Michigan Horticultural Society, which had been organized by Don Hazelswart and a group of his gardening friends and associates in 1981, was trying to find a suitable site for a botanical garden near Grand Rapids. As early as 1986, Howard Subar, a member of the society, had approached Fred about the availability of that particular piece of Meijer property in the city. The company was planning to put a store there, so Subar's request came to nothing. By 1991, Betsy Borre, the president of the Horticultural Society, had embarked on a campaign to increase awareness of the need for a botanical garden, and to raise the necessary funds. The group had already identified a location, given to them by Kent County, just to the north of the city. When the Horticultural Society asked Fred if he would be willing to support the creation of a botanical garden, he agreed to do so. Borre suggested a possible location as well, the property known as Wahfield Park, on Alpine Avenue.

Fred then talked for a while about the sculptures he and Lena had been collecting. They owned one of the largest collections of work by the Michigan artist Marshall Fredericks, and they thought that many of them might fit well in a garden setting. The idea, then, was to combine two functions in one spot: the joining of a botanical garden and a sculpture park. The idea was not quite as unprecedented as combining groceries with general merchandise, but it seemed to be a good way to attract a wide variety of visitors, and to showcase Fred and Lena's interests. She loved gardening and he loved sculpture.

Arend Lubbers

When the idea of a botanical garden was first being considered, Fred wanted to show me a potential location on the north side of Grand Rapids. The location did not look particularly attractive, so, as politely as possible, I encouraged him to continue looking.

On another occasion, he took me to a warehouse where he had some sculptures stored. He said he wanted to add them to the new botanical garden. He went on to explain that Lena loved plants and flowers, and he hoped the sculpture would enhance the park. Once he settled on making the Meijer Gardens a sculpture park as well, he let those who knew sculpture influence him in his buying decisions, and gave them credit. What a jewel in the crown for West Michigan!

The north-side location was eventually dropped from consideration, and Fred began to think it might be possible to put a public garden into the plot of land behind the envisioned retail outlet.

"I know I'm a very small part of the corporate team now," he says, "because I'm basically retired. But you don't give up your emotions of seventy years just because you're retired. So that's what I'm doing with the Gardens, because I have more fun here than being in Florida or someplace else. I think I could scrape up enough to have a cottage in Florida, but I haven't had the desire. Lena hasn't had the desire. We're very happy to be helping develop the Gardens, and will be happy to be as much a part of the future as possible."

This new project was very much like starting another business: it required imagination, cooperation, and input from a host of other people, fundraising to find donors, discreet inquiries about who would make a strong team for this new project, and the thousands of details that lie behind every successful enterprise. Of crucial importance was the fundraising campaign. The initial estimate was that it would take $13 million to build a suitable facility; and for a while it looked as if that amount could not be attained. Fred says that in the back of his mind, he was prepared not to go forward with the project. "But at some point," he says, "out of loyalty or respect, Earl Holton volunteered to head the capital campaign. I thought he might be banging his head against a wall, but he was determined to make it work." And he did. "Without Earl's involvement," Fred concludes, "I don't think the Gardens would be here today."

It was Earl's decision to involve Meijer's vendors in the campaign, and to see what they would be willing to do. They came through with both capital contributions and a host of in-kind donations, and before long it was clear that the Gardens would indeed become a reality. Fred began to involve himself with every aspect of the activities.

One of the early backers was the environmentalist and philanthropist Peter Wege. Both Fred and Peter had spoken to a large gathering in the Grand Rapids Civic Center on the first Earth Day, April 22, 1970.

Peter Wege with Fred at the future site of the Meijer Gardens

A commitment to the wise use of earth's resources has been important to both of them. In the summer of 1993, the two long-time acquaintances walked over the grounds of the proposed site for what was then called the West Michigan Botanic Garden. Peter used a cane to support an ailing knee, and Fred limped slightly on his artificial hip, but their energy was unflagging.

Peter M. Wege

I had first met Fred at the Kent Country Club, as I recall it. Even though he doesn't play golf, he lived nearby. Fred and I shared an interest in the environment, so we've had some interesting conversations over the years. We often joked together, especially when he bought a golf course — considering his complete lack of interest in the game. I remember walking over the land that became the Meijer Gardens and suggesting the nature trail to him. There was a pond on the right, lots of native trees and wild grasses. It was pristine.

The nature trail named for him grew out of this suggestion, as the FMG's Wege Library grew from his support for improved understanding of environmental issues.

Bill Martindill

Part of the property that is now the home of the Frederik Meijer Gardens and Sculpture Park had originally been planned for a new store. However, when a new site was found on Knapp, welcomed by the municipality, Fred and Lena donated this additional parcel of prime real estate for the expansion of what was then the Michigan Botanic Garden (later renamed in honor of Fred). At the grand opening for the Knapp's Corner store, Fred made clear that he thought the new location was a win-win for everyone involved.

"We have a bigger store in a better location," he said. "But more importantly, the gardens and trails will be bigger and better for future generations. This Meijer store won't be here forever, but hopefully one hundred years from now people can still visit the gardens to refresh their souls."

As plans were developing, groups of people involved in the project met regularly at a temporary office space in the Atrium Building. One day a group of a dozen or so was examining blueprints for the planned

The Knapp Corner Meijer store *(Photo courtesy of Bob Strodtbeck)*

construction, which was to begin in a few months. The huge glass conservatory was to anchor the west end of the complex, but Fred noticed that a row of support greenhouses, pictured on the previous blueprint, had been eliminated from this one. He asked about the change, and was told that the $13-million budget didn't allow for the support greenhouses. Costs had gone up, and something had to be cut.

"But you can't really do a good job with the conservatory," he interjected, "if you don't have those smaller greenhouses." He was told that it would be harder, but the staff would find a way to manage.

"How much would it cost to put them back into the plans?" he asked no one in particular. One of the architects said he could get a very good estimate within a week or so. Fred had an immediate response: "Could you get a fairly good estimate within ten minutes?"

Within ten minutes the fairly good estimate had arrived: it would cost an additional $2 million dollars, more or less.

"Well then, let's do it," said Fred. "We need to make sure our people have what they need to succeed."

Many of the people involved in the early stages of planning expressed the opinion that botanical gardens don't typically need large parking lots. When someone suggested that a single parking area, with room for perhaps 200 cars and buses, would probably be sufficient, Fred immediately questioned the assumption. "I'd like to think we know something about filling parking lots," he said, smiling. At that point, he was still nursing plans for the Meijer store on the front part of the property, and had arranged for extra parking spaces behind the store — to accommodate overflow from the botanical gardens.

From the beginning, Fred worked with the board to hire a superb staff, and he listened carefully to the advice of people whose expertise he trusted. Though it is a nonprofit organization, he has always been determined to see that it is managed with the best business practices.

Once the project was well underway, Fred asked a number of supporters to accompany him on a visit to the Missouri Botanical Gardens in St. Louis. He thought that since it was one of the oldest botanical gardens in America, it could provide the group with ideas and help set an example for one of the newest. He was greatly impressed by the beauty and maturity of the gardens, by the wide expanses of space, and by the geodesic dome that served as the main conservatory. He enjoyed the small sculpture collection, which, coincidentally, was the work of Carl Milles, friend and mentor of Marshall Fredericks.

He was less impressed with what he perceived as a lack of business acumen. While talking to an employee about the gift shop, he was informed that the shop had just finished a very successful year, providing an income of more than a hundred thousand dollars.

"And what are your expenses?" he asked. "How much of a margin is there on your inventory? What are the employee costs?"

"Oh, we don't keep track of things that way," the employee replied. "We're just proud to make our contribution to the budget."

From the outset, Fred had assigned several key people from the Meijer corporate offices to help establish policies for the Gardens. Now he was even more determined to see that all of its operations, including the gift shop, would conform, as much as possible, to the best available practices of a well-run business.

But even he might have had trouble believing that, within ten years of its founding, it would welcome more than a half million visitors annually, making it the second-most popular cultural destination in Michigan, trailing only the Henry Ford Museum and Greenfield Village in Dearborn.

Volunteers at Meijer Gardens *(Photo courtesy of Bob Strodtbeck)*

Nancy Ferriby, *Executive Assistant, Frederik Meijer Gardens*
and Sculpture Park

Fred was here visiting with Lena and, I believe, a cousin of hers. The ladies were in the gift shop and Fred was sitting in a chair in the main
entry area. One of our facility attendants happened by and said hello,
whereupon Fred engaged her in conversation. He asked her a question
related to one of the sculptures, which she didn't know the answer to,
but she told him she'd find someone who did. She relayed the question to me. I found the answer, and since the attendant had something else to do, I welcomed the opportunity to talk to him. I headed
upstairs and found him sitting casually in one of the comfy chairs. I sat
beside him and introduced myself. We'd met before, but I know he
meets an enormous number of people, so thought it best to reintro-
duce myself.

He looked at my name tag and asked me the ethnic origin of my
last name. I told him Ferriby is my name by marriage, and that it is of
English origin. He asked about my maiden name, Malthaner, which is
German. This is the part where I remember the conversation took a
very interesting and humorous turn. He proceeded to talk about history, the world wars, and some interesting ethnic traits. He said he is
Dutch, but he's now part German — because of his recent hip replace-
ment. Then he mentioned that certain cultures have a bent pinky finger, so we started talking about that. It was just really entertaining to
me that I was sitting there for probably twenty minutes, talking about
German hips and bent pinky fingers and babies that resulted from the
big wars. He gave me some great laughs, and what I sense was a good
history lesson.

Fred loves it that the beautiful themed gardens and special exhibits
bring people in. The permanent sculpture collection, augmented by
visiting shows, gives them a second level of experience, something
else to learn about. There are also outdoor concerts in the evenings
throughout the summer. As a result, the gardens have multiple fea-
tures to appeal to every kind of visitor, and to expand their sense of the
world.

"My grandmother Meijer had many problems," Fred reminisces,

"but she said this: *De oog wil ook wat hebben* ('the eye wants something, too'). She meant that there has got to be more to life than just eating, sleeping, and going to work." The world of art has proven to be especially interesting to Fred. Art not only provides solace to the eye, it is a uniquely human way of playing games with ideas of shape, form, and substance. Though its subject may be almost anything, from the trivial to the profound; though its materials may be anything — bronze, language, music, paint, or living plants; though its moods may encompass the extremes of human emotions, the essence of art is celebration and joyfulness.

Jeanette Pigorsh

Every time I see a stump fence, I think of Fred. Having grown up in the country, I am familiar with stump fences even though they are becoming a thing of the past. Realizing this, Fred commissioned Tom Hillis, a local sculptor, to create several life-sized bronze stumps. He had these placed in the Meijer Gardens to preserve this piece of small-farm history.

Tom Hillis's bronze stump sculpture, replicating stumps from Lena's family farm

Jim Hilboldt

It has been pure pleasure to watch the commitment by Fred and Lena to take the Meijer Gardens from an idea to an international reality for all to enjoy. It's a wonderful example of their dedication to the community, to the environment, and to society.

Fred has always wanted the sculpture gardens to be world-class. There are many decorative, lighthearted, whimsical pieces in its collection, especially in the farm gardens and the Lena Meijer Children's Garden. However, there's also a superb and growing nexus of works by some of the world's most distinguished artists, ranging from Auguste Rodin to Henry Moore to Magdalena Abakanowicz.

Mary Ann Keeler

Fred, Lena, and a few others, including visiting artists, would sit around our dining room table and share childhood experiences about our families, and I always remember Fred's stories of traveling with his parents in Europe, taking in the sculptures in the plazas, and maybe a concert or two in a concert hall. My stories about my mother's determination that all five of her children would learn a musical instrument brought forth a smile from Lena when she told about her father saying to her, "If you will take music lessons, I'll buy you a piano."

When he was young and lived on the farm in Greenville, Fred says, "we probably had thirty different horses, because we were trying to get a better one every time, and every time the dealer was smarter than we were. We went backwards. We got a bad deal. I've ridden bad horses, lousy horses, terrible horses. I remember one I had to ride bareback when he wouldn't take a saddle. And that sucker didn't spill me. I mean, he was surprised. The last time I rode a horse I was eighty years old and I was in a barrel race in Colorado. I just loved horseback riding. I loved skiing. I loved bicycling. Of course, I don't do any of that stuff now, because it's too dangerous at my age."

That long experience with horses may help explain why Meijer stores have always kept their penny pony rides for children. It may also explain the rather large number of horses to be found in the sculpture collection of the Meijer Gardens. There's not only the 24-foot bronze done by Nina Akamu in homage to Leonardo Da Vinci's monumental unfinished horse from the Renaissance; there are a variety of other horses on the premises, ranging from draft animals in the farmyard to the engaging "Cabin Creek" by the distinguished American sculptor Deborah Butterfield.

Caleb Brennan, *Conservator/Assistant Curator of Sculpture, FMG&SP*

Before the monumental *American Horse* was unveiled, they put a curtain around it, to shield it from the general public. A security guard was posted with a list of names of those people who were approved to view it. Unfortunately, Fred's name wasn't on the list, so when he came there one day, he was almost turned away.

"May I see the list?" he politely asked the guard. He then wrote his name at the bottom, and was promptly allowed in.

Nina Akamu's *American Horse,* tribute to Leonardo Da Vinci *(Photo: Bob Strodtbeck)*

Dave Meinke

I was given the assignment of photographing every phase of the Leonardo Da Vinci horse, from the Tallix foundry in Newburgh, New York, to the dedication at the Frederik Meijer Gardens. Because of its enormous size, it came in parts on flatbed trucks. As the head, body, legs, and tail were being assembled, I couldn't help but feel an overwhelming sense of history in the making knowing that one of Leonardo Da Vinci's masterpieces was finally coming to life here in Grand Rapids.

As this massive piece of art was nearing completion, but before the head was attached, I thought I would toss my business card into the body of the horse as a personal token of my experience in the project. Later that day, I happened to be standing next to Fred and Lena when someone came up to Fred and said, "Someone put their business card inside the horse." I was embarrassed, but admitted I had done it. Fred thought that was a good idea and he wanted to do the same thing. He asked the construction workers to lift Lena and him on a scissored lift platform above the open head cavity. He took out a business card and a Purple Cow ice cream card, and in a grandiose fashion, dropped them into the horse while the onlookers and news media cheered.

The unveiling of Akamu's horse in 1999 celebrated the five hundredth anniversary of the destruction of a clay equestrian statue Leonardo had intended to cast in bronze for the Sforza family of Milan. His plans were destroyed by the arrival of a French army, which ended Sforza influence in Lombardy, and which also, cruelly, used his clay model for target practice, reducing it to rubble.

Though he knew relatively little about sculpture when he began, Fred was willing to trust others who did know something about it. He responds strongly to works that have stories connected to them. He has a preference for art that can be explained and discussed. However, if the sculpture committee wants to buy a work Fred doesn't like on first viewing, he's invariably open-minded and willing to learn more. It is the quality of curiosity, in addition to his energy and his financial support, that makes the Gardens such a success. The *Wall Street Journal* characterized the work on display at the Frederik Meijer Gardens as "the most important sculpture collection west of the

Kroller-Mueller." In 2002, Fred and Lena, with a group of others, went to the Kroller-Mueller Museum, located outside the Dutch village of Otterlo, in an attempt to see firsthand whether the *Journal's* assessment was accurate.

Mieke ten Harmsel

While we were touring the museum's outdoor sculpture exhibit, comparing its collection to the works on display at the Frederik Meijer Gardens, Fred was full of practical questions, as always. How much money did the government put into the museum? How much came from the admission fees? How much from private donors? But he was also intensely interested in the sculpture he saw. Works by Henry Moore, beautifully situated, drew a strong reaction. He loved the ethereal floating swan-like piece by the Hungarian Marta Pan, slowly drifting on a pond in the light breeze.

He was especially struck by a tall slender tower made of a delicate lacing of cables and stainless steel tubes by the American Kenneth Snelson, so he went over and lay on his back beneath it. Asked why he was doing that, he replied, "I want to see if it moves in the wind." He lay there a while, looking up into the sky, and we asked him what he had concluded. "Can't tell," he said. "The clouds are moving, too." A few minutes later, still filled with an antic spirit, he saw a bronze tree displayed on a path in the woods, and went over to hug it. "The world," he said, "can always use another tree-hugger."

Later that day, we visited the Museonder, an underground museum. The entrance is basically a huge stump. When we walked inside, we could see that the root system had been cleaned and maintained, and the dangling roots filled the air for five stories downward. A spiral walkway led us to the bottom, and while walking we passed a number of wall displays illustrating different natural events that occur underground — things like decomposing leaves, animal activity, water tables, molten lava, bedrock, and sediment. The museum is in essence a study of the geological past of the Netherlands.

Shortly after entering, Fred noticed two young boys down on their knees, looking at an exhibit. He got down next to them to see what had caught their attention. They immediately began explaining what they were looking at, full of excitement, speaking in Dutch at a break-neck speed. He apologized to them in his halting Dutch, saying he couldn't understand them very well. Immediately, they switched to English, and explained it all once again, almost as quickly. Then they ran off, smiling and chattering, further down the long curving ramp.

Fred's endless curiosity got the best of him. He assumed that everyone in West Michigan would share his — and the young boys' — interest in the underground museum. He devoured it all, and before long was asking aloud what it would cost to re-create such a place in Grand Rapids. Lena whispered to me, "This may turn out to be the most expensive trip we've ever taken."

Although Nina Akamu's *American Horse* and Alexander Liberman's *Aria* are currently the largest pieces of sculpture in the Gardens, there were plans at one time for another monumental work, to be executed by Arnaldo Pomodoro, perhaps the most distinguished Italian sculptor of his generation. His polished globes can be seen, among other places, in the central courtyard of the Vatican Museums in Rome and in front of the United Nations building in New York City.

Hank Meijer

One time, while Dad was visiting Pomodoro in his studio outside Florence, he asked him whether there was any major project he had wanted to do but had been unable to consummate. Immediately Arnaldo launched into a description of a work he had wished to do for the church in his hometown. It was an imposing wall of bronze cut into a grassy hillside, creating a walkway below the level of the ground. The bronze wall would hold containers for human remains. From the center of the opening would rise a massive structure, roughly in the shape of a volcano, which visitors could enter. This bronze cone, open at the top, would also hold human remains.

For a variety of reasons, the church had decided not to go forward with it. Dad liked the idea, and for some time we investigated the possibility of commissioning it for the Gardens. It would have been a columbarium, intended for cremated remains. The Gardens even went

Fred and Lena and visitors to the Meijer Gardens *(Photo courtesy of Bob Strodtbeck)*

so far as to obtain a cemetery license from the state of Michigan. However, problems arose here, too, as they had in Italy, and Arnaldo's dream was not realized.

Although Pomodoro's columbarium did not materialize, Fred and Lena decided that they wanted the Gardens to be their final resting place, and a spot was designated near the Farm Gardens, not only for them, but also for Harvey Lemmen, as well as for Earl and Donnalee Holton.

Fred and Lena make regular visits to the Gardens, where on even the most bitterly cold day of winter they can enjoy the warmth of schoolchildren rushing about, of visitors being pushed in wheelchairs, of people from every walk of life being uplifted by the beautiful butterflies in the Lena Meijer Conservatory, or the latest exhibit in the sculpture galleries. They invariably check in with David Hooker to ask how everything is going, and to see what attendance has been like lately.

David Hooker, *President and CEO, Frederik Meijer Gardens and Sculpture Park*

Something that told me a lot about what Fred would like me to work on here happened soon after I began. We were standing at the front desk, Lena was in the gift shop, and we were chatting about one thing and another. "You know," he said, "growing old is tough. I'm getting older all the time, and some day I won't be here. Your job, really, is to figure out what to do with this place once I'm gone."

On another occasion, within a month of starting this position, I walked with Fred to his car, where his driver, Carol Alexander, was waiting for him. As we moved out onto the sidewalk, he stopped. He placed his walker down, looked at me, and said, "You know, some people think that the only reason I've created this whole institution is as a legacy, so people will have something to remember me by." He paused for a second, and then said, "They're right." He smiled and got into the car.

Chapter Twenty-six

That's Just Fred

> Trade always weakens dogmatic belief because it makes men realize that people with different beliefs have common needs, and that people with beliefs which one has been taught are wicked may be leading a life which one has been taught is good.
>
> — W. H. Auden

> We humans are just one kind of being in a very complex universe, and what we know about the universe is only one little part of what is out there. We shouldn't get too excited about our own importance.
>
> — Fred Meijer

Fred has an astonishing memory for people he's known and worked with all his life; he brings up hundreds of individuals in a series of interviews. He not only remembers their names, he also knows quite a bit about them — their families, where they live, what schools their children go to, the things he and they have in common or disagree about, the things they've done together, the good times they've had. This kind of ability requires a good memory, of course, but it's more than simple memory. It stems from genuine respect and concern for their lives, and from the recognition that they are important to his life. They form a gargantuan extended family gathered over the course of nearly ninety years, and he tries to celebrate in each one of them the uniqueness of the human spirit.

That sort of respect, that brand of humanity, cannot be faked. Someone who says "I can never remember names" would be, to his way of thinking, like someone who says "I can never get around to taking a bath." It's a matter of choice, of deciding to take the time and to make the effort.

He has always carried a little notebook in an inside pocket, into which he makes entries all day long. The day isn't really over until he's gone through his notes, passed on what can be relayed to someone else, re-emphasized the names and places and ideas for himself, shared important information with Lena, and repeated significant items until they have lodged themselves in his memory.

Throughout his business life he has demonstrated the ability to work with many people. In addition to that quality, he somehow encourages them to do their best, to become more than they had thought they could be. He is able to instill loyalty and affection in the people he works with, along with respect.

"It's important to keep the right kind of perspective about yourself," he says. "You may be the manager of a large store of ours, and therefore to us you are a very important person, the key person in the community of the store. But in the larger scope, that bagger you hire is

Greenville,
where it all
began

just as important a human being walking across this earth as you are. Treat him or her that way, and you will see dignity in action."

It's common in America to see corporate heads as ego-driven souls who may well be respected but are not often looked on with affection. That has never been the case with Fred. He's a walking refutation of Machiavelli's advice to would-be princes that it is "better to be feared than loved."

Not a Billionaire

On December 7, 2006, the *Greenville Daily News,* Fred's hometown paper, published an editorial commemorating the four Greenville men who were at Pearl Harbor when it was attacked. The article noted that the day was also the birthday of Fred Meijer, whom it identified as the "billionaire owner" of the company listed by *Forbes* magazine as America's tenth-largest private company. A photocopy of the editorial was sent around the office, and a few days later carried notations and initials showing that it had been read by Pam (Kleibusch), Rob (Ver Heulen), Doug (Meijer), Hank (Meijer), and Fred. Across the top of the page, in Fred's distinctive handwriting, is a small inscription: "Billionaire — Not True."

The disclaimer is typical. Years ago, when he was first included on the *Forbes* list of America's wealthiest people, he called the magazine and spent a good bit of time explaining to them that he was not as wealthy as they thought. He had distributed the ownership throughout the family, along with several foundations and charitable trusts, he told them, and thus could not honestly be on their list. For several years it worked, and he was spared the embarrassment of being included on the *Forbes* list. After all, he prided himself on running a business that was careful about its expenditures, and he did not wish to be included on a list that often featured people thought of in the public imagination as big spenders and high rollers. But in 2007 he was back on it, with an estimated worth of $2.2 billion. The *Forbes* people's caveat was that they listed "Frederik G. H. Meijer and Family" rather than Fred himself. But they published his picture, not a family portrait. And their estimate this time may have been a bit short of the mark.

Fred gave up his argument with them, but he has never felt like — or lived like — America's stereotype of a billionaire. For most of their married life, he and Lena resided in a fairly modest house, which was built for them by a relative. They do not have a summer home on a lake, a chalet in the Alps, or a Florida mansion — let alone a yacht or a private jet. Fred has often said, with a typical twinkle in his eyes, that he could easily have lived in a double-wide trailer. This brings out a knowing smile from Lena. But he means it.

He buys his clothes at Meijer stores, keeping an eye out for a good deal, and the idea of a two-hundred-dollar haircut makes him smile condescendingly. Another example is cars: for much of his adult life Fred has avoided new cars. The notion that prestige could attach itself to an object whose purpose was to get people safely and efficiently from one place to another is utterly foreign to him. Prestige, for him, has other, deeper sources.

Not a Crusader

Meijer stores sell lottery tickets, and in Michigan their lottery sales are larger than those of any other business — providing a significant source of revenue to the state. Fred has occasionally toyed with the idea of stopping the sales on moral grounds. But the company goes on selling them, having decided that it is not the place of a retail business to legislate morality.

His stores also sell alcoholic beverages, tobacco products, and coffee. These are also things Fred himself never touches, though not for reasons of morality. It's just a matter of what he prefers. As a child, he had heard stories about his Meijer grandparents' problems with alcohol, and those stories probably played a part in his decision not to touch strong drink.

No Smoking

In the 1960s, years before other companies had such policies, Meijer banned smoking in its corporate offices. Although Fred has never smoked, and opposes the practice on every conceivable ground, he and his father allowed it in the company's private offices for some years. Especially in the early years of the business, a sizable majority of the men in the company smoked. However, there came a time when a number of women who worked in the office wanted a place to do the same thing.

"A lady named Marge Teachout — I have often wondered where she is now. Her husband was a taxi driver, and she worked in the office. You have people who are quiet in the office and you never get to know them, and you have people who are vocal and disagree with you, and that is how you get to know them. Marge came to me, speaking for some of the other women, and said, 'Fred, we want to smoke. The men do it in their private offices, so you should give us a private office where we can smoke.' I said I'd have to think about it, although I couldn't see any reason why they couldn't, since the men were doing it. I called together several of the men who were smokers, and they said, 'We don't want those women sucking on cigarettes.' I told them I really had no choice. I had to let the women smoke if the men did it. So they said, 'We'll quit smoking.' They may not have meant it, but I took them at their word. I went back to Marge and told her, 'Okay, you've got equality.'

"'When can we start smoking?' she asked. 'You can't,' I said. 'The men quit. Now nobody smokes.'

"There is no smoking here," Fred concludes with a smile, "because of women's liberation and my belief in the equality of people."

Travels

Fred has taken countless trips for both business and pleasure, and it's often difficult for him to separate the two. There were many family vacations spent skiing or horseback riding. He and Lena have traveled to Israel several times, pursuing a desire to know more about the Holocaust and its aftermath. They have gone to Taiwan, China, South America, Africa, throughout Europe and the Mediterranean — in fact, to almost every region of the earth except India and the North and South Poles.

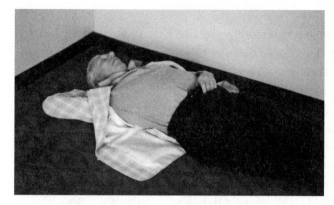

Fred taking a catnap between flights at the Melbourne, Australia, Airport, 1980

Doug Meijer

My parents, especially Dad, like to travel. They enjoy learning about the history and culture of other countries. Their parents immigrated from Germany and the Netherlands, so they liked to go to Europe to explore their roots and see family members. Dad even bicycled around Holland not too long ago. Dad has been on every continent and probably a hundred countries and territories.

Fred aboard local transportation in Southeast Asia

Bill Schroeder

Even though his is a fast-paced world, Fred knows how to slow down and smell the roses. This is nowhere more evident than when on vacation he enjoys taking roads less traveled, and as such, hiking and biking often replace the high-speed modes of "just getting there."

It's fun to watch him interact with locals on their turf, regardless of the country, all the while soaking up their customs and culture. He is always flexible, knowing that a sudden change in plans can lead to an unexpected adventure.

Since we share the same philosophy, I have had the privilege of accompanying Fred on bicycle trips through the Netherlands, Nova Scotia, Colorado, and elsewhere. We've hiked the rugged Milford Track in New Zealand, floated on a barge down the Rhone in France, and sailed on the Great Barrier Reef in Australia.

Fred and Lena have often visited the Netherlands, to see relatives and to encounter that country's art as well as its bountiful array of flowers. On these far-flung rambles, whenever he was not accompanied by Lena, Fred would make a point of writing her each evening to talk about the events of the day.

Fred and Lena, with friends Bill and Barbara Schroeder, bicycling in the Netherlands

Bob Tobin, *CEO of Stop and Shop and Ahold U.S.A.*

On one occasion, Audrey and I were in the Netherlands for a huge tulip festival. There were hundreds of acres and thousands of people. I saw a man sitting on a bench quite a distance away. I said to myself, "That guy looks just like Fred Meijer. I'll bet it's one of his distant relatives." As I moved closer, all of a sudden I saw Lena, and the mystery was solved. The world indeed is a small place. Fred very much enjoyed being Dutch, and cherished his heritage and roots. No one should be surprised that being a dairyman and a merchant came naturally to him through his genes.

Ralph Hauenstein

Fred can defend himself in three languages — his native English and also Dutch and German. At a gathering of friends one evening, he spoke to me in German. Apparently he expected a quick reply, since my name is of German origin. When I said nothing, he ribbed me for not being able to do so. I told him I could speak any language except Greek and asked him to say something in any language he chose. He again spoke to me in German, and I immediately replied that it was Greek to me. It was the first and only time I've seen him speechless, and it didn't last long.

Bud Stehouwer

In 1989, a group of us were planning a bike trip through the Netherlands. I asked Fred if he wanted to go, and even though he was sixty-nine years old at the time, he didn't hesitate. His cousin Willie Mantel joined us there. We averaged thirty miles a day and stayed at small, quaint hotels along the way. I remember that every night Fred would wash his shirt and wrap it in a towel to dry.

He liked to stop and talk to the locals whenever he had a chance. He passed out Purple Cow ice-cream cards. I wonder how many of those found their way back to the United States.

Fred and Lena's most recent trip to the Netherlands, in 2002, was punctuated by visits to a sprawling flower exhibit and an internationally renowned sculpture park at the Kroller-Mueller Museum in Otterlo. They had just returned to Amsterdam, after a day spent in museums and flower shows, when the Dutch politician Pim Fortuyn, who had seemed sure to be the next prime minister of the Netherlands, was assassinated. Suddenly, the hotel was abuzz with hushed conversations and anguished questions. This was the first political assassination in Holland since the sixteenth century, and it was initially met with astonished disbelief. How could it be? people wondered. But it was true, and it was a sobering reminder of the nearness of political violence, even in a country renowned for its peaceful, nonviolent approach to life.

Rich De Vos
> I had the privilege of traveling with Fred and Lena as part of a tour group to Italy. There was a lot of walking involved, and I was amazed at their energy. One day we hiked several miles up a mountain trail in the Cinque Terre, and they never seemed to tire. One time I watched as they approached the edge of a cliff, soaking up the scenery, seemingly oblivious to what a difference a couple more steps would make.

One Kind of Crusader

For most of his adult life Fred has fought a battle with architects and contractors over a very basic element of every modern building: restroom design. When it comes to bathroom doors, he's every inch the crusader. He argues that the doors of a restroom should always, always — always — open outward, so that a person does not have to use a handle or doorknob. The restrooms in all Meijer stores are designed that way: thus, when someone has finished using the facilities, has washed his or her hands, and is ready to leave, it's a simple matter of pushing with a shoulder or elbow, and they're out, clean and ready to return to work or to shopping. There's no potentially germ-ridden door handle to grab, no unpredictable contamination from the hands of anyone who might have exited the room earlier. The only better solution would be to have restrooms without doors, using an internal wall as a visual barrier, so that one could freely walk in and out. As a matter of fact, that is now becoming a standard in many public places, including several of the newest Meijer stores. But for years the issue has gnawed at Fred.

This may seem like a small matter, but in a store where people buy their food, in a public place with thousands of guests and associates constantly on the move, Fred sees it as a very serious issue, right up there with strict cleaning standards. Doors that open inward, allowing people easy access into a bathroom, have the wrong idea, he insists. You don't need an easy way in; you need an easy way out, without having to put your hands on germ-ridden surfaces. This is a battle Fred has fought for decades, for the sake of both the employees and the customers.

He's incensed whenever he sees blueprints with the doors opening the wrong way; of course, it's standard in most of America for restroom doors to open inward. The primary reason is space: doors that open outward can block hallways and impede traffic around them. But that's no reason to spread infection, as Fred sees it. So he's been a restroom crusader, knowing full well that it might seem to some people as though he's tilting at windmills.

"I remember a fellow from Philadelphia who said to me, 'Fred, if you haven't got anything more important to talk about than toilet doors that open out, it isn't very important.' Well, he went broke. Out of business. Now I'm sure toilet doors didn't do it, but I'm also sure that paying attention to the details of what is good for the customers, whether they know it or not, is good business."

Years ago he was talking to a group of Meijer associates when, among other things, he explained why the bathroom doors in all the company's stores open outward. A woman who worked in a new store in Indiana spoke up. "Not in our store," she told him. "Ours has a door that you push to get in and pull to get out." By the end of the day, Fred had contacted the store director and discovered that the woman was correct: there was a Meijer restroom with its doors opening the wrong way.

He immediately asked himself where he had gone wrong. For all these years he'd been preaching the gospel of bathroom doors, and somehow the message had not gotten through. Didn't the architects know how he felt? Of course they did — he had told them a hundred times. Didn't the company executives know? Of course they did. Store directors? Of course. So what went wrong in Indiana? By the time he got home, he was stewing. Lena asked him what was wrong, and he retold the whole story, implying that heads were going to roll.

"You should have a sense of humor about it," she cautioned.

Fred generally takes Lena's advice to heart. It doesn't hurt that he seems to have an inherently sunny approach to almost everything about life. Even restroom doors, now and then.

It turned out that there was a simple explanation. The architects had specified the door correctly in their drawings, but the local carpenter, who had evidently never worked on a Meijer store before, saw the blueprint and decided there was a mistake. He reversed the door on his own, and nobody else had noticed. The solution was equally simple. Call the carpenter back and have him reverse his earlier decision. The work was done in less than a day.

"It's always a good idea to have a sense of humor," Fred concludes, "because you might not know the whole story."

Capital Punishment

In 1846, Michigan became the first English-speaking government in the world to outlaw capital punishment. Between 1683 and 1836, there had been about a dozen executions in what would become the state of Michigan, and only two since statehood was granted in 1837. Of those fourteen executions, seven of the condemned were Native Americans, and four — two women and two men — were African-Americans. This pattern made it clear to the citizens of the early state that there were many possibilities for injustice in the practice, and in May 1846 the legislature signed the prohibition into law. It's a decision Fred agrees with completely.

"I'm totally opposed to capital punishment. A powerful state has other ways to keep criminals off the street without killing them. And then, if there's been a mistake, it's not fatal. My wife asks, 'Why do you reiterate that?' I say, because of other people. Two-thirds of the people in Michigan would probably vote for capital punishment today if some of us didn't speak up and express our views."

Religion

"For a while when I was a kid," Fred recalls, "I went to Sunday School at the Congregational Church in Greenville, where Rev. Sy Parsons was the preacher. I sang in the choir and went to Sunday school there. But as far as I'm concerned, they broke their word. I was a good student. Many of the other kids were shooting paper wads and tearing up the wooden chairs, while I was doing my lessons and learning my Bible verses. When the year was over, we all got up in front of the church. All the other kids got a Bible, which we had been promised for doing our work. I didn't get one, because we weren't registered members of the church.

"I never dare to bring that up in public speeches, because I'd get fifty Bibles tomorrow, and I've already got five or ten. Don't need any more. Religion does fascinate me. You can learn from all of them. I've read the Bible from cover to cover, the Torah, and other religious writings, including some of the Koran. But there have always been bad people in some of the churches, leaders who take advantage of sincere people and their innocent faith."

Persiflage

Todd Gray

I had asked Fred for an interview on a project I was working on. As we were walking to his office, he asked if our meeting would involve persiflage. My hesitation led to his next question. "Do you know what persiflage means?" I said I didn't, so he went to get a dictionary and looked it up for me.

Persiflage: A light, flippant style of conversation or writing. Obviously, it's a word I'll never forget. I thought at the time he should have been a schoolteacher.

Sue Veeneman

Fred's passion for knowledge is inspiring. He enjoys discovering new words, and sharing them with others. One of the first times I worked directly with him, he asked me if I knew the meaning of "bucolic," and proceeded to explain that it meant rural or countrified. He then used the example of our corporate offices, since we could see cows grazing in a pasture just west of the offices. To this day, I smile whenever I hear the word.

Mary Radigan

Over the years, as business writer for the *Grand Rapids Press,* I have had a chance to interview Fred on numerous occasions. I always enjoyed listening to his witticisms. Here are a few:

"For the concert of life, no man has a program." To which he adds, "But you can help write the music."

"I value my sons' advice, even when I don't follow it."

"My parents raised me in the way the world was going, not where it had come from."

"I wish I were fifty years younger. I see a whole new world opening up that I will not be a part of."

"Anyone who thinks he can function at full tilt when he's eighty is crazy."

Frugality

Larry ten Harmsel

During the summer of 2007, at the age of eighty-seven, Fred decided to have his eight-year-old artificial hip replaced with another one. The original implant was not well seated, and was giving him a great deal of pain when he walked. He arranged to have the surgery at Spectrum Hospital, where everything went well. He was then sent to Mary Free Bed, a hospital that specializes in rehabilitation.

I visited him there a few days after the operation. Walking down the hallway toward his room, apparently looking a bit lost, I was asked by one of the nurses if she could help me. I gave her the number of the room I was looking for. "Oh," she said, "Fred's room." She pointed the way.

When I walked in, he was full of good cheer, saying that the hip pain was pretty much gone. He'd been up and around for much of the day, assisted by a walker and by Lena, who was sitting at the bedside with him. Harvey Lemmen was also there visiting. What struck me immediately was that the room was not a private one. The other bed was occupied by a young boy from Greenville, who had been in a terrible auto accident. He was out of the room while I was there, or Fred would certainly have introduced him.

He may have saved a bit of money by having a double instead of a private room, but he also enjoyed having company. Frugality or taste? Hard to know.

Portofino Ice Cream

Peter Secchia, *Former U.S. Ambassador to Italy*

In the early nineties, we were invited to cruise in the Mediterranean with Rich and Helen De Vos aboard their yacht. Fred and Lena were two of the other guests. Joan and I came up from Rome, and boarded Rich's yacht. We anchored off Cinque Terre, a series of five villages on the side of mountains across the bay from Portofino.

Portofino, northeast of Genoa, is the most famous boating destination and most often photographed harbor in Italy. Cinque Terre is on the west slope of the Apennines, and these five villages are connected by a difficult mountain trail.

Some of us decided to hike from one village to the next. We all knew there was a very narrow trail high on a cliff. There were some areas where you hardly had room to pass anyone else. And it was sometimes a quarter of a mile straight down to the Mediterranean. It was a risky situation. Fred and Lena surprised us by deciding to hike with us.

Well, after a while they started falling behind. Sometimes the rocky steps were pretty steep, and they needed some help. Because my wife and I were the only ones who spoke Italian, we stayed in the front of the pack, and we kept leaving behind some of the others, who were a bit slower. I asked Dr. David Moore to stay behind with Fred and Lena. I wanted to go ahead to find a place where we could stop, sit in the shade, and have a cold lemonade. It was the middle of the day, and it was hot.

So as I was walking along the trail, I came up with this fun idea. Fred, for years, would come to parties we hosted, and he would pass out his little ice-cream card, so everybody could turn it in at the Meijer store for a free ice-cream cone. We often had funny stories about those, as it was his tradition.

I found some calling cards, crossed out the front, and wrote on the back: "Free Ice Cream Cone for any friend of Peter the Ambassador when you are in Portofino."

We knew the Ristorante Stella because it was owned by a friend of ours. The gelateria next door was managed by our friend's daughter. So I took these cards, wrote them out, and then stopped an Italian I met on the trail coming toward us, who I knew would pass Fred and Lena. I asked him to pass them to Fred and Lena, after describing them and Dr. Moore.

Joan and I went on to the village. Fred and Lena came down a few minutes later, saying, "We got the cards you sent us."

I replied, "What do you mean, cards I sent you?" He showed me the cards. I said, "Oh, those. They're from the local gelateria. Any friend of mine gets free ice-cream there." Fred didn't believe me at all. He smiled.

I knew in advance exactly where Rich was going to dock when we got back to Portofino, because there's only one place in the harbor where his boat will fit. It's right near the Ristorante Stella and the gelateria.

When we got there and tied up, Fred and Lena were the first two off the boat. I called ahead on the cell phone, and told the young lady that a friend of mine was coming in with a card. She should act like she sees them every day.

They walked toward the restaurant, saw the gelateria, and went inside. Now, good Hollander that he is, he was determined to turn in that card and get a free ice-cream cone. But somehow he thought he could prove to me that this wasn't a valid card.

He was unaware that I knew these people. So there they go off the boat, and I'm sitting there watching them, and he and Lena bolt right to the gelateria. He came back with a big cone and a grin on his face.

"How did you make that happen?" he asked.

"It's just something I do for all my friends in Italy," I replied. If we had been going to any other village, I wouldn't have been able to pull it off, but it was a "gotcha" for all our friends who ate cones as Fred's guests.

Just Too Conservative

Duncan Littlefair was for decades the senior pastor at Fountain Street Church in Grand Rapids, a church known for its Unitarian-Universalist theology and for the wide variety of liberal, cultural, and social causes it championed. It was a surprisingly vibrant institution in a city often seen as a bastion of theological and cultural conservatism. The first time Fred met Duncan socially, they chatted for a while. Then Duncan asked whether Fred might be interested in joining Fountain Street.

"It's good of you to ask," replied Fred, "but I think you're just too conservative." A criticism Duncan had never heard before, this remark took him by surprise. Fred didn't join Fountain Street, or any other church. In fact, however, the two men hit it off, and their conversation marked the beginning of a friendship that lasted more than forty years, until Dr. Littlefair's death in 2004 at the age of ninety-one.

Emotion or Pragmatism?

In 1984, while celebrating fifty years of business, the Meijer Company decided to expand its Greenville store. That store had long been located on land that was formerly the Meijer family's farm. The house Fred had been born in still stood there. Unfortunately, that was the most sensible place to put the 60,000-square-foot addition to the store. What to do?

"We had no choice but to build where the family house stood if we wanted to expand the store," Fred said later. "We could have moved it, but if you move it, then what do you do with it?" So his birthplace was torn down. "I couldn't think of a more practical way out," he concludes. By coincidence, the garden center of the expanded store (no longer in use) occupied the same plot of land where his mother had once planted her vegetable garden.

Fred tries to be frugal and practical in his decisions. If he does something for show, it's usually modesty or pragmatism he wishes to emphasize, not ego. Another story Peter Secchia tells illustrates this quality perfectly.

Peter Secchia

One time Fred and Lena were in Rome, and Joan and I had them for lunch. Since Fred was such a famous retailer in my part of the world, I invited some of the more successful Italian retailers to this lunch, figuring that maybe they could share some stories. I invited folks who spoke English quite well, thinking they would love Fred's fabulous stories on retailing.

If you know anything about Italian business, you know that those who are at the top of the economic ladder are dressed very well, are very cultured, and are not often without name-brand ties, clothing, watches, jewelry, and so forth. They all look as if they are expecting *Gentleman's Quarterly* to be on site.

We had the typical conversation before lunch. When we sat down to lunch, we put Fred at one table with my wife, and Lena at the other table with me. The discussion was about retailing, and both tables participated. They discussed what was going on at various stores, and the Italians were talking about how they marketed the very top-of-the-line products — Rolex, Gucci, and Bvlgari watches and other kinds of high-end jewelry that they ran through their stores.

There are no big-box stores in Italy, such as Meijer or Home Depot, just traditional small department stores with very large jewelry sections. As they talked, the conversation drifted off to watches. And Fred became excited, and showed his table his watch, which he had just bought at a Meijer store for five ninety-five.

"Five hundred ninety-five, signore?" asked one Italian gentleman.

"Five dollars and ninety-five cents," Fred said proudly. Lena waved from the other table and said, "I have one, too. They were on sale."

The Italian marketers were all silent; they didn't know how to react to this.

When Joan and I stopped laughing, we continued our lunch. After lunch they all asked me, "Is this for real? He buys a watch for five dollars and ninety-five cents? He waits till they go on sale? Does he pay for them? In his own store?" Then they understood.

Fred always has a message. Whether you recognize the message right away or not, you'll learn it later. I might think of three or four messages here: Fred pays for everything he takes from his store, something he wants his employees to know; he has an efficient operation — he can market watches that work well for less than six dollars; he got his wife what he wears himself — they share a sense of values; and they have patience, so they waited for it to "go on sale."

You gotta love the guy. I just thought it was a riot, and we enjoyed explaining to our Italian guests the easiest message: "That's just Fred."

Afterlife

When Lena's mother, after a long illness, knew she was not going to live much longer, she began talking quite openly about her impending death to Fred and Lena on their visits to her. On one occasion, she asked Fred point blank whether he thought she would go to heaven. His mother-in-law had been a faithful member of the Lutheran Church all her life, and had shown complete sincerity in both her faith and her life.

Fred wondered how he could answer such a question truthfully. He couldn't simply say yes.

"Grandma Rader," he replied, "if anyone goes to heaven, it will be you."

Really Retired

Whenever someone asks Fred if he's really retired, he brings up a story about a crusty fellow in Maine who is asked by a tourist if he has lived there all his life. "Not yet," the old codger replies.

Index

NOTE: Page numbers in **boldface** represent photographs and captions.

March on Washington (1969 Vietnam War protest), 271
Martindill, Bill, **283**, 310
Mary Free Bed Hospital, 286
Matthews, Buck, 179-80
McCarthy, Jack, 208
McCormack, Joe, 187-88, 208, 244-45, 252
McIntyre, Dave, 155
McLane, Drayton, 272
Meadowfield Street house (Grand Rapids), 64, 71, 74-76, **75**, 87-88
Meed, Dan, 52
Meijer, Douglas Frederik, 78, 327; childhood/young adulthood, **74**, 74-90, **75**, 77, **83**, **85**, **86**; and family business, 89, 96, 99, 102-3, **158**, 324; on father's personal frugality, 198
Meijer, Fred: altruism and quiet generosity, 275-81; approach to having fun, 236-50, **237-39**; attention to detail, 174, 202-10; charitable giving and community projects, 282-304; and college education, 21, 52, 92, 166-67, 214, 270-71; and corporate sense of family (testimony by employees and customers), 99-108; dancing talent, 60-61; Depression-era childhood, **6-8**, 7-19, **11**, **16**, **18**, 315; excellent memory, 52, 270, 322-23; and family life, 65-67, 69-90, **75**, **83**, **86**; family vacations, **84**, 84-87, 197-98, 248, 326-30, **327-28**, 335-37; grandchildren, 89; human rights and civil rights concerns, 258-68, 297-98; leading by example (testimony by employees and managers), 178-91; legacy, 304; and Lena Rader, 46-47, 61-63, **64**, 65-69, **67**; management style and the Meijer culture (testimony by employees and managers), 158-77; marriage, 62-63, **64**, 66-69, 71-72, **256**; meetings with world leaders, 251-55, **288**, **291**; member of Improvement Club, **283**; military service, 50-52; musical interests, 13, 85; opposition to capital punishment, 332; passion for knowledge, 333-34; personal frugality, 196-200, 325, 334-35; reflections on things he might have done differently, 269-74, **270**; religious views, 333; and sister Johanna, 94; and skiing, 87, 137; and small children, 254-55, **255**; and sons, 74-90, **75**, **83**, **86**, **89**, **158**; young adulthood at the family's grocery, **18**, 18-19, 20-31, **29**, **51-52**, 52. **See also** Meijer family business
Meijer, Gezina (Zien) Mantel, 1-8, **2**, **6**, 15-18, **79**; death of, 65; and family business, 18, 20, 69, 79, 263; and grandsons/family life, 75, 78, **78**, **86**; immigration to U.S., 1-2; political radicalism, 48-49
Meijer, Hendrik (Fred's father), 1-8, **2-3**, 12-18, 53-54, 77, **93**; death of, 115; and fire at Greenville store, 70-71; and first Greenville store, 17-18, 20-31, 44, 46-47, 53-60, 70-71; and grandsons/family life, 75, 77, 78, 114-15; and Greenville barbershop, **3**, 3-4, 7, 15, 17, 56-57, 112, 114-15, 259, 276; and Greenville Hospital, 7, 61-62, 282-83; and human rights, 258-59, 260-61; as immigrant farmer, 4-5, 13-17; immigration to U.S., 1-2; and low-price gospel, 192-96; partnership with Fred, 29-30, 53-54, 95-96, **98**, 181, **181**, 214; practical jokes, 181, 238-40; and shoplift-

ers, 206-7. **See also** Meijer family business

Meijer, Hendrik (Hank): childhood/ young adulthood, 64, 72-90, **74, 75, 83, 85, 86**; and family business, 72, 89, 96, 99, **158**, 324; having fun, 238, **238**; and March on Washington (1969), 271; and Meijer Gardens, 319-20; and Saigon staircase, 291-92

Meijer, Johanna: and the Cedar Springs store, 48, 55-56, 59, 263; childhood, 3, **6**, 15-17, **16**, 18; and the family business, 20, 48, 55-56, 59, 92-94, 263; University of Michigan education, 21, 48, 52, 270. **See also** Magoon, Johanna Meijer

Meijer, Lena Rader, 32-47, 63-67; early employment at Meijer Thrift Market, 44-47, 56, **57**, 69; family life, 64-67, **67**, 75, 81-90, 326-30; and family vacations, 87, 326-30, **328**; growing up in Amble, 12, 32-43, **35-37, 40, 42-44**; marriage, 62-63, **64**, 66-69, 71-72, **256**; meetings with world leaders, **252**; personality, 65; piano playing, 40, **41**, 43, 85

Meijer, Mark Donald, 85-87, 291-92; ambulance business, 88-89, **89**; childhood/young adulthood, 74-90, **75, 83, 85, 86**

Meijer auto centers, 220, **221**

Meijer Broadcast Center, Grand Valley State University (GVSU), 166, 285, 294

Meijer Community Parties, 179-80

Meijer Credit Union, 220, 277

Meijer family business: approach to having fun, 236-50, **237-39**; building and marketing the Meijer brand, 128-39, **132, 134-35**; buyout offers (declined), 222, 230-31, 272, 273; and changes in supermarket technology, 211-14; charitable giving, 97, 282-304; company cars, 189-90, 198-99; and competitors, 224-35, 273; the corporate sense of family, 99-108; culture of respect and teamwork, 159-63; customer satisfaction and refund policy, 133-34, 137-38; and details determining profits in grocery business, 203-8; the discounting movement, 110-15, 123-25; diversification, 217-20, **221**; downsizing and layoffs, 273-74; early meat departments/managers, 163-65; and early supermarket idea, 142-43; employee hiring and promotions, 96-97, 163-67; employees and the color barrier, 259-61, 264-65, 297; employee wages and benefits, 200-201; former and current team members (2008), **145**; freshness, **134**, 134-39, **135**; gas stations, 128-29; going public (thoughts/speculations about), 97, 222; grocery distribution centers, 216-17; and hypermarkets/supercenters, 145-50, **148**, 234; leading by example (testimony by employees and managers), 178-91; leases and buildings, 151-54; the low-price gospel ("Why Pay More?"), 192-201; and the Magoons, 71, 92-94; the Meijer culture (testimony by employees and managers), 158-77; Meijer label products, 133; and new general-merchandise stores (1960s), 109-15, 123-25, 137; one-stop shopping, 113-15, 130, 138, **144**; and other family-owned businesses, 91-92, 95, 158-59; and paradigm shifts in retailing, 140-50,